GURU NANAK

His Mystic Teachings

J. R. Puri

RADHA SOAMI SATSANG BEAS

Published by:
J. C. Sethi, Secretary
Radha Soami Satsang Beas
Dera Baba Jaimal Singh
Punjab 143 204, India

Fourth edition 2004

12 11 10 09   8 7 6 5 4 3 2

ISBN 978-81-8256-040-6

Printed in India by: Lakshmi Offset Printers

CONTENTS

PREFACE

GURU NANAK is another volume in our Mystics of the East Series. All the monographs previously published in this Series have been well received; hence, need was felt for a monograph on Guru Nanak, one of the greatest saints of India. Like the other volumes in the Series, Guru Nanak brings out the same essential features that are inherent in the teachings of all true saints. The author ably expounds some important aspects of Guru Nanak's teachings that are generally ignored. Thus, although there are already many books on Guru Nanak, we hope this book will have special interest for those with some background in the subject who are imbued with a seeking spirit.

Guru Nanak differs from the rest of the Series in its exposition at some length on the meaning and significance of mysticism for human life. The author also attempts to bring out the close relationship of mystical experience to ethics as well as religion, drawing on his background in Western philosophy. He has made a lifelong study of the teachings of the saints, and has a deep and penetrating insight into the essence of their teachings. It is hoped that his discussion of the universal truths taught by perfect masters of different countries and different ages will be found most fascinating.

The greatness of the saints lies in their achievements in the realm of spirit, and it will be seen that this great saint of the Punjab, Guru Nanak, reached heights of spiritual exaltation rarely achieved in any age. We hope that every genuine seeker and aspirant for God-realization will derive much benefit from the study of Guru Nanak's mystic teachings.

S. L. Sondhi
Secretary
January, 1982

FOREWORD

BACK IN 1969 I contributed a paper entitled "Mystical Teachings of Guru Nanak" to an international seminar organized by Punjabi University, Patiala, on the occasion of Guru Nanak's quincentenary celebrations. A few years later some friends suggested that I might get some reprints of the article for the benefit of people interested in Guru Nanak's mystical philosophy. The seed of this suggestion took some time to germinate and grow in my mind. In the process I was advised to expand the scope of the article to include a biographical chapter on Guru Nanak's life. Later still it was impressed on me to add some of his hymns to give a flavour of his own writings, albeit in translation, to the reader. I was also prevailed upon to add a few subsections under the head 'Teachings', as also to give a few quotations from the other Gurus in the House of Nanak to support and elaborate Guru Nanak's teachings. So, what started as a humble project of a small article has now assumed the dimensions of a book.

I am deeply beholden to Prof. K.S. Narang, who has not only taken a keen interest in the project but has also given valuable suggestions in the writing of the book. My thanks are also due to the various members of the Dera Publications Committee who helped finalize the manuscript; to Mrs. Beverly Mansukhani and Mrs. Kamla Samtani for typing it; to Miss Anthea Guinness for going through the manuscript and preparing the press copy; to Gopi Gajwani for designing the cover; and to Miriam and Wayne Caravella who saw it through the press, guided by Miss Louise Hilger with her usual care and devotion.

J. R. Puri
8 January, 1982
Dera, Beas

SECTION ONE

Life

Life of
Guru Nanak

FACT AND FICTION are so interwoven in the life stories of saints and prophets that it is almost impossible to separate them completely. This is particularly true of Guru Nanak, in whose biographies truth and fable are so mixed that it is hard to bring out his true image from them. Therefore, in spite of our best efforts to make the account of his life as objective as possible, the subjective elements cannot be entirely excluded.

Sources

The oldest authentic record of the life of Guru Nanak is to be found in the *vars** of Bhai Gurdas. But Bhai Gurdas' primary interest was in the teachings of Guru Nanak rather than in his life, and he has, therefore, left behind an inadequate biographical account. Moreover, his *vars* are much more eulogistic than descriptive.

Guru Nanak has often been associated with performing miracles, but as Bhai Gurdas says, apart from the miracle of the true Name, Guru Nanak chose not to work any wonders.[1] In fact, "he derided those who did, as deriving powers from evil spirits."[2]

---

*For explanation of terms, see Glossary.

The *janamsakhis* constitute the major source of information in regard to the incidents of Guru Nanak's life. A *janamsakhi* literally means 'birth story', though the term has generally been used for a life story. There is neither any logical connection between the *sakhis*, nor much literary merit in them, although they are supposed to have been put together in chronological order. It has been said that they were "written by semi-illiterate scribes for the benefit of a wholly illiterate people."[3] In their original form, nothing is mentioned about their authors, nor about the dates of their composition and the primary sources on which they were based. In all probability, they passed through several hands and went through a process of change, involving additions and deletions at different stages.

Early writers on Sikh history attach great importance to the *sakhi* attributed to Sewa Das. Macauliffe considers it "beyond dispute the most trustworthy detailed record we possess of the life of Guru Nanak."[4] It contains much less mythological matter and is a much more rational, consistent and satisfactory narrative. This *janamsakhi* has two versions: one found in the India Office Library and known as *Vilayat Vali Janamsakhi*; the other found at Hafizabad and known as *Hafizabad Vali Janamsakhi*. The two differ only slightly and represent a single work of which the original has been lost. The two together have come to be known as *Puratan Janamsakhi*.

Before the discovery of this *sakhi*, the ground was held by the *sakhi* ascribed to Bhai Bala. Even the appearance of the *Puratan Janamsakhi* has not completely dislodged it.

Another *janamsakhi* is attributed to Meharban, who was a grandson of Guru Ram Das. Meharban's father, Prithi Chand, was the eldest son of Guru Ram Das, and was superceded on the issue of succession by his younger brother, Arjan. This led to a long hostility between, on the one hand, Prithi Chand and his followers, known as the Mina sect, and Guru Arjan Dev and his successors, on the other. This hostility was supposed to have been reflected in Meharban's account of Guru Nanak's life. For this reason, many scholars have evinced little interest in it. Thus Macauliffe says that in Meharban's *Janamsakhi* his father was glorified, and "there was ample opportunity for the manipulation of details."[5] McLeod, however, is of the view that "Meharban has been largely misjudged – the tone, far from being one of denigration, is manifestly one of enthusiastic homage and places this *janamsakhi* firmly within the same hagiographic category as the other *janamsakhis*."[6]

The *janamsakhi* called *Gyan Ratnavali* is attributed to Bhai Mani Singh of Guru Gobind Singh's time. *Var 1* of Bhai Gurdas served as the basis of his narrative. Its language is comparatively modern and it was composed after the tenth Guru's time. It also includes large borrowings from the *Puratan* and the *Bala Janamsakhis*, thus making it a heterogeneous collection. It has, therefore, hardly any independent value of its own.

The historical value of these *sakhis* is questionable. The stories of miracles are inconsistent with the Guru's own teachings. There are also references to and descriptions of incidents that are partly or wholly improbable from the modern point of view. If some miracles did occur in Guru Nanak's life, they were the expression of the deep concern of the Master for some devoted disciple. They were of direct interest only to the particular individual, and not meant as an ostentatious display for the laity.

Verification through comparison with other independent sources is a useful technique, but unfortunately such sources are scanty. Practically the only internal evidence in the case of Guru Nanak are a few references in the Adi Granth; and then there is the epigraphic evidence from Baghdad. Recently, however, some authentic evidence relating to Guru Nanak's travels in Orissa and Sri Lanka has come to light.

In the present stage of our knowledge, it would not be advisable to reject outright an incident mentioned in a *janamsakhi*. Notwithstanding some erroneous or improbable details it might contain, it may be worthy of our acceptance in general, if it is otherwise probable.

The earliest Muslim account of Guru Nanak is found in the famous work *Dabistan-i-Mazahib*, attributed to Mohsin Fani or Mobid Zulfiqar Ardastani.[7] In spite of the great popularity of the work, it cannot be considered very reliable. For one, it is not by an independent witness. For another, the author was a "garrulous and a somewhat credulous Mohammedan," as described by the later English historians such as Malcolm and Cunningham.

Macauliffe took upon himself the task of making "some reparation to the Sikhs for the insults which [Trumpp had] offered to their Gurus and their religion." He wrote his book from "an orthodox Sikh point of view, without any criticism or expression of opinion of his own." He thus included the various miracles reverently accepted by the Sikhs.[8]

The above brief survey of the main available sources should serve to warn the reader that he should not expect full and authentic details about the life of Guru Nanak. The historian is not yet in a position to offer more than a bare outline.

Advent of Guru Nanak

Guru Nanak was born in 1469 A.D. There is, however, no unanimity regarding the date or month of his birth. According to *Puratan Janamsakhi*, Meharban's *Janamsakhi*, *Gyan Ratnavali* and *Mahima Prakas*, Guru Nanak was born on 15 April 1469 (*Vaisakh Sudi* 3, *samvat* year 1526). On the other hand, the *janamsakhi* of Bhai Bala gives a date corresponding to a day in November 1469 (*Kartik Sudi* 15, *Puranmasi, samvat* year 1526). As late as 1815 (*samvat* year 1872), the anniversary fair of Guru

Nanak's birth was celebrated in the month of *Vaisakh* (April) at Nankana Sahib. The date of celebration was shifted to *Kartik* (November) in the time of Ranjit Singh, at the instance of Bhai Sant Singh Gyani. A possible motive for this change of date was to avoid a clash with the celebration at Anandpur of the birth of the Khalsa, in the same month. Moreover, the agricultural Sikh community could hardly afford to attend two fairs during the wheat-harvesting season.

According to the *janamsakhis* and *Mahima Prakas*, Guru Nanak was born in his father's house in a village called Talwandi Rai Bhoi, later known as Nankana Sahib, about forty miles from Lahore (now in Pakistan). Another belief holds that he was born in the house of his maternal grandfather in a village called Kahan Katcha or Chahal. This view is in accordance with an old tradition prevalent in the Punjab, as also in some other parts of India, that the wife returns to her parents' home for confinement. The name Nanak suggests that the birth took place at the residence of the *nana* or maternal grandfather, and it is possible that the Guru's elder sister was also born in their *nana's* house, as she was called Nanaki. The *janamsakhis*, however, unambiguously state that the Guru was born in the house of Mehta Kalu Bedi of Talwandi Rai Bhoi.[9]

The chief of village Talwandi at the time of the Guru's birth was Rai Bular, who was a well-wisher of Guru Nanak and who later became his follower. The Guru's father, Kalu, was a Khatri by caste and a Bedi by subcaste. He was a village accountant or *patwari*. The name of the Guru's mother was Tripta, and she is remembered for her devotion to her son. As stated above, the Guru had an elder sister named Nanaki.

Education
The early life of the Guru relating to his childhood does not lend itself to historical verification. There is, however, a general

agreement in the various accounts that he preferred the study of divine knowledge to secular studies. His educational career was brief and not marked by careful attention to the usual curricula. There was not only a lack of interest in secular studies, but also a lack of opportunity to acquire such knowledge. Talwandi was a small place that could not boast of a Jogi *math* or a Muslim *khanqah*, which were the usual centres of advanced study in those days.

Rai Bular, the kindly landlord, promised to appoint Nanak as the village accountant, in succession to his father, provided the boy qualified himself by learning Persian, in which all official accounts and documents were written at that time. That Guru Nanak acquired some proficiency in Persian is evident from the liberal use of Arabic and Persian words in his hymns. Different sources give the names of his Persian teachers as Rukn-ud-Din, Qutb-ud-Din and Sayyid Hasan. It is also said that he was taught accounts in Hindi by one Gopal Pundit.

Quest for Truth
Whatever secular knowledge Guru Nanak might have acquired in his early years, his quest for divine knowledge led him to various centres of religious learning. In this search he came in contact with ascetics and anchorites, who were supposed to have acquired divine knowledge by study, meditation, and exchange of ideas with religious teachers in other parts of India. Some of Guru Nanak's writings – the *Japji*, *Asa-di-Var*, and *Sidh Gosht*, for example – reveal not only contact with such people, but also a profound study of scriptural literature, for the sound grasp of religious problems that he displays could hardly have been acquired by mere oral exchange with hermits and mendicants at various places during his travels.

Sacred thread ceremony

An important incident in Guru Nanak's childhood was his investment with the sacred thread at the age of nine. He did not consider the ceremony sacred, as he plainly told the family priest, Hardial. The story narrated in the *janamsakhis* seems to be suggested by the Guru's words in *Asa-di-Var*:

> When making the sacred thread, the *janeu*,
> See that the following rules you pursue:
> Out of the cotton of compassion
> Spin the thread of tranquillity;
> Let continence be the knot
> And virtue the twist thereon.
> O pundit, if such a sacred thread there be
> Around our neck, we shall wear it willingly.
> A thread so made will not break,
> It will not get dirty, be burned or lost.
> O Nanak, thou shalt see
> Those who wear this shall blessed be.[10]
>
> *Asa, M.1, p.471*

Marriage and family

Some time between his twelfth and sixteenth year, Nanak was married to Sulakhani, daughter of Mula, a resident of Batala in Gurdaspur District, Punjab. From the different *janamsakhis* we can infer that the Guru's marriage took place between 1481 and 1485. It was in all probability his brother-in-law, Jai Ram, who had him married. Left to himself, says Macauliffe, he would not have been interested in performing this part of a man's duty after entering government service in Sultanpur.[11] In the course of time he had two sons, Sri Chand and Lakshmi Das.

Profession

Kalu Bedi intended his son to lead a normal worldly life, but Nanak's interests lay elsewhere. He associated continually with religious men. Anxious to divert his attention to secular interests, Kalu Bedi tried to keep him engaged in such activities as herding buffalo, cultivating land, shopkeeping, and dealing in horses. But Nanak's heart was not in these occupations, and owing to his unusual behaviour, he was considered quite abnormal.

Nanak's obduracy in refusing to take up any of these professions drove his father to despair. He tried his best to cut off the young man's contact with the ascetics and the anchorites in the forests around Talwandi, but none of his efforts proved of any avail. The members of his family began to feel that Nanak had lost his reason:

> Some take me as one under an evil spell,
> Others say that I am 'out of tune',
> Some call me a man forsaken and woebegone;
> But I am mad after my Lord
> And I know of none but Him.
>
> *Maru, M.1, p.991*

The next attempt of Kalu Bedi to get his son settled was to send him to Chuharkhana (in the district of Gujranwala, now in Pakistan) to work as a merchant. On his way, he spent the money given to him on feeding starving holy men. He then returned to Talwandi, where his father "cuffed him for disobedience." Jai Ram, however, saved the situation by persuading Kalu Bedi, with the support of Rai Bular, to allow Nanak to accompany him to Sultanpur.

The Sultanpur phase of Guru Nanak's life is without much controversy. On Jai Ram's recommendation, Nanak was employed as a storekeeper by Daulat Khan Lodi. Although Nanak accepted this secular occupation, his mind did not change at all. He performed his duties during the day to the best of his ability, but during the night he was engaged in meditation.

Crucial mystic experience

It is during this period that we have the first recorded evidence of his mystic experience. Early one morning after bathing in the Kali Bein, a rivulet flowing by the side of Sultanpur, he disappeared in the nearby forest and, according to *Puratan Janamsakhi*, he was taken to the presence of the Lord *(dargah parmeshar ki)*. God offered him a cup of nectar *(amrit)* and charged him with the mission of preaching the glory of His Name. He returned to Sultanpur after three days, to the delight of the local people, who had assumed that he had been drowned in the stream.

This account obviously refers to the realization of God by Guru Nanak within himself through a mystic trance. When his soul current was withdrawn from within his body through concentration *(simran)*, it formed contact with the divine melody within *(Shabd)* and he had what is generally called the enlightenment experience. Guru Nanak, in his hymns, has identified the Supreme Being with *Shabd*, as is apparent in the following hymn in *Rag Maru*:

> Thou art the timeless Being
> And Time (Kal) is not on Thy head.
> Thou art invisible, unfathomable and peerless.
> Thou art the blissful melody *(Shabd)*,
> Calm and tranquil.
> One is attuned to Thee
> By immersing oneself in *sahaj*.
>
> *Maru, M.1, p.1038*

The process of withdrawal of the soul current from within the body is virtually the process of dying. The mystic, who has mastered this technique of inducing voluntary death, has indeed triumphed over the phenomenon of death, for he can vacate his body and return to it at will. As St. Paul says, "I die daily."[12] Such a person will no longer have any fear of death. What fear will exist in one who can die every day and return to life whenever he likes?

Guru Nanak exhorts the spiritual aspirant to attain this state during his lifetime. He says:

> Where thou hast to go after death,
> Oh, go thou to that home while living.
>
> *Sri Rag, M.1, p.21*

The cup of nectar offered by God to Guru Nanak, as stated in the *Puratan Janamsakhi*, also refers to the inner beatific experience that transforms one into an immortal being.

> Within the body is the true *amritsar*
>   (pool of nectar),
> And through love and devotion
> Doth the mind drink of it.
>
> *Maru, M.3, p.1046*

This great mystic experience of Guru Nanak was the turning point in his life. Henceforth he was no longer a mere seeker after Truth, but a realized master who had been endowed with the clear vision of disseminating it to the multitude.

Did Guru Nanak have a master?

Opinions differ in regard to the question of whether Guru Nanak had a master. The traditional view of the Sikhs is that he had no master. They believe that the Guru was commissioned by God during his crucial mystic experience in the forest near the Kali Bein to preach the glory of His Name and to disseminate spiritual knowledge.

Some scholars, however, assert that Guru Nanak did have a master. In *Siyar-ul-Mutakharin* it is mentioned by its author, Ghulam Husain Khan, that Sayyid Hasan was the master of Guru Nanak.[13] In a recent publication a scholar has confirmed this fact with the statement: "One new point mentioned by Ghulam Husain Khan about Guru Nanak is that the latter had, during his boyhood at Talwandi, a teacher by the name of Sayyid Hasan, a Muslim scholar and dervish."[14]

The Kabir *panthis* in general claim that Guru Nanak got his light from Kabir. "Among those who acknowledge their indebtedness to Kabir as a spiritual guide are Nanak Shah of the Punjab, the founder of the Sikh community."[15] Another scholar writes that Kabir's name "is unmistakably associated by all writers with Nanak."[16] Continuing his account he mentions A.S. Garden and J.N. Farquhar as advocates of the view that Guru Nanak was a disciple of Kabir.[17]

Beale, apparently accepting the view that Guru Nanak had a master, writes that Sayyid Husain was his master. He adds that according to some, Kabir was his master.[18] Still another eminent scholar recalls Guru Nanak's visit to Baghdad, where an inscription reads, "Guru Murad died. Baba Nanak Fakir helped in constructing the building which is an act of grace from a virtuous follower. 927 A.H."[19] So, according to this inscription Guru Murad was Guru Nanak's spiritual guide.

Most scholars, on the other hand, deny that Guru Nanak's inspiration came from any of the names mentioned above.[20]

Some other scholars quote Guru Nanak to show that he left his home in search of a master and that through this master he attained God-realization.

I left my home to look for a *master,*[*]
The desire to see the Lord made me a hermit.

Ramkali, Sidh Gosht, M.1, p.939:18

O Swami, hear thou:
This is how I tamed my mind.

I attached myself to the Word
Given by *my Master*
And, through his grace,
The Lord united me with Himself.

Ramkali, Sidh Gosht, M.1, p.994:58

Still others point out that some verses of Guru Nanak indicate references to his own master, especially when he uses the word *my*:

Let my life be extinguished without Thee,
I have made sure by asking it of *my Master*;
There is no abode for me save Thine, O Lord.

Sri Rag, M.1, p.14:1:P

I am a sacrifice to *my Master*
A hundred times a day,
Who made angels of men
And, lo, without delay.

Asa-di-Var, M.1, p.462:1

If one cannot see the Lord,
What can one say of Him?

---

[*] Italics in these quotations are mine.

I am a sacrifice unto *my Master*,
Who hath shown Him to me
Within my heart.

Ramkali, Dakhani Onkar, M.1, p.937:52

I ask from *my Master*,
For I do as he directs.
All praise to the Word,
For if it takes abode in the mind,
The agony of ego is burnt down.

Sri Rag, M.1, p.58:5

I bow low at the feet of *my Master*,
By whose grace I have seen the Lord.

Asa, M.1, p.353

My *compassionate Master* ever remains
Merged in love of the Lord;
Day and night he is attuned to the One
And believes in Him
Since he hath seen* Him.

Ramkali, Dakhani Onkar, M.1, p.907:1:P

I am a sell-off to thee, *O Master*,
How fortunate am I that I am thy slave!
In exchange for thy Word, *O Master*,
I've sold myself at thy shop,
And now I go the way thou biddest.

Maru, M.1, p.99:1

---

*His belief in God is not blind faith, but is based on personal experience.

> Brother, I have no sanctuary
> Save His Name;
> It is my only treasure.
> *My Master* gave it to me;
> I am forever beholden to him.
>
> *Sri Rag, M.1, p.58:1:P*

I have not researched this issue in depth or in detail, since the main object in writing this book is to expound the mystic philosophy of Guru Nanak. It is not my intention to enter into this controversy, which is concerned only with the historicity of its peripheral aspects.

Transformation

It is said that on his reappearance after the divine transformation at the River Bein, Guru Nanak relinquished all his possessions and observed a general silence. Mardana became his constant companion at this time. There was one cryptic sentence that he frequently uttered: "There is no Hindu, there is no Muslim." He said little else.

This simple statement only signified his cosmic vision and universal love; nevertheless, it offended many. Members of the ruling race were especially cross at his equating Hindus with Muslims. A complaint was made before Nawab Daulat Khan, the governor.[*] He dismissed it by saying that Guru Nanak was a faqir whose words they did not easily understand.

The qazi, the expounder of Muslim law, was also present and supported the complainants. He requested the Nawab to send for the Guru. When Guru Nanak arrived, the governor offered him his homage and seated him by his side.

---

[*] Bhai Gurdas in his *Vars* mentions Daulat Khan Lodi as one of the disciples of Guru Nanak.

It was now time for the Muslim afternoon prayer. All arose and went to the mosque. The Guru accompanied them. When the *qazi* conducted the service, the Guru kept standing and did not kneel, as expected. The *qazi* found in this further ground for complaint. He brought the lapse to the notice of the Nawab. When asked to explain, Guru Nanak said, "The *qazi's* heart was not in the prayer. His mind constantly wandered to the newborn foal he had let loose in his yard before coming to the mosque. He kept remembering there was a well nearby and feared the foal might fall into it."

The *qazi* admitted as true what the Guru had said and fell at his feet. The Guru then uttered the following:

> He is a Muslim who effaceth himself,
> Who maketh truth and contentment
> His holy creed, his *Kalma*;
> Who neither toucheth what is standing,
> Nor eateth what hath fallen –
> Such a Muslim shall go to paradise.[21]

There is another noteworthy story relating to the period of Guru Nanak's service at Sultanpur. He was accused of negligence of duty in performing the function of the governor's storekeeper. The actual charge was that he gave people more than they were entitled to get. This resulted in loss to the government granary. If the charge had been proved, he would have been severely punished. However, when investigations were made, the governor found that the store was not only sufficient, but there was actually a surplus. This incident need not necessarily be considered a miracle. A plausible explanation might be that Guru Nanak, who received his salary in kind, spent very little of it on himself. The rest he put in the official stock, thereby showing excess in the government granary.

We do not know the exact dates of the Guru's arrival at Sultanpur and his departure from there. The duration of his stay there most probably fell within the period of Daulat Khan Lodi's administration at Sultanpur. The upper limit of the Guru's stay, therefore, would be 1500, when Daulat Khan Lodi was promoted and became governor of Lahore. The Guru might have left Sultanpur sometime around 1500.

Missionary journeys

The next date about which we are definite is 1520. In that year we find Guru Nanak at Sayidpur. The intervening years (1500–1520) he spent in journeys known as *udasis*.[22] The term *udasi* has been given to these journeys because Guru Nanak travelled like a person who has renounced the world. He put on the dress of a pilgrim, which varied according to the nature of the place that he was visiting and the people whom he met. Thus, on his South Indian journey he "wore wooden sandals, took a stick in his hand, twisted a rope round his head as a turban, and on his forehead put a patch and a streak."[23] While proceeding to the north, Guru Nanak is said to have worn "leather on his feet and on his head, twisted a rope round his body, and on his forehead stamped a saffron *tilak*."[24] When he went to Mecca, it is said that he "disguised himself in the blue dress of a Muhammadan pilgrim, took a faqir's staff in his hand and a collection of his hymns under his arm. He also carried with him in the style of a Mussalman* devotee a cup for his ablutions and a carpet whereon to pray."[25]

From this, it may be safely inferred that the Guru identified himself with the people whom he visited in different places and whose religious garb he adopted. This must have naturally

---

* Muslim.

facilitated him in disseminating his divine teachings to the multitudes.

Guru Nanak appears to have led the life of an ascetic, at least for a short period. Bhai Gurdas says:

> His food was sand and the pod of the *ak*,
> And his bed he spread on stones.
> He performed great austerities,
> To the supreme satisfaction of God.[26]

In the *Dabistan*, it is written:

Nanak underwent severe austerities. At first he reduced his food, and after some time, he depended upon drinking a little of cow's milk. After that he lived on *ghee* and then on water. Lastly, he lived on air like those who, in Hindustan, are called *pavanharis* or consumers of air alone.[27]

No definite and precise record of the various *udasis* of Guru Nanak is available today. The account given in *Var 1* of Bhai Gurdas is doubtless the earliest and most authentic of all sources, but though descriptive, it is not an exhaustive coverage. The *Puratan Janamsakhi* speaks of five journeys – four major and one minor – and mentions many places. The *Meharban Janamsakhi* reduces the number to two, although the places named are numerous. The main omissions in this list are Kamrup, Baghdad and Nanakmata. Moreover, the *Puratan* and *Meharban* versions differ in the sequence of the Guru's visits to various places, as also in the details concerning them. Again, there are obscurities and incongruities regarding geographical locations. In spite of all these difficulties, we shall endeavour to give as coherent and clear a picture as possible of the missionary tours of Guru Nanak covering a period of two decades. For this purpose, we shall draw upon the *Puratan* and *Meharban Janamsakhis* to reconstruct the framework, and supplement it with such data as are available from Bhai Gurdas.

First journey

Guru Nanak's first *udasi* began from Sultanpur Lodi after he had stayed there for some years. Mardana, his faithful companion and minstrel, accompanied him on this tour. According to the chronological scheme suggested above, the first journey could not have started after 1500, and in all probability a few years earlier. The *Puratan Janamsakhi* states that it lasted twelve years, after which the Guru returned to Talwandi.

Bhai Gurdas, in his graphic description of this tour, says that the Master visited many places of pilgrimage, especially on festival days. He saw the people performing the rituals related to their orthodox religions, but devoid of any loving adoration. These external observances earned them no merit. Since the love of God was not preordained for them, the Guru found them reading the Vedas and the Smritis.

Continuing his account, Bhai Gurdas states that during this tour Guru Nanak met ascetics, yogis, *siddhas, naths*, gurus and disciples. He also saw crowds praying to gods, goddesses and other minor deities. During his entire round of the pilgrim centres, he searched but found no true devotee or believer. Hindus and Muslims, he saw them all, with their *pirs* and pundits, but he found that the blind were thrusting the blind into a well.[28]

From Sultanpur, Guru Nanak and Mardana went towards the west. In the forests adjoining Sayidpur (now Eminabad in Pakistan), the Guru remained engrossed in meditation for several days, and according to Bhai Gurdas he "attained perfect union." Then he entered the city along with his companion and took shelter in the house of a carpenter called Lalo. This infuriated a local official, Malik Bhago, whose invitation to a great feast had been declined by the Guru. The offended host remonstrated with Guru Nanak against it and said that he had been greatly insulted. The Guru took Lalo's coarse bread in one hand, Malik Bhago's refined one in the other, and squeezed them both. From Lalo's bread oozed milk and from Malik Bhago's, blood. The difference was explained by the Guru that while Lalo's bread had been earned by honest hard work, that of Malik Bhago was the result of bribery and oppression.[29]

There is nothing improbable in the story, apart from the miracle of milk and blood flowing from bread. It brings out an important precept in Guru Nanak's teachings, that one should earn one's living by honest labour:

> If out of wealth amassed through deceitful means
> One offers propitiation for his ancestors,
> The Lord knows it all and even the ancestors
> Have to suffer for it;
> Nay, even the priest as go-between
> Gets his hands chopped off.
> Thus are the ends of the Lord's justice served.
> Nanak, he alone receiveth honour,
> Whose earnings are acquired through hard work
> And honest living.
>
> *Asa-di-Var, M.1, p.472*

From Sayidpur, the Guru and his companion went to a solitary forest. During this journey they reached the house of a thug named Sheikh Sajjan. He hatched a plan of throwing the guests into a well, but his evil designs were frustrated by his contact with the Master and his spiritual influence. Sajjan confessed his wicked intentions, as also his earlier sins, and eventually became the Guru's disciple. The first *dharamshala* was constructed where this incident occurred. This story is mentioned in all the *janamsakhis*, although it differs in details.

Kurukshetra was another important halt in this tour of Guru Nanak.[30] He arrived there on the occasion of a solar eclipse, possibly with the purpose of preaching the futility of such practices as the worship of eclipses. He succeeded in converting many people to his views.

At Panipat, according to the *janamsakhis* (except that of Meharban), Guru Nanak met the local *pir* called Sheikh Sharaf. Since this *pir* had died much earlier, the Guru apparently met his contemporary successor. This discrepancy need not make us reject the entire story, as there is a natural tendency in a writer to associate the acknowledged great in his narrative, in order to enhance the effect of his assertion. It is said that the *pir* was totally converted and he "kissed the Guru's hands and feet."[31]

Delhi was the next stop where, however, Guru Nanak did not stay long, nor did any noteworthy incidents happen there. From Delhi he proceeded to Hardwar. Here he saw many pilgrims throwing water towards the east for the manes of their ancestors. On seeing this, the Guru started throwing water towards the west. When asked to explain, he said that he was watering his fields near Lahore. They asked how such a thing could be possible, and he replied that if water could reach the other world, surely it could reach Lahore, which was much nearer.[32] Here again the Guru's purpose was to bring out the futility of rituals.

The next place Guru Nanak visited was Gorakhmata (now called Nanakmata).[*] A number of *siddhas* met him here, took

---

[*]Located northwest of Pilibhit in Uttar Pradesh. The name was changed in memory of Guru Nanak's visit to the place (Macauliffe, *The Sikh Religion*, I:59).

him as a good aspirant for yoga and invited him to join their order. The Guru answered with the following hymn:

Religion lies not
In the yogi's patched garment,
Nor in his staff,
Nor in besmearing the body with ashes.
Religion lies not in suspending large rings
From split ears,
Nor in shaving the head,
Nor in the blowing of horns.
To live uncontaminated
Amid worldly temptations
Is to find the secret of religion.

Religion lies not in empty words.
He who regards all men as equal is religious.
Religion lies not in wandering outside
To tombs and places of cremation,
Nor in postures of contemplation.
Religion lies not in roaming abroad,
Nor in bathing at places of pilgrimage.
To live uncontaminated
Amid worldly temptations
Is to find the secret of religion.[33]

Suhi, M.1, p.730

The *siddhas* made their obeisance to the Guru in reverence. His teaching delivered many in this region from superstition.

From Gorakhmata, the Guru went to Prayag (modern Allahabad), a centre of Hindu pilgrimage on the confluence of the Ganges and the Jamuna. A large number of pilgrims were taking a holy bath in the river, as it was a day of religious importance. Sitting in the midst of the milling crowds, Guru Nanak raised a song in praise of the Divine. Several of the pilgrims were attracted by him and stood enthralled by his sweet music. A priest who had been watching the scene came hurriedly to the Guru and said, "Time is running out, and you have yet to take your bath. Let not this opportunity slip away, lest your sins should remain unwashed." In reply, the Guru asked, "By bathing the body, how does one wash away one's sins? How will the impurity of the heart be cleansed by it?" And then the Guru broke out into another song: "Who was ever made pure by washing the body? They are truly pure in whose heart dwells the Lord...."

The sacred city of Benares (now called Varanasi) was the next important halt. Here Guru Nanak saw learned pundits reading scriptures with pupils sitting around them. He also saw Vaishnavites worshipping stones and bare-bodied ascetics practicing various forms of penance. Some sat in postures of meditation in the cemetery.[34]

Guru Nanak's apparel attracted notice, for it was neither of a householder, nor of a hermit. A leading pundit, Chatur Das, approached him with the question: "What faith do you profess? You neither wear the necklace of *tulsi* (holy basil), nor do you carry any *saligram* (the devotee's stone). You have no rosary to count the beads, nor a mark of white clay on your forehead." In answer the Guru uttered the following hymn:

> Let God's name be the *saligram* thou adorest,
> And good deeds the rosary of *tulsi* beads
> Around thy neck.
> Seek divine grace
> And let this be thy raft's anchor.
> Why waste thy time watering barren land
> And plastering walls built on sand?

Let good deeds be the string of vessels
To draw water from the well
And yoke thy mind to the wheel.
Distil the nectar
And irrigate with it the land.
Then wilt thou be owned by the Gardener.

Basant Hindol, M.1, p.1171

Chatur Das, still proud of his learning, invited the Guru to stay in Benares and learn the various branches of secular knowledge. The Guru replied that for him only one Word was of real significance, to realize God within oneself.

The famous long composition of fifty-four stanzas called *Dakhani Onkar* was uttered at Benares, according to *Puratan Janamsakhi*. It enunciated the nature of the true One and of His creation. This gave a new understanding to Chatur Das, who fell at the Guru's feet and became his follower.

There is a tradition that Guru Nanak met Kabir. According to *Meharban Janamsakhi*, they met at the time of the Guru's Benares visit. The Kabir Panthis also believed that the two knew each other. If there ever was a meeting between them, Benares was the most likely place.[35] Another view is that the meeting took place in 1506 near Pusa.[36] Macauliffe, however, does not subscribe to the belief that the two ever met. He holds that Kabir was "dead but not forgotten" when the Guru arrived at Benares. The meeting involves no chronological difficulty, although positive evidence is lacking.

After Benares, Guru Nanak went to Patna, Ayodhya and Gaya.[37] He held discourses with *bhagats* and pundits at Ayodhya. He spoke at Gaya on the futility of the Hindu ceremonies for the benefit of ancestors.

The *janamsakhis*[38] lead us next to a country called Kauru or Kavaru, ruled by a queen named Nur Shah. This country was dominated by women well known for their skill in magic and incantation. It is said that they tried their black magic on the Guru, but it had no effect on him because of his spiritual power. Eventually, the queen and the magicians became his disciples. Kauru is usually identified with Kamrup, situated in western Assam. The tradition about Guru Nanak's visit to Assam is a strong one, despite the incongruous details given by credulous narrators of later times.

Guru Nanak's visit to Puri is mentioned in all the *janamsakhis* except the *Puratan*. Here, according to *Chaitanya Bhagvat*, he met Sri Chaitanya Mahaprabhu, the well-known Vaishnavite saint.[39] The two together led the congregation in devotional music or *kirtan*. The Guru was accompanied by his disciple Sarang.* Rup and Sanatan, two brothers, and Jagai and Madhai also participated in the *kirtan* and divine dance.[40]

Some other names mentioned in *Chaitanya Bhagvat* of those who joined the congregational singing are Nagar Purshotam, Jangli, Nandni and Gopal Guru. For the last mentioned, the Guru is said to have developed deep affection. There was also Nityanand Prabhu, who was considered to be an incarnation of Balram, the brother of Lord Krishna.[41]

The meeting between Guru Nanak and Sri Chaitanya appears to have left a deep impression on Vaishnavite scholars, and its memory lingered for over a hundred years, as is clear from the following invocation:

Salutation to Guru Nanak, who is the enlightened and learned in all scriptures, and is the Guru of all gurus.[42]

---

*The name 'Sarang' probably refers to Mardana as the *sarangi* or rebec player. His proper name was unlikely to be known to the Bengali author.

Guru Nanak seems to have halted in the district of Balasore in Orissa, either on his way to Puri or on his return
journey to the Punjab from Puri. There is a local tradition
that Guru Nanak visited a village called Sangat near Bhadrak
in the Balasore district, as seems evident from the name of
the village.

Soon after his departure from Puri, in about 1510, Guru
Nanak probably returned to Talwandi. This tallies with our
chronological scheme and also with the twelve-year sojourn
mentioned in the *Puratan Janamsakhi*. However, he did not
return to his father's house, nor did he see his wife. Accompanied by Mardana, he again set out on his travels. This time he
decided to cover a part of the Punjab before starting for distant
parts of India. Crossing the rivers Ravi and Chenab, he made
his way to Pakpattan. Here, it is said, he met Sheikh Brahm
(Ibrahim), the incumbent and twelfth in line of Sheikh Farid
of Shakargunj, and delivered discourses.[43] Nanak next moved
to Dipalpur, Kanganpur, Kasur, Patti, Goindwal, Sultanpur,
Vairoval, Jalalabad and Kari Pathandi. At the last mentioned
place, many Pathans became his disciples.[44] He then went to
Batala, from where after a short stay he visited Pasrur, Sialkot,
Mithankot and eventually Lahore.

Lahore was the concluding point of his first *udasi*. According to the *Puratan Janamsakhi (Hafizabad Vali)*, Guru Nanak
settled for some time in a village called Kartarpur, on the
right bank of the Ravi, which was founded by a 'millionaire
official'.[45] It is said that the Guru wanted to provide a home
for his family before going out of the Punjab on another
long journey. The family had been staying so far at Pakhoke
with his father-in-law.[46] Here, he met Bhai Buddha, who was
then a child. Also, it was possibly here that he composed the
Barah Maha.

Second journey

Guru Nanak's second journey was to the South, according to *Puratan Janamsakhi*. He is said to have been accompanied by two *Jats* named Saido and Gheho. Some fanciful stories, which seem to be based on curious ideas of the distant lands in the South, have been woven around this visit by the authors of the *janamsakhis*. It is said that the Guru's companions met a mythical Muslim saint, Khwaja Khizar, in Dhanasari, an unidentified country. Guru Nanak himself held a discourse with a Jain priest. Subsequently, he went to an island in the ocean, ruled by a tyrant who tried to cook the Guru in a cauldron. Later, Guru Nanak had an encounter with a hypocritical *pir*, whom he admonished about the futility of barren formalism.

These stories may not have any historical value, but they aim at impressing on the reader the strange and hostile environment in which the Guru and his companions moved.

Guru Nanak's visit to Sri Lanka, however, is based on firm ground.[47] Sri Lanka was not unknown to enterprising Indian merchants by this time. Before the Guru arrived there, one of them had established his residence in the country and had translated a hymn of Guru Nanak for the benefit of the king. The ruler of the island at the time of the Guru's visit was Dharmapara-kramabahu. Epigraphic evidence shows that a religious teacher by the name of Jinacharya met the king and tried to convert him. The king agreed to embrace his creed provided he succeeded in defeating in debate Dharmakirti-sthavira, who was *sanghraj* or high priest of the country.

It is said that in a public debate on the supreme personal deity and on the eternal nature of the soul, Jinacharya defeated his adversary by a majority of the votes of those who formed the audience. Later, however, the Brahmins ranged themselves against Jinacharya, for various reasons. He insisted on monotheism and denounced idol worship. Moreover, he refused to recognize the superiority of the Brahmins, based on the caste system. Eventually, he left the capital and the question of the king's conversion did not arise.[48]

Although in the epigraphic account the name 'Nanak' does not appear, there is little doubt that the episode relates to the Guru's experience in Sri Lanka.

Guru Nanak concluded his second journey by returning to the Punjab along the west coast. On his return journey he addressed congregations at various places.[49] The *Meharban Janamsakhi* mentions visits of the Guru to Ujjain, the Vindhya Mountains, the Narmada River, Bikaner and Saurashtra. However, the other *janamsakhis* are silent about all these places except Bikaner.

Third journey

The third *udasi* of Guru Nanak was towards the north. On this journey he was accompanied by Hassu, a smith, and Sihan, a calico-printer. Achal Batala* was the Guru's first halt, according to Macauliffe. Here he held a long discourse with the *jogis* and composed the *Sidh Gosht*.[50] Bhai Gurdas, however, does not subscribe to this view and holds that this incident occurred much later, after the Guru's tour in the west.

According to *Puratan Janamsakhi*, Guru Nanak proceeded from Achal Batala to Srinagar in Kashmir. There he stayed for some days and many became his followers by coming in contact with him and listening to his discourses.

From Srinagar the Guru penetrated the Himalayas, and scaled many high peaks on his journey. Tradition says that he reached Ladakh and Tibet, but there is not yet any epigraphic confirmation of these visits.[51] The *Puratan Janamsakhi* states that the Guru reached Mount Sumeru, where he held

---

* About four miles east of Batala, Gurdaspur District, Punjab.

a discourse with *siddhas*. Bhai Gurdas has also given a long account of this discourse. All the important *janamsakhis* accept this encounter, although there are minor differences in regard to detail. Despite this unanimity of description of the main incident, McLeod wholly rejects it. He stresses that Mount Sumeru has no real existence and is found only in legend. He rejects the identification of Mount Sumeru with Mount Kailas or some other peak, not realizing that it would be unfair to expect exact knowledge of the geography of the Himalayas from either Bhai Gurdas or the authors of the *janamsakhis*.

Fourth journey

The Guru's fourth *udasi* commenced with his visit to Hasan Abdal,* from where he proceeded westwards.[52] At Hasan Abdal, it is said that the Guru raised his hand to stop a rock that was rolling down the hillside with great force. The rock had been pushed loose by an angry Muslim faqir. Tradition says that an impression of the Guru's hand was left on the rock, and the place came to be known as Panja Sahib (the holy palm). McLeod rejects outright the entire story as "without features which suggest a substratum of truth."[53]

For nearly a century, Guru Nanak's visit to the Arabian countries has been looked upon with scepticism. Recently however, evidence confirming the fact that he did indeed visit this region has become available.[54] Bhai Gurdas has given details about the Guru's activities in Mecca and Baghdad, and there is a mention of Medina as well.[55] In the *Puratan* and *Meharban Janamsakhis*, however, there is no reference to Medina or Baghdad, but a visit to Mecca is mentioned. But Baghdad figures in the *Gyan Ratnavali* as well as in the *Bala*

---

* A village in Attak District in Pakistan.

tradition. Macauliffe has accepted the traditional version of the visits to Mecca, Medina and Baghdad.[56]

The account given by Bhai Gurdas of Guru Nanak's visit to Mecca is both graphic and authentic. He states that the Guru proceeded to Mecca in the garb of a Muslim faqir. He was attired in blue garments, carried a staff in his hand, a book under his arm, a water mug, and a prayer mat. When he reached Mecca, he 'sat in a mosque', and at night while sleeping he put his feet towards the *mehrab*. A man named Jivan[*] pointed out to him that it was a 'sinful posture'. "Please turn my legs in the direction in which God does not exist," said Guru Nanak. All were astounded by his words of profound wisdom, and paid homage to him. The Muslim divines then began to question him on religious matters. One of the questions they asked was, "Who is greater, the Hindu or the Muslim?" He replied, "Without good deeds neither of them is a true Hindu or a Muslim, and neither will find refuge in God's court. In ignorance the Hindus and Muslims are jealous of each other, not realizing that Ram and Rahim are one."

According to Bhai Gurdas, Guru Nanak went to Baghdad from Mecca. Although we have no reliable account of his activities there, this should not put any doubt in our mind about his visit to Baghdad. The testimony of two inscriptions found recently is sufficiently convincing. One of them, on a wall behind a platform, has been translated as follows:

In memory of the Guru, that is the divine Master Baba Nanak Fakir Aulia, this building has been raised anew, with the help of seven Saints. [Chronogram] The blessed disciple has produced a spring of grace – year 927 A.H. (1520–21 A.D.).[57]

---

[*] Rukn-ud-Din, according to *Puratan Janamsakhi*.

The second inscription was found by Swami Ananda Acharya in a shrine outside Baghdad. He has translated it as a part of one of his poems:

> Here spake the Hindu Guru Nanak to Faqir Bahlol, and for these sixty winters, since the Guru left Iran, the soul of Bahlol has rested on the Master's word like a bee poised on a dawn-lit honey rose.[58]

A visit to Medina is practically implied in the visit to Mecca. There is no valid reason why the Guru should have left out the one holy city after visiting the other. Bhai Gurdas makes a short reference to it: "Having subdued the fortress of Baghdad, he overcame all, in Mecca and Medina." No further details are given.

The Guru had virtually reached the concluding part of his last *udasi*. He returned to Kartarpur and put aside his garments of renunciation.

It is widely believed that Guru Nanak was present at Sayidpur when the town was sacked by Babar in 1520. The main source for this view is Guru Nanak's own hymns in the Adi Granth, collectively known as *Babar Vani*.[59] The Guru's intense sensitivity to human suffering has brought forth words of compassion articulated in forceful verses of poignant feeling marked with a tinge of protest. In one of the hymns he expresses himself thus:

> The tresses that adorned these lovely heads
> And were parted with vermilion,
> Have been shorn with cruel shears:
> Dust has been thrown on their shaven heads.
> They lived in ease in palaces,

Now they must beg by the roadside,
Having no place for their shelter....
Their beauty and wealth
Were once their greatest assets,
Their beauty and wealth
Are their greatest enemies now;
Barbarous soldiers have taken them prisoner
And disgraced them....
Desecration and desolation
Follow in the footsteps
Of the great Mughal, Babar.
None, none in Hindustan
Can eat his supper in peace.
For the Muslim woman
The hour of prayer is past,
For the Hindu
The time of worship is gone....
Few, some very few,
From this havoc return home....
Many are lost forever,
And weeping and anguish
Are the lot of those who survive.
Ah, Nanak, how completely helpless
Mere men are.[60]

Asa, M.1, Ashtpadi, p.417

So impressed is McLeod with this true-to-life picture of the great holocaust that he says:

There is in his description of agony and destruction a vividness and a depth of feeling, which can be explained only as expressions of a direct personal experience.[61]

Final years

The last period of Guru Nanak's life covers the years 1520–1539, from the time of the sacking of Sayidpur to the time of his death. He spent this entire period at Kartarpur on the banks of the Ravi, where he led the life of a teacher of Truth in the garb of a householder.

As Bhai Gurdas says:

> He gave utterance to words of divine wisdom,
> Bringing light and driving away darkness.
> He imparted understanding
> Through discourses and conversation;
> The unstruck music* of devotional ecstasy
> Resounded endlessly![62]

"Those who followed him cast off the burden of the Atharva Veda."[63] He now lived in the highly exalted condition known as *sahaj*.

Mention may be made here of two features of far-reaching import associated with the last phase of the Guru's life. They are the institutions of *langar* or community kitchen, and of *seva* or voluntary physical labour. The *langar* symbolized equality, humility and brotherhood. All who engaged themselves in one task or another in community service ate a common meal together, sitting in rows without distinction of caste or creed, rich or poor. Even the visitors to the colony joined them, thus making a fraternity with an intensely religious outlook. *Seva* consisted of such activities as drawing water from the well, bringing fuel, grinding corn, cooking food, distributing it, washing utensils and sweeping floors; and the most menial chore was considered the most rewarding.

---

* Anahad Shabd.

No dramatic incidents took place during this last period of the cloistered life of Guru Nanak. Nothing occurred that could serve as material for the storytelling proclivities of the authors of the *janamsakhis*. Only two events have been considered noteworthy. The Guru lost his faithful companion Mardana; and he found a devoted disciple in Lehna of Khadur, whom he eventually nominated as his successor.

Mardana, who was now in his seventy-sixth year, fell ill and grew so weak that all hope of his recovery was lost. Guru Nanak asked Mardana, who was born in a Muslim family, how he wished his body to be disposed of. He replied that it be disposed of as the Guru wished. Then the Guru said, "Shall I make you a tomb, so that you become famous in the world?" Mardana answered, "When the Guru is releasing me from the bodily sepulchre, why should he entomb me in stone?" The following morning he passed away, and his body was consigned to the River Ravi.[64] Thus ended the remarkable career of the minstrel who had spent forty-seven years of his life in the company of his Guru, and had roamed the four corners of the world as his shadow. So close was he to Guru Nanak that "the association of none other in Talwandi, whether of the family or a neighbour, pleased him more than Mardana's."[65]

Guru Arjan gave Mardana signal honour by including three of his hymns in the Adi Granth. Here is one of them:

> In the vat of *kalyug*
> Lust is the wine
> And mind is the one
> That drinks it.
> The cup of anger
> Is abrim with attachment,
> And one's ego
> Is the cup-bearer;

In the false company of avarice
One comes to ruin.

Make good deeds your vat,
Truth the molasses
And *Nam* your wine;
Let virtue be your bread,
Continence your butter
And modesty your meat.
This, O Nanak,
Is the true spiritual food;
Received through the Guru,
It cleanses the mind.

Var Bihagara, Mardana, p.553

The arrival of Lehna at Kartarpur occurred in an auspicious manner. Born at Sarai Naga, near Muktsar, he moved in his early life to Khadur, a village about sixty miles from Kartarpur. In Khadur lived a devotee of Guru Nanak named Jodha, on whose lips the word 'Guru' was frequently heard by the residents. They generally made fun of his piety, for they were worshippers of the goddess Durga.[66] Every year they made a pilgrimage to Jawalamukhi, in the lower Himalayas. One day Lehna heard Jodha recite the Guru's hymns and was greatly moved. He decided to stop at Kartarpur while on his way to Jawalamukhi along with the rest of the party.

In his very first meeting with the Master all his questions and doubts were resolved. He found in the Guru's company a solace and a joy that he had never known before. His quest and journeyings came to an end. He threw away the jingle bells with which he used to dance before the goddess. The Guru asked him his name, and he replied, "Lehna." "Your debt was here, so God has brought you hither," said the Guru.[67] The word *lena* in Punjabi means 'to receive', and from the Guru, Lehna received what was meant for him alone. In course of time, he was installed as the Guru's successor. "As Guru Baba Nanak was, even so Lehna became. As was the Guru, so was the disciple."[68]

Departure from the world

The account of the departure of Guru Nanak from this world is given in a graphic manner in the *Puratan Janamsakhi*. When the Guru was advanced in years, he seemed to have made up his mind to leave the world. Appointing Lehna his successor, he addressed him as Angad ('part of himself').[69] The news spread that the Guru was about to leave on his final journey. People began to gather for his last darshan.

Guru Nanak's wife and others – relatives as well as disciples – were filled with grief, and began to weep. The Guru pacified them and exhorted them not to weep. He uttered the following hymn:

> Hail to the Creator, the eternal Sovereign,
> Who hath put each one in the world to his task!
> When the span is run out
> And the measure is full,
> The soul departeth the body.
> As the word arriveth and the soul leaveth,
> All family and friends weep.
> The body and soul become separated
> When the days are at an end, O mother.
> By thy deeds as thou acquired in the past,
> So hast thou received thy portion now.
> Hail to the Creator, the eternal Sovereign,
> Who hath put each one in the world to his task!

Remember the Lord, brothers;
This is the way all must go.
Transient are the attachments of this world,
Certain is the journey henceforward.
Certain is the journey henceforward
Like a guest's;
Then why abide in ego?
Repeat the Name of Him alone
By cherishing whom
Thou shalt meet happiness
In the end.
Ranks of this world
Will not be recognized in the next;
None knows what will befall him there.
Remember the Lord, brothers;
This is the way all must go.

What pleaseth the omnipotent Lord shall happen,
This creation is but His instrument.
The Creator who is eternal pervadeth
Sea, land and space.
The Creator who is eternal
Is unknowable and infinite,
And none can know His limit.
Fruitful indeed is the coming of those
Who give themselves single-mindedly to Him.
He destroyeth and He Himself createth,
And by His order He adorneth.

That weeping is acceptable, O Nanak,
Which is in love for Him.
Vain is the weeping, unmindful the world,
Which weepeth for earthly attachment.

In such weeping one torments the body
Without understanding.
Whoso cometh here must also go,
Vain it is to dwell in ego.
That weeping is acceptable, O Nanak,
Which is in love for Him.

Vadhans, M.1, pp.578–579

Then the disciples gathered there began to sing hymns. The whole atmosphere was filled with the resonance of holy music. The Guru went into a trance and then, according to *Puratan Janamsakhi*, uttered the hymn called *Barah Maha* (twelve months). This poem depicts the intense longing of the soul for union with the Lord, in lyrical verse. The main symbolism is that of the bride's yearning for her husband.

After the singing was over, the Guru handed the book of his hymns to Guru Angad. The night was now turning into dawn. The last moments of the Guru are described in the *Janamsakhi* thus:

The Muslims began to say, 'We shall bury him.' The Hindus said, 'We shall cremate him.' The Guru spoke, 'Put ye flowers on both sides – those of the Hindus on the right and those of the Muslims on the left. They whose flowers remain fresh will have the choice.' Then he asked the *sangat* to recite God's praises. The *Sohila* was read:

Where the Lord's praise is sung
And where men contemplate on Him,
There shouldst thou go
And sing the song of praise
And remember the Creator.
Sing thou praise of my fearless Lord.

How precious to one is the song
Which bringeth everlasting comfort!
Day in, day out He looketh after His creation,
The universal Giver careth for one and all.
None can appraise His gifts,
Then who can appraise the Giver Himself?
Fixed is the year and the day of the marriage;
Friends, pour oil upon the threshold
To welcome the bride,
And pronounce blessing for me
That I may meet the Lord too.
The writ goeth round every house,
And every day men are called forth.
May we remember Him
Who hath the authority to summon,
For the day, O Nanak, is not far.[70]

Sohila, Gauri, M.1. p.12

In the end, the epilogue of the *Japji* was recited. "The Guru then pulled the sheet over himself and lay down. The assembly paid obeisance. When the sheet was lifted, there was nothing but the flowers. The flowers of both the Hindus and the Musalmans remained fresh. The Hindus took theirs and the Musalmans theirs. The whole *sangat* fell on their knees."[71]

On September 7, 1539,* Guru Nanak gave up his mortal frame, leaving a rich spiritual heritage for the succeeding generations to draw upon.

---

*This date tallies with the date in the Kartarpur manuscript of the Adi Granth, which is the original copy of the scripture as compiled by Guru Arjan. Moreover, by tradition, it is on this date that the death anniversary of the Guru is observed at Dera Baba Nanak. The *janamsakhis* give varying dates of his death, but 7 September 1539 is accepted by the *Bala Janamsakhi*, as also by McLeod in *Guru Nanak and the Sikh Religion* (p.101).

The devotees of the Guru raised some monuments in his memory, but they were all swept away by the encroaching Ravi. It is said that it was in accord with the Guru's own wish. His followers and descendants then built a new town, called Dera Baba Nanak, on the other side of the river, and began to live there. Most of the present inhabitants of this town owe their origin to those founding fathers.

Teachings

Teachings of
Guru Nanak

Seeing without eyes,
Hearing without ears,
Walking without feet,
Working without hands,
Speaking without tongue,
Thus dying while living,
O Nanak, know this
As the way unto the Lord
To be attained through His cosmic law.

Majh-ki-Var, M.1, Shalok, M.2, p. 139

From *Shabd** cometh the earth,
From *Shabd* cometh the sky,
From *Shabd* emanateth all light;
The whole creation resteth on *Shabd*,
And this *Shabd*, O Nanak, resideth within man.

Puratan Janamsakhi, p.137

Without the *Satguru* no one ever found God,
Without the *Satguru* no one ever shall.

Asa-di-Var, M.1, p.466

---

* For explanation of terms, see Glossary.

Revolt against ritualism

When the world is engulfed in the darkness of ignorance and caught in the thraldom of passion, saints and prophets appear to redeem it from these evils. Guru Nanak was born at a time when the true spirit of religion had vanished. The Hindus and the Muslims alike had come to identify religion with rituals and ceremonies. Practices such as wearing the sacred thread, applying streaks of saffron to the forehead, mechanical telling of beads, repetition of prayers without understanding them, and cruel sacrifice of animals and even of human beings to appease gods and goddesses had come to acquire the connotation of religion. The unity of Godhead had been lost in the worship of numerous small deities. Guru Nanak strongly denounced idol worship and begging, which he considered not only futile, but detrimental to the human spirit:

> In your house you keep an idol
> With its attendant gods;
> You wash it and worship it;
> You offer it *kungu*, sandal, and flowers;
> You fall at its feet
> And propitiate it to the utmost;
> Yet it is by continually begging of men
> That you clothe and support yourself.
> For such foolish acts you will receive
> The punishment of the foolish.
> The idol gives you not when you are hungry,
> Nor preserves you from death.
> It is like a foolish quarrel among the blind.
>
> *Sarang-ki-Var, M.4, Shalok M.1, p.1240*

Many Jains and Buddhists, too, were not quite free from these actions, where the concept of religion had been reduced to mere ritual. They had, as it were, lost the kernel of religion and had become content merely with its husk.

Guru Nanak came in the line of the great saints who emphasize only personal experience of the Divine as the core of true religion. He repudiated all caste distinctions, all narrow parochial divisions, and the ceremonial aspects that had come to characterize the religions of his time. He came to clear the minds of men of the cobwebs of superstition and bigotry. Nor was this all. He did not merely introduce reason into the examination of religious beliefs, which might have ended in the blind alley of scepticism. He had a positive message to give. This message was one of hope and cheer to dispel the all-pervading gloom of the skeptic and the cynic.

Supremacy of man

Guru Nanak gave a meaning to human life, and his teachings gave a direction to the attainment of the ultimate goal. Perhaps this message was not new, for it was ingrained in the scriptures and culture of ancient India, but gradually it had been lost over the centuries. He revived it in a manner that was both refreshing and emphatic. He impressed on his contemporaries that human life is not aimless like that of animals, which are born, which grow and then die. That, indeed, is not the purpose of human existence. Out of the myriads of biological species, it is given only to man to find a way out of the recurring process of birth, according to the theory of reincarnation and transmigration of the soul. There are eighty-four lakh forms of living beings and they are all going round in the never-ending cycle of birth and death. Indeed, the whole creation could be compared to a huge mansion with eighty-four lakhs of different apartments, none of which has an outlet except one. This one outlet is the human form. Thus, in the vast prisonhouse of this world, man alone has been endowed with the possibility

of finding release from it. Man is, then, qualitatively superior
to all other living species:

> Out of all the eighty-four lakh life forms
>   He created,
> To man He hath given the pride of place;
> For whosoever slippeth
> From his rung of the ladder
> Continues to suffer
> From the pangs of birth and death.
>
> *Maru, M.5, p.1075*

> Even the gods and goddesses pine
> For the human body,
> For within this body
> Resideth the Lord Himself.
>
> *Bhairo, Kabir, p.1159*

Not only does God live within the human body, but it
is only within this body that He manifests Himself. Thus it
is doubly blessed, for it contains Him and it reveals Him.
The Adi Granth says: "The temple of God is this body which
manifesteth the rarest gems of knowledge; but worldly men
know not at all that man can be the temple of God" (*Parbhati*,
M.3, p.1346). Likewise, "The human body is a beautiful town in
which you obtain the divine nectar" (*Kalyam*, M.4, p.1323).

It is, thus, folly to look for the divine Being outside. All
attempts to seek Him in temples, mosques and churches, in
forests and mountains, in plants, birds and animals are bound
to end in failure. Guru Nanak denounces all such attempts in
strong terms. As Guru Ram Das says: "Whosoever seeketh the
Lord elsewhere, and not in his own body, is verily a fool; in
delusion doth he wander from place to place, like the deer who,

in quest of his own musk, looketh into bushes and shrubs" (*Gauri-ki-Var*, M.4, p.309).

This assessment of the human form is not confined to Guru Nanak or even to the Indian scriptures. It is quite prominent in the Quran, for it puts man at the "top of the creation." Likewise, the Old Testament says, "God created man in His own image."[72] Thus Guru Nanak brought to the surface a truth that has been stated by almost all the great religions of the world, but which perhaps had been temporarily forgotten.

Mysticism

The focal point that lies at the centre of Guru Nanak's teachings is personal experience of the Divine. It is this experience that leads to the consummation of all desired ends. It takes one beyond the realm of time and space and all its attendant evils. It gives one release from the negative experiences of sorrow and suffering, gives release from the cycle of birth and death, and produces the positive states of bliss, beatitude and eternal peace. Since it is a state of timelessness, it is a state that has no beginning, no end, no growth, no decay. And since this consciousness transcends time, of necessity it also rises above the level of cause and effect, for these terms signify nothing but events that occur earlier and later in time.

This personal experience of the Divine, often called 'religious experience', is what the philosopher calls 'mystic experience'. Now what exactly is meant by mysticism? The word 'mysticism' is often used in a variety of ways that are loose and incorrect. For instance, it is sometimes identified with anything that is misty, foggy or vague. It is absurd, as Stace says, to associate mysticism "with what is misty" because of the similarity of sounds, for there is nothing misty, foggy or vague about mysticism, as it has a precise meaning.

Another absurd association is to relate mysticism with mystery-mongering. There is, of course, an etymological connection between 'mysticism' and 'mystery'; nevertheless, mysticism is not a kind of hocus-pocus. It has nothing to do with claims to the elucidation of sensational mysteries. Again, mysticism is not the same as what is commonly called the 'occult'. Nor has it anything to do with spiritualism or ghosts or table-turning. Nor does it stand for what are commonly called parapsychological phenomena, such as telepathy, telekinesis, clairvoyance or precognition. It is possible that mystics may sometimes claim to possess such powers, but even when they do, they are well aware that such powers are not part of the mystical experience. Such powers, if they exist, could be possessed by persons who are not mystics.

Finally, visions and voices are not to be included among mystical phenomena, though it may be that mystically inclined persons also see visions and hear voices. For instance, certain persons in history, such as Socrates, Mohammad and Joan of Arc, are supposed to have heard voices; however, these occurrences cannot be classed as mystical experiences. If these persons are to be considered mystics, they are not to be classed as such because of these voices. In fact, mystics who also saw visions did not themselves regard such visions as mystical experiences. A case in point is St. Teresa of Avila, who frequently had visions, but knew they were not the experiences she desired.

William James, in his book, *The Varieties of Religious Experience*, has suggested that our normal consciousness is one particular kind of consciousness; all about it, but parted from it by the flimsiest of screens, lie potential forms of consciousness entirely different. This statement quite fits mystic consciousness, for it is quite unlike our everyday consciousness and is wholly incommensurable with it. Our ordinary consciousness is like a building with three floors. The ground floor consists of physical sensations – sights, sounds, smells, tastes, touch sensations and organic sensations. The second floor consists of images that we believe to be mental copies of our sensations. The third floor contains the intellect, which is the faculty of conceptualising. This level is characterized by reasoning and abstract thinking. Now all these three levels constitute the entire cognitive aspect of ordinary consciousness. Arising from these basic cognitive elements and dependent upon them are emotions, desires and volitions. In order to have a name for this entire structure, we call it our 'sensory-intellectual consciousness'.

Now, mystic consciousness is qualitatively and radically different from this kind of consciousness. It is not merely that it involves different kinds of sensations, thoughts or feelings. For instance, some insects, such as the bee, can perceive ultra-violet and infrared; some animals, such as the dog, can hear sounds that are inaudible to the human ear; and some animals even have a sixth sense different from any of our five senses. These are no doubt sensations different from any that we have, but they are still sensations. The mystical consciousness, however, is devoid of any sensation at all, as also of concepts or thoughts. It is not a sensory-intellectual consciousness at all, and so it cannot be described or analysed in terms of any of the elements of the sensory-intellectual consciousness, with which it is totally unrelated.

This, indeed, is the reason that mystics always say that their experiences are ineffable. All our words in all languages are the product of the sensory-intellectual consciousness, which expresses its elements or some combination of them. But since none of these elements is found in mystic consciousness (with the doubtful exception of emotions), it is felt to be impossible to describe mystic experiences in any words whatever.

The mystic experience

So far we have confined our account primarily to what mysticism is not. We shall now try to seize upon, in a positive manner, the common characteristics that are fundamental to all true mystical experiences. Although mystics are born in different parts of the world, in different ages and in different cultures, the 'mystic experience' they describe in their writings is identical. The descriptions of the mystical experience may differ superficially in terms of the particular imagery used by mystics of different cultural backgrounds, but the agreements are more basic and important, while the differences are superficial and of relatively little importance.

The most important, the central characteristic, in which all fully developed mystical experiences agree, is that they involve *an ultimate non-sensuous unity in all things*, a oneness or a One, which the senses or the reason cannot penetrate. This may be considered to be the definitive characteristic that serves to distinguish mystic consciousness from all other forms of experience. To quote Guru Nanak: "One alone pervadeth, O Nanak, no second was there, nor ever shall be" (*Gauri-ki-Var, M.1*, p.250). In no less emphatic terms, Namdev says: "All is God, all is God; without God is naught" (*Asa, Namdev*, p.485). Similarly, Rumi says, "He Himself is the pot, and Himself the pot-maker, and Himself even the clay of the pot."[73]

It may be pointed out here that to call the mystic experience an apprehension of the Unity is considered by some mystics an inadequate, if not an incorrect expression, since it supposes a division between the subject and the object. They insist that we should say that the experience is of oneness. For instance, Plotinus writes:

We should not speak of seeing, but instead of seen and seer, speak boldly of a simple Unity, for in this seeing we neither distinguish nor are there two.

Another salient feature of all true mystic experience is that it is accompanied by a strong affective tone, which is generally described as bliss, blessedness or beatitude. Guru Nanak describes it thus:

> They who are imbued with the Name
> Remain intoxicated with bliss night and day.
> Through the Name alone do they find peace.
> *Ramkali, Sidh Gosht, M.1, p.946*

> Says Nanak, Thy devotees hunger to praise Thee;
> Thy true Name is their mainstay.
> They are in a state of beatitude day and night.
> I am the dust of the feet
> Of these virtuous ones.
> *Asa-di-Var, M.1, p.466*

This feeling is qualitatively different from empirical pleasure. For the pleasures of the senses are both limited in their range and relative in their scope. They soon satiate, and indeed they can change into painful states. Moreover, they are always relative to certain unpleasant conditions. For example, the pleasure of eating is relative to a state of hunger, which is not pleasant. In contrast to this, mystic bliss is both unlimited and absolute. It suffers no satiety or decline. It has the character of 'permanence' in it. And it is absolute, because it is not subject to or preceded by an unpleasant state.

Finally, the mystic experience is marked by a sense of supreme value. It gives the mystic the realization that he has attained the ultimate Truth. Guru Nanak says:

Rare is the one who practices the Truth,
By the guru's grace;
Thus cease his comings and goings.

Parbhati, M.1, p.1344

Unutterable is the Word of God,
Which leads to the state of nirvana;
And rare is the one who realizes it
Through the guru's grace.

Bilawal, M.1, p.844

The mystic then feels that for the first time he is truly alive. Simultaneously it dawns upon him that this sensory spatio-temporal world is unreal, a mere appearance, which he often calls an illusion or a delusion:

He alone lives in whom the Lord abides;
None else is alive, O Nanak.

Majh, M.1, p.142

The world's a pasture
Where we spend a few days,
Playing and enjoying
In utter darkness;
The juggler juggles away,
Like a sleeper
Murmuring in his dream.

Maru, M.1, p.1023

Compared to the reality he has now experienced, the phenomenal world is a passing shadow:

In the true palace
The master has revealed
The Imperceptible to me;
Eternal is that palace,
No shadow of *maya*, this.

Gauri, m.1, p.228

Spinoza has remarked that the path to salvation lies on the razor's edge, but then what is ultimately attained is of supreme value and is worth all the trouble that one has to undergo. As Guru Nanak puts it, the mystic experience enables one finally to overcome all the barriers and impurities associated with the mind:

The five restive thieves*
Are kept in check,
The ego is eliminated,
Sinful seeing and evil thoughts
Flee away;
Such is the effect
Of mystic knowledge.

Parbhati, m.1, p.1324

Philosophers generally distinguish between two main types of mystical experience. This is the view both of Walter Stace and Rudolf Otto, for instance, as expressed in their books, *Mysticism* and *Philosophy and Mysticism East and West*. They are called 'extrovertive mystical experience' and 'introvertive mystical experience', and both these varieties are found in all the higher cultures. Both of them are apprehensions of the One, but they

---

* The five senses of perception.

reach it in different ways. The extrovertive way looks outward through the physical senses into the external world and finds the One there. The introvertive way looks inward through introspection and finds the One at the bottom of the self. The latter is far more important than the former and is the major strand in the history of mysticism.

The extrovertive mystic, with his physical senses, continues to perceive the world as a multiplicity of objects, but he sees these objects transfigured in such a manner that the Unity shines through them. This is the nuclear point, around which all other common characteristics revolve. This implies a second universal characteristic, namely that the experience has an objective reference and is not merely an inner and subjective state of the mystic. This is what James calls 'noetic quality'. A third universal characteristic is paradoxicality. It seems to disregard the commonly accepted laws of logic. The fourth characteristic is bliss, beatitude or joy, and a sense of supreme value. Along with it is the feeling that what is apprehended is holy, sacred or divine. This is what makes the mystic take the experience as experience of God. And last, it is said to be ineffable. Such expressions as 'inexpressible', 'unutterable', 'impossible to describe', occur frequently in mystic writings all over the world.

Introvertive mysticism*
The basic psychological facts about the introvertive type of mystical experience are in principle easy to state and undoubtedly

---

* It may be noted that on pages 56–67 of this book, the late Prof. Puri quoted from *Mysticism and Philosophy* by W. T. Stace and paraphrased his thinking on the subject, though differing from him in some key areas. The publishers acknowledge the work of Stace that has supported Prof. Puri's work: pp. 85–88 in Stace's section on introvertive mysticism, pp. 326–329 in his section on mystical theory and ethics, and pp. 341–342 in the section on mysticism and religion.

in essence they are the same all the world over, in all cultures, religions, places and ages. They are, however, so extraordinary and paradoxical that they are bound to strain belief when suddenly presented to one who is not prepared for them.

The introvertive mystic claims that he closes the outlets of the physical senses so that no sensations can reach consciousness. This would seem to be easy in the case of the eyes, ears, nose and tongue, but would be difficult in the case of the sense of touch and the organic sensations. However, the mystic claims to achieve this by constant and hard practice.

Having eliminated all sensations, the mystic next excludes from consciousness all sensuous images, and then all abstract thoughts, reasoning, processes, volitions and other particular mental contents. One may ask, what then would be left of consciousness? In the absence of any mental content whatsoever, there would be a complete emptiness, a void, a vacuum. One would suppose *a priori* that consciousness would then entirely lapse and one would fall asleep or become unconscious. But the introvertive mystics unanimously assert – and there are thousands of them all over the world – that they have attained to a complete vacuum of particular mental contents, and what then emerges is a state of pure consciousness. It is pure in the sense that it is not the consciousness of any empirical content. It has no content except itself. And this self-realization is often eventually spoken of as God-realization.

Jalal-ud-din Rumi describes the same process when he says:

> O close thou thine eyes, thine ears and thy lips, and if thou
> dost not behold the secret of God; then laugh at me.[74]

Guru Ram Das likewise refers to the insipid pleasures of the senses and points to the bliss that transcends them when he says:

Nine doors there are,
And tasteless are all the nine,
For the real nectar droppeth
Inside the tenth.

Kalyan, м.4, p.1323

The paradox involved in this experience of the undifferen-tiated Unity is that there should be a positive experience that has no positive content – an experience that is both some-thing and nothing. Stace calls it the plenum-vacuum paradox of mysticism.

The mystic also sometimes expresses it by saying that he gets rid of the stream of consciousness, only to bring to light the Unity that holds the manifold of the stream together. This undifferentiated Unity is the essence of the introvertive mysti-cal experience.

All this goes against the philosophy of David Hume, who stresses that the self is to be known as some particular mental content, for "I can never catch myself at any time without a perception."[75] Hume concludes from this that there is no such thing as a self or ego, and that a person is "nothing but a bundle or collection of different perceptions."[76] The substantial self, which the mystic affirms and Hume denies, is what Kant called the transcendental unity of apperception.

How can we reach this extraordinary psychological condi-tion? Methods and techniques for attaining it were not only discovered, but worked out in detail in India long ago, even before the age of the Upanishads. These techniques comprise the various practices and kinds of yoga. Apart from certain physical disciplines, such as breathing exercises, there has to be a great and continual effort at the control and discipline of the mind. In the West among mystics, these methods have not been basically very different. Of course, Christian mystics, such as St. Teresa, have emphasized the importance of prayer or 'orison', but this does not consist in begging favours but in strenuous efforts to obtain a direct experience of the divine Being, in mystical ecstasy. And, according to them, union with God normally occurs when all the empirical contents of mind have been eliminated and the empty ground of the self in pure consciousness has been reached.

From the above it is obvious that the introvertive type of mystical consciousness is usually acquired after long years of effort and does not come spontaneously. In rare cases, spontaneous introvertive experiences do occur, but they are not the rule.

Some Western thinkers, such as Walter Stace and Rudolf Otto, seem to hold the view that the two kinds of mystic consciousness, extrovertive and introvertive, are quite different and perhaps mutually exclusive. It appears to me that they are mistaken in their view. It is my contention that after experiencing the introvertive type of consciousness, which is by far the more important, the mystic also begins to experience the extrovertive type. For having divested himself of all empirical contents in a state of introvertive consciousness, the mystic not only discovers the undifferentiated Unity within himself as a reality, but of necessity he will also find outside an overriding unity behind all multiplicity. Without the inner experience of the One, he cannot see that all multiplicity as well as all movement of change is mere appearance. An example will illustrate the point. If a person has never seen the process of forming water by combining hydrogen and oxygen in certain proportions, he will have good common-sense arguments to support his doubts. For instance, hydrogen burns, and oxygen is an excellent supporter of combustion, while water is something that neither burns itself nor permits anything else to burn in it. Likewise the mystic who has had a vision of the undifferentiated Reality within himself will begin to see the hollowness of the 'many' that he perceives through his senses, and will start perceiving an all-pervading unity.

Almost all the general characteristics of the extrovertive type are common to introvertive mystic consciousness, except that the latter is experienced as unitary consciousness, from which the multiplicity of sensuous, conceptual or other empirical content has been excluded. This, of course, is the one basic, nuclear characteristic from which all other characteristics follow. From this also comes the second difference, that introvertive consciousness is non-spatial and non-temporal.

Although there is no clear-cut line of demarcation between the mystics of the East and the West in regard to the extrovertive and introvertive types, yet it is true that, by and large, the mystics of the East lay emphasis on the introvertive. They seem to hold the view that once that elevating state of unitary consciousness is attained through certain practices or yogas, all the rest will follow naturally. For instance, the perception of an all-pervading unity behind the apparent multiplicity of the world will be a natural consequence of inner realization. And this introvertive experience of the One, which transcends phenomena, is in turn the source and basis of all ethical and moral values.

Mysticism and ethics

The question of the relationship between mysticism and ethics may be divided into two parts – the philosophical and the historical or sociological. The philosophical problem is: What is the source of ethical rights and duties? The mystic claims that the ultimate source of ethical value lies in mysticism itself. The word 'source' is used here in the psychological rather than in the logical sense. This theory maintains that mystical experience is that part of human experience from which moral feelings flow. The second problem is concerned with the actual influence that mysticism tends to have, or actually has had, on leading a good life. Does it serve as an incentive for leading a noble life, or does it serve as an escape from its responsibilities?

The basis of the mystics' claim that the mystic experience is the source of all ethical values rests on the assertion that in such an experience the separateness of the individual self is abolished. It is the feeling of separateness that produces egoism, which is the source of much evil – conflict, avarice, aggressiveness, selfishness, hatred, malice, and the like. The necessary emotional counterpart of the separateness of the self is that basic hostility, which is characteristic of Hobbes's view of the inherent selfishness of man. On the other hand, the natural emotional counterpart of mystic consciousness is love, for there is no separateness of 'you and I' or 'you and he', and we are all one in the universal Self. And love, according to this theory, is not only the sole basis but also the sole command of morality. In the rapture of love, Guru Amar Das exclaims: "Say, whom shall we call good or bad, when all creatures are Thine?" (*Asa*, M.3, p.425).

An objection could be raised against this theory. The vast majority of men do not profess to have attained the mystic experience. In fact most are quite skeptical about it. Yet, such men not only exhibit love and unselfishness but in general lead highly ethical lives. How is this to be explained in terms of the ethical theory based on mysticism? Is there not a gap in the theory?

The theory explains this gap by saying that ethical feelings arise from a faint infiltration into their normal consciousness of a mystical core that remains latent in men but that influences their feelings and lives without their knowing or understanding it. Thus, if a debased man exhibits in his life any feelings of affection, sympathy or kindness, these must have their source in the mystical side of his nature. Such a mystical sense perhaps lies far below the threshold of his surface consciousness. Thus, to make the theory complete, it must be held that but for mysticism, whether latent or explicit, there could not be love or even mere kindly feeling in human life.

Moral action sometimes seems to be motivated by a sense of duty rather than by the feeling of sympathy or love for those whom it is intended to benefit. Kant, for instance, is of the view that a sense of duty is the only genuine source of morality. But it seems he did not make a proper analysis of the moral motives. For whatever Kant may have thought, it would seem that the sense of duty must ultimately be rooted in sympathetic feelings. Towards the suffering of those who are in close proximity, a sensitive man will feel intense sympathy. But, as the distance increases, the emotional feeling of the man will decrease proportionately. In the case of a wide social reform, such as the abolition of slavery, the initiator cannot visualize the individual sufferings of the numerous distant men whom he hopes to benefit. Since personal feelings of sympathy are impossible, it may be that the man must act on the principle of duty. The principle, adequately stated, would be: One should treat all individuals, even those who are wholly unknown to him, as if he felt personal love for them. The principle is a rational extension of feeling, which is possible because "reason is universal and is independent of proximity or distance, whereas feeling is particular and local." The point at issue is that a cruel and cold man, who is incapable of feeling love – if such a man could exist – would also be bereft of the sense of duty that so impressed Kant. This sense of duty is itself rooted in genuine love and sympathy, and is a kind of indirect or rationalized form of it.

It may therefore be said that love and compassion are necessary and immediate accompaniments of mystical experience. But this is not sufficient to establish the mystical theory of ethics. What is required to be shown is not only that love flows from mystical consciousness, but that it is the only source from which love flows into the world. It must be the sole fountain of love. It will not do to show that mysticism is one of the several sources from which love comes into men's hearts.

It seems to be impossible to prove this thesis. Men seem to love, for instance, their children or friends quite naturally and without being aware of any mystical elements in their natures. Even animals feel love for their young and act altruistically towards them. Now, it would look fantastic to attribute the feelings of love in a horse or a dog to mysticism. And yet Plato propounds this theory in some of his *Dialogues*. For instance, in the *Republic* he suggests that the 'Good', the *summum bonum*, is that which every soul possesses as the end of all her actions, dimly divining its existence, but perplexed and unable to grasp its nature.[77] In the *Symposium*, Plato suggests that in all living beings, including birds and beasts, the desire for procreation could be traced to the urge for making themselves immortal through generation, because "love is of the immortal…and generation always leaves behind a new existence in place of the old."[78] Thus, the source of all appetition in men as well as in animals is hunger for the immortal, the Good, the One.

Thus, the mystical theory of ethics maintains that all love, whether in men or animals, arises from the mystical experience, either explicit or latent. The mystical theory, then, supposes that mystical experience is latent in all living beings, but that in most men and animals it is profoundly submerged in the unconscious. However, it throws up influences above the threshold in the form of feelings of sympathy and love. These feelings partially break down the barriers that separate the individual selves. And if this breakdown were complete, it would lead to an actual identity of the 'I' and the 'he'. Guru Nanak describes it thus:

> He eliminates his ego from within himself,
> He effaces the sense of the other
> And becomes one with the Lord.
>
> *Ramkali, M.1, p.943*

> She alone is the true wife
> Who loses herself in the Lord.
>
> *Tukhari, M.1, p.1108*

> We attain the treasure of love through the guru
> By dwelling on the Essence;
> By decorating herself with the Word,
> The bride merges herself in the Lord –
> She finds her Spouse in her very own home
> Through the infinite love of the guru.
>
> *Sri, M.1, p.61*

Love therefore may be considered a dim groping towards that disappearance of the individual into the universal Self. We normally do not recognize our feelings of love as mystical because "the experience of the union of all separate selves in the one cosmic Self is hidden from most of us in the abyss of the subliminal."[79] The innate yearning of the soul for union with the Divine, filters through to our consciousness as a desire for fulfilment on a human level. Worldly love is in no way a precondition for experiencing divine love; but the imagery of lover and beloved, wife and husband, is used by mystics like Guru Nanak since it conveys, however inadequately, a dim reflection of that ultimate experience – the merging of the individual into the Divine:

> She who is the beloved of her Lord, O Nanak,
> Is a happy wife, she is a queen among women;

She is intoxicated with the bliss of *sahaj*
And is merged day and night in love.

Tilang, M.1, p.722

Who can unite her with her Lord,
When she has been abandoned by Him?
It is through the Word,
And by immersing herself in His love
That she can meet her Lord.

Gauri, M.1, p.243

Let us now turn to the second question: What influence has mysticism actually had on leading a good life? The commonest moral accusation against mysticism has been that it functions in practice merely as an escape from life and its active duties, into an emotional ecstasy of bliss, which is selfishly enjoyed for its own sake. Thus, mysticism is denounced as a flight from life and from the urgent work of the world. This charge has particularly been levelled against Indian mysticism by the Western critic.

This reflection, on the whole, is based on a misunderstanding, and one can meet the criticism effectively. In the first instance, it may be noted that it has consistently been the practice of the Indian mystic to pass on the torch from man to man through the instrumentality of gurus and ashrams. Thus, he does not remain in solitude, unaffected by the suffering of others, but he seeks to show them the path of salvation that he has found. As a teacher of what he conceives to be a good life, he cannot be called selfish. Second, the Indian mystic has a different set of values. To him, spirituality is of far greater value than the satisfaction of material needs or even the alleviation of material suffering. Hence, to pass on the torch of spirituality to other men is regarded by the Indian mystic as the supreme altruistic action. And third, there is perhaps a basic difference in the philosophic approach of the Indian from that of the Westerner. The men of the West think that it is theoretically possible to alleviate, if not altogether remove, material misery through schemes of social reform. But according to the Indian mystics, such as Guru Nanak and the Buddha, suffering is inherent in life and cannot be removed by any action so long as the individual retains his separateness from the ultimate Being. Guru Nanak says: "The whole world is suffering, O Nanak" (*Ramkali-ki-Var, M.3, Shalok M.1*, p.954). "He alone is in bliss who is imbued with the Name" (*Ramkali, Sidh Gosht, M.1,* p.941:31). Suffering is a consequence of finitude, and will, therefore, persist so long as the finite does not merge into the Infinite.

Mysticism and religion

It has been a common assumption that mysticism is a religious phenomenon. And this assumption is not unjustified, if we understand by the religious feeling, the feeling of the holy or the divine. For the mystic refers always to the timeless or the eternal, which he experiences also as supremely noble, transcending altogether the transient world of flux, vanity, frustration and sorrow. He experiences this state as 'peace which passeth understanding'. Hence, in this sense, mysticism is rightly regarded as religious in essence.

But if we take religion to be a creed or set of dogmas or an institution, then mysticism need not be religious. Thus considered, Plotinus was a non-religious mystic. The intellectual framework in terms of which he interpreted his experience was a system of philosophy and not religion. Even Buddhism in this sense is not religious, because it does not refer to the experience of the undifferentiated Unity as 'union with God'. Mysticism does not favour any one particular creed or world religion more than another.

Instead of asking whether mysticism is essentially religious, the question may be raised whether all religion is essentially mystical. It can reasonably be answered that most of the world religions and all the well-established Indian religions are essentially mystical, because their source and centre is the enlightenment experience. It seems these religions were originally mystic schools. However, in the course of time, true and practicing mystics disappeared, and along with them the mystic practice was abandoned.

Guru Nanak's advent was marked by the resurgence of the true religious spirit in India. Before he arrived on the scene, men's minds had been enclosed in the rigid framework of rituals and ceremonies. Groups and factions based on different sets of dogmas and creeds had emerged. Divisions had arisen between various classes of people. Religion, which was supposed to bring out the best and the noblest in man, had produced the contrary. No wonder many had become sceptical, if not contemptuous, of all that religion stood for. Guru Nanak, however, taught a spiritual practice that was free from all rituals and ceremonies. The goal of this practice was union with God, the 'enlightenment experience', and therefore had nothing to do with dogmas, institutions or external divisions. Guru Nanak came and revived the faith of man in man, and the faith of man in God.

The mystic schools

There are a large number of mystic schools, which differ not only on the basis of practices involved, but also on the aspects on which emphasis is put. In regard to the mystic practices, different schools select different parts of the body on which concentration is to be fixed, and different exercises – both mental and physical – are to be gone through. It is not possible to give a detailed account of all the schools in this short outline. All that I propose to do is name some of the important schools and give the central idea on which each is based. These are *Karma Yoga, Upasana Yoga, Laya Yoga, Raja Yoga, Tapasya, Hatha Yoga, Pranayam, Jnana Yoga* and *Bhakti Yoga.*

Karma Yoga is not exactly a method of concentration. It is the belief that salvation can be attained through performing right karma or actions, and doing one's duty without desire for reward. This school is generally associated with Sri Krishna, who advocated it in the Bhagavad Gita.

Upasana Yoga is based on the method of worship, whether of material images of the devotee's deity, or inner mental worship. In *Laya Yoga* the individual tries to collect all his conscious current within himself through the inner repetition of some holy name. This enables him to withdraw all his mental contents into their source. This method gives the devotee a taste of the inner spiritual bliss and some supernatural powers.

Raja Yoga is said to have been practiced in olden times by kings and rulers. Here, the devotee resorts to the repetition of some name to collect his attention behind the two eyes. In this practice, importance is given to the feeling of detachment from the material world *(vairagya)* and the power of discrimination between the real and the unreal, between what is good and what is evil, and such other concepts (i.e. *viveka*).

In *Tapasya*, the element of asceticism is predominant, involving cruelty or torture to the body. Along with the repetition of a holy name, some limbs of the body are put in painful positions, such as holding the arm up in the air for a long time, with the result that either it dries up or it becomes lifeless. By thus tormenting the body, the individual hopes to achieve victory of the spirit over the flesh.

Hatha Yoga, too, lays great emphasis on the body. It involves various practices to cleanse the body and some difficult postures which protect one against various bodily diseases. The course is quite long, tedious and difficult.

Pranayam is primarily concerned with holding and controlling the breath. This practice culminates in the individual merging himself in that subtle essence of breath, which is the source of all the kinds of air.

Jnana Yoga believes in securing salvation and access to higher spiritual planes through knowledge *(jnana)*. It constantly contemplates the great mystic truths, such as the nature of the soul and its oneness with God. For instance, Sri Krishna says to Arjuna:

Nor at any time was I not, nor thou, nor these princes of men, nor verily shall I ever cease to be hereafter.[80]

About the soul, he further says:

Never is it born, nor doth it die, nor is it such that being once, it should cease to be. Everlasting and eternal, even with the destruction of body, it doth not die.[81]

Bhakti Yoga is based on the principle of love, devotion and faith. The devotee is intensely attached to the beloved Lord and is completely resigned to His supreme will, for he has faith in His perfection, kindness and loving nature. Bhakti has sometimes been classified into two kinds, mixed and pure. In 'mixed bhakti', desire for some sort of reward lingers in the mind of the devotee, whereas in 'pure bhakti' there is no such desire, only an urge for service for the sake of service, and devotion for the sake of devotion. Bhakti here is not a means to an end, but the end itself.

Spiritual practice
The spiritual practice attributed to Guru Nanak may be called *Surat Shabd Yoga*. It has also been described by other names,

such as *Shabd Yoga*, *Sahaj Yoga*, or *Shabd Abhyas*. In this practice, the individual withdraws his attention and soul current from throughout his body to a point behind the two eyes, called the 'third eye'.* He must shut all his sense organs, which serve as windows for the outside world. The third eye focus is the seat of the soul in the waking state. By assiduously concentrating his attention at this centre, which might be called the 'headquarters of the soul', the devotee is able to attain the state of *samadhi*, or spiritual trance, which is a state of pure consciousness and which yields bliss and peace. This process of transmitting the soul current through the tenth door or eye centre, and untying the knot of the soul and mind, is referred to frequently in the Adi Granth. The Gurus and Bhai Gurdas have referred to the eye centre using various terms. Among other words they have called it *daswan*, 'the tenth'; *til ghar*, 'the home of the eye'; *ghar mandir*, 'the temple of the home'; *ghar*, 'home'; *dibb drishti*, 'divine eye'; *dar ghar* and *ghar dar*, 'door of the house'; *dar*, 'door'; *sodar*, 'that door'; *mukat duar*, 'door of liberation'; *til*, 'sesame'; and so on.

Guru Amar Das says:

> Close thou the nine doors,
> And collect thou thy scattered mind
> In the tenth *(daswan)*,
> Which leadeth thee to thy true home;

---

* Various other names have also been given to it. It has been called the 'inner eye', the 'single eye' or the 'eye'. Tulsi Sahib describes it as *khas-khas ka dana*, 'poppy seed'; *sui duar*, 'eye of the needle'; *dur bin*, 'telescope'; *mahin dana*, 'minute seed'; *mukar*, 'mirror'; and *til*, 'sesame seed'. The Hindu mystics have named it *shiv netra*, 'the eye of Shiva'; *dibb chukshu*, 'divine eye'; or *tisra til*, 'the third eye'. The Muslim mystics have termed it *nuqta-i-suvaida*, 'the black spot'. Rene Descartes, the French philosopher, probably meant the same point when he referred to the pineal gland.

There ringeth the transcendent music
Day and night,
Which thou canst hear with the help
Of a mystic adept.

Majh, m.3, p.124

Nine doors He manifesteth,
But the tenth *(daswan)* He keepeth hidden.
Through devotion to a mystic adept,
To some He showeth the tenth door,
Which opens out forms of wondrous beauty
And the nine treasures beyond description.

Ramkali, Anand, m.3, p.922

Calling it the 'temple of the home', the 'home of the eye' or simply 'the home', the Adi Granth says:

My mind wanders much,
Moment after moment
In delusion after delusion;
It stays not in the home *(ghar)*
Of the eye *(til)*.
Only with the goad of the Word,
Through the guru,
Does it abide in the temple
Of the home *(ghar mandir)*.

Basant Hindol, m.4, p.1179

O my foolish and ignorant mind,
Stay thou in thy home *(ghar)*;
Repeat thou the Name of the Lord,
Attuned from within to Him.

Maru, m.1, p.1030

Where dost thou wander, O mind?
Abide in thine own home *(ghar)*.
Through the guru, with ease,
Thy search will give thee
Salvation of the Lord's Name.

Asa, M.1, p.414

If the mind were to shed its passions
And abide in its home *(ghar)*,
Dyed in the fear of the Lord,
It would enjoy the nectar of divine knowledge
And would hunger no more.

Sri, M.1, p.21

Elsewhere in the Adi Granth, it is called 'divine vision' or 'eye', 'door to the house' or 'door of salvation':

He who is a customer for the Lord
Obtains the jewel of discrimination;
He opens up the eye of divine knowledge *(dibb drishti)*
And beholds the treasure of salvation.

Asa, M.3, p.425

His divine vision *(dibb drishti)*
Is awakened and he is rid of delusion;
Through the grace of the guru
He attains to the sublime state of bliss.

Maru, M.3, p.1016

The *gurmukh* alone tastes the divine nectar;
He is received with honour
At the door of the Lord's mansion *(dar ghar)*.

Asa, M.1, p.415

Which is the door *(dar)*
That leads to the Lord's abode?
Let someone come and point out
That door *(sodar)* to me,
For which I go about sadly.

Ramkali, M.1, p.877

He alone knows the door of his home *(ghar dar)*
Within the temple *(mandir)* of his body,
Who has been enlightened
Through the perfect master.

Maru, M.1, p.1039

Nanak, the door of salvation *(mukat duar)*
Is extremely narrow;
Only if you become very small can you enter.
The ego of the mind is gross;
How can it pass through?

Gujari-ki-Var, M.3, p.509

Bhai Gurdas, whose writings are considered the key to the
Adi Granth, writes in this connection:

The soul, that had become defiled in the company of the
mind and the senses, became dazzlingly beautiful after it
withdrew itself from them, reached the *til* and adopted
Shabd as its lord and spouse. Just as a woman whose
husband is alive puts a vermilion mark on her forehead,
likewise the soul that has withdrawn itself from the nine
doors and entered the tenth within to meet its lord, puts
the mark of its good fortune on its forehead. (In other
words, the soul has entered the third eye.) This eye has
marvellous beauty. Myriads of brilliant lights are hidden

behind its veil. The soul that enters it becomes the bride of the Lord of countless universes.

The glory of the auspicious mark on the forehead is so enhanced when the *til* has been awakened in the bride, that the brightness of other women becomes pale in comparison.[82]

Again he says:

> The *til* has primeval purity and is intensely attractive. It is impossible to describe the glory of the soul that has been adorned with the *Shabd* after entering the *til*. The sanctity of the *til* exceeds the merit of bathing in myriads of holy Ganges. Millions of moons cannot equal its matchless brilliance. It is this magnetic power of its beauty that automatically pulls souls practicing withdrawal from the nine doors.[83]

Shabd

What are we to understand by the term *Shabd*? Literally it means 'word' or 'sound'. It also stands for a religious song or hymn. But for the mystics it is a superconscious transcendent entity. "It can neither be heard with the ears, nor uttered by the tongue. Pen cannot write it, language cannot describe it." It transcends human understanding, goes beyond all duality and relativity. And it penetrates all things and beings. "Without *Shabd*," says Guru Nanak, "there is darkness within us. Without *Shabd*, neither can this physical covering be removed, nor can we end the cycle of birth and death."

The *siddhas* ask Guru Nanak:

> Where doth that *Shabd* abide which taketh us
> Across the ocean of the world?

Ten kinds of air we have,
On which doth it depend?

And the Guru answers:

That *Shabd* abideth within, transcendent;
I behold it wherever I look.
The source of all air is in Sunn
But this *Shabd* doth not depend on anything.
Ramkali, Sidh Gosht, M.1, p.944:58–59

The word *Shabd* has been expressed by many other terms in the Adi Granth, such as *Nam* and *Bani.* *"From age to age existeth the *Bani* known as the *Shabd* or *Nam*, sweet and dear" (*Sorath*, M.3, p.602). It has also been called *Hukam*, as is clear from these verses:

True is Thy *Hukam*;
Through the guru is it known.
Through his instructions,
When the ego is eradicated,
Truth is realized.
Majh-ki-Var, M.1, p.144

On all the four sides
Works Thy *Hukam*, O Lord;
On the four sides
Even of the underworld
Pervades Thy *Nam*;

---

* "In Sri Guru Granth Sahib *shabd* has mostly been used for *nam*. Whatever is the meaning of *nam* in Guru Granth Sahib, that very meaning is carried by *shabd*.... In many places the meaning of *shabd* is *hukam*" (Bhai Vir Singh and Gyani Hazara Singh, *Sri Guru Granth Kosh*, pp.225–226).

The *Shabd* pervades all.
Through Thy own grace
Do we meet Thee.

Malar, M.1, p.1275

In the following verse, Guru Nanak has identified *Nad*, *Shabd*, *Dhun*, *Sach* and *Nam*:

Within one resounds, O Nanak,
The pure *Nad-Shabd-Dhun*,
And he merges in the *Sach-Nam* of the Lord.

Maru, M.1, p.1038

The Gospel of St. John calls it the 'Word': "In the beginning was the Word, and the Word was with God, and the Word was God."[84] In the Vedas, it has been termed *Nad* or 'heavenly sound'. The Muslim mystics have called it *Kalma*, the 'Word'; *Nada-i-Asmani*, *Bang-i-Asmani*, the 'heavenly sound'; or *Isam-i-Azam*, the 'highest name'; and *Sultan-ul-Azkar*, the 'king of words'.

Shabd, the Word, has two aspects, *sound* and *light*, as is clear from the following verses of Guru Nanak:

Within us is the light
And from within the light
Emanates the sound;
We are attuned to the true Lord
Through the Word.

Sorath, M.1, p.634

He within whom is lit
The divine light
And within whom resounds
The divine melody,

Is emancipated from suffering
By his master.

Gujari, M.1, p.489

Within one rings
The unstruck melody
Of the lute,
And within every body
Shines Thy light.

Ramkali M.1, p.907

Both light and sound are essential in the spiritual practice for the aspirant to reach his destination. Just as a man who has lost his way is helped to determine his direction by the sound coming from a distance, so also the sound of *Shabd* draws the disciple towards its source. And just as light helps one to avoid pitfalls in the darkness, so does the light of *Shabd* on the inner journey save the disciple from obstacles on the way by illuminating the path.

The rays of Thy light spread out
And there is illumination within;
The compassionate Lord Himself
Creates and beholds it all.
The sweet unstruck melody
Rings ever within one,
And he is rid of fear and doubt.

Maru Dakhani, M.1, p.1033

This spiritual 'sound current' emanates from the Supreme Being and creates and sustains all planes. If we were to compare the absolute Lord to a spiritual ocean and our souls to drops of it, then this spiritual current would be a vast river which flows out of the ocean and waters all the lower regions.

Thus *Shabd* is God's very being and essence. It reverberates in all planes and is the source of all life and the fountainhead of all consciousness. It may be taken as the omnipresent form of God. And since in essence the soul and *Shabd* are one, it draws the soul upwards as a magnet attracts a needle. That is why this method is called *Surat Shabd Yoga*, i.e., the union of the soul with the transcendent *Shabd*.

Speaking of this method, Guru Nanak says: "By *Surat-Shabd* do thou cross the ocean of phenomena, O Nanak, by uttering his *Nam*" (*Ramkali, Sidh Gosht, M.1*, p.938:5). And again: "How can the mundane find the *Surat-Shabd*? Without *Surat-Shabd*, they keep on coming and going" (*Maru, M.1*, p.1042). The Muslim mystics have expressed the same idea in almost similar terms. "Listen thou to the eternal Word, which will give thee deliverance from birth and death."[85] And Jalal-ud-din Rumi has this to say in this context:

> Bring the firmament under thy feet, O thou brave one, and then listen thou to the divine melody coming from the heavens above.[86]

And again:

> Many a kind of delicious music and many a sweet melody did I hear, and then for me the temple and the mosque both became heretic.[87]

Dying while living
It is a commonly held belief among Indians that we can attain salvation after death, provided we have led a virtuous life in this world. The question arises, can we not attain this state of transcendent consciousness in this very life? Can we not cross the portals of death during our lifetime? Though the world says

no, Guru Nanak assures us that we can. He himself realized it, and he teaches us how it can be attained. For unless the goal is reached while we are still living, where is the guarantee that it will be reached after death?

From the Guru's writings, it is obvious that he could go beyond the gates of death and come back as often as he liked. This is how he puts it:

> Every day do I die and every day do I come back to life; such is the method which my Guru hath taught me.[88]

This ability to cross the portals of death at will is, indeed, common to all higher mystic teachings. The ancient Indian scriptures right from the time of the Upanishads testify to it:

> If a man realizeth not his self during his lifetime, from life to life in a series of births and deaths he needs must go.[89]

And again:

> If a man knoweth not his self during his lifetime, the ills that may be in store for him after death, he cannot even imagine.[90]

The Sufi scriptures give the same counsel: "Before thy death do thou die."[91] Rumi exhorts thus: "Rise thou, O soul, and come thou up before thy death, and behold thou thy kingdom and thy eternal home."[92]

The process involved in realizing this transcendent experience is analogous to the process of dying. That is why Guru Nanak calls it 'dying while living'. In death, the soul current gradually withdraws from the body, starting from the extremities. The mystic in his spiritual practice and in the proc-ess of concentration aims at the same objective, but he does it voluntarily. The ordinary man's death, on the other hand, is an event over which he has no control. Moreover it is painful and there is no reverse process, for he cannot come back to life. But, as it has already been pointed out, the mystic has mastered the method or technique of conquering death. Thus Guru Nanak says: "Where thou hast to go after death, oh conquer that realm while living" (*Sri, M.1,* p.21). "Such a yoga do thou practice, O Nanak, that thou diest even while living" (*Suhi, M.1,* p.730).

A voluntary death of this kind, which means an ascent into higher spiritual realms, gives release from bondage, the bond-age of sorrow and the bondage of reincarnation. "One who dies or merges into the Shabd," stresses Guru Nanak, "dies eternally from this phenomenal world, and will know no second death" (*Sri, M.1,* p.58). This truth has been emphatically brought out not only by Guru Nanak, but by other mystics also. In regard to this, Rumi has to say: "Of dying before death the secret is this, that after such a dying divine blessings dost thou receive."[93] And another Sufi mystic writes: "If before thy death thou dost die, this dying shall bear fruit."[94] Nor is this assertion confined to the mystics of the East, for Jesus Christ speaks of the neces-sity of being "born again" in this lifetime in order to enter the kingdom of heaven,[95] and says that he has the power to leave the body when he wants to, and take it up again at will:

> No man taketh [life] from me, but I lay it down of myself. I have power to lay it down, and I have power to take it again. This commandment have I received of my Father.[96]

Similarly, Socrates said in his epistles that he could come out of his body and go back into it as a man comes out of a house and enters it again, and this gave him intense bliss and peace.

God is within

The finite contains the Infinite. The transcendent Absolute is screened in flesh and blood. The Supreme Being is concealed in the human body. This fact is constantly repeated in Guru Nanak's teachings:

> Think not the true Lord to be far;
> He is right within us.
>
> *Asa, M.1, p.421*

> Within every body
> Is the Lord hidden;
> Within every body
> Is His light.
>
> *Sorath, M.1, p.597*

> Searching his body, his home,
> By the master's instructions one finds
> The Name revealed within.
>
> *Maru, M.1, p.1013*

When Guru Nanak says that God is within man, he does not mean that He is a part of the physical frame of man. Otherwise, doctors would find Him when they perform post-mortems. But God is subtle and spiritual. Thus although He is inside us, by killing the body we do not kill Him. The death of the mortal frame does not touch Him, for He is transcendent. In fact, God is not part of our body for the same reason that He is not to be found in the material world. By saying that He is within us, Guru Nanak means that we can realize Him by concentrating within ourselves.

> In the body resideth He Himself,
> The transcendent divine Being,

But the gross-headed man of the world
Knoweth it not,
And seeketh Him outside.

Suhi, M.3, p.754

As the scent is in the flower,
And the reflection is in the mirror,
So is God within thee.
In thine own body do thou seek Him,
O brother.

Dhanasari, M.9, p.684

By the grace of guru do thou behold
That within thyself is the temple of God.

Parbhati, M.3, p.1346

It is a well-known principle in psychology that the organ of knowing must be suited to the object of knowledge. For instance, our eyes cannot see in light that is too bright or too dim. Similarly, our ears cannot hear sounds that are too loud or too low. For sounds beyond the range of our ears, we use scientific instruments to make the sounds audible. Similarly, we use the microscope or the telescope to see very minute or distant objects. Now this happens on the same plane of experience, viz., the physical world. If we wish to know something on the subtle plane, we have to become subtle. The absolute Reality is extremely subtle and therefore to know it we have to recede within our subtle, transcendent self.

Guru Nanak said that phenomena conceal from our view the essence of Reality. The Upanishads state that *maya* or illusion hides from us the fact of Brahm. We have to pierce through the cover of phenomena or the veil of *maya* to be able to behold the Reality beneath.

Moreover, when Guru Nanak says that God is within us, he does not mean that He is not without. By saying that He is within, Guru Nanak means that unless we realize Him within, we cannot know Him outside. So the difference between the introvertive and extrovertive mystic experiences is not so absolute as some of the Western thinkers have taken it to be. As has already been said, the extrovertive type is only secondary and is, in fact, dependent on the introvertive kind of mystic consciousness.

The master

Mystics might differ in minor details of their accounts of mysticism, but all great mystics are unanimous in their estimate of the need and the role of a guru or enlightener. They all agree that in the entire spiritual process culminating in the realization of God, the guru or the master plays the crucial role. Without him, the desired end is impossible to attain. In fact, a mystic school is not to be judged by its tenets or principles of belief only, but essentially by its adept and his internal spiritual reach.

To learn any ordinary skill or art, two factors are needed: effort, and direction or method. If we wish to reach a destination, we can never reach it unless we move, and if we want to learn an art, we cannot learn it unless we practice it. The same is true of mystic transport. Without effort and practice, the transcendental experience cannot be attained.

But mere hard work itself is not enough. Unless effort is made in the right direction and along the right lines, it will not only be futile, but may prove positively harmful. Suppose we have to reach a railroad station and we begin moving, and moving fast; but if we have taken the opposite direction, the more we move, the farther we go from our destination. Now, many an ardent seeker has an intense desire to know Reality, but he does not know the proper method. Thus Guru Amar Das says: "They worship, but they know not the way" (*Ramkali, m.3*, p.910). If for a commonplace task a teacher or a guide is necessary, he is much more so for treading the spiritual path, which is not only different from any that the traveller has known, but is also beset with many dangerous pitfalls. A Persian mystic writes:

> Dye thou thy prayer cloth in wine, if thy Master asks thee to do so, for ignorant he is not of the ways and customs of the path that he hath traversed.[97]

And Jalal-ud-din Rumi has given a more elaborate account in this context:

> Find thou a guide, for beset with perils and dangers is this journey. Whosoever without a Master journeyeth on this path, the evil ones lead him astray and cast him into the well of misery. If thou hast not over thy head the protecting hand of thy Master, devilish doubts shall forever keep thee perplexed. Many a man wiser than thou has tried to tread the path by himself, but has come to grief through the evils of Satan.[98]

Guru Nanak says that the fact that we are still subject to the cycle of birth and death, and suffer ceaselessly, shows that by our own efforts alone we cannot liberate ourselves. Guru Arjan writes:

> If by ourselves we could attain
> Union with God,
> Why should we have suffered
> The pangs of separation?

Nay, only through mystics
Do we realize Him, O Nanak,
And experience the rapture.
Majh, Barah Maha, m.5, p.134

Guru Nanak's hymns – as indeed the songs of the Adi
Granth as a whole – are replete with love for the Guru. In the
words of Prof. Puran Singh, "After Guru Nanak, all the mystics
and devotees of the Punjab have sung Punjabi songs in the
Master's tunes."[99] The theme of the poetry of Bhai Gurdas has
the same dominant strain. It tells of the inner illumination that
is kindled at the touch of the Master; grossness vanishes and the
subtle light shines on the path of the life in one unbroken spell
of love. Awake, yet asleep, the disciple is pure as God, by the
grace of the Guru. To Bhai Gurdas, the disciple is unthinkable
without the Guru, as the two together make the Godly life on
earth. Wherever his eyes fall, he sees the same life. All things
are words for him to express his love – the love of the disciple
and the Guru. The Master is before him in the form divine of
man and his mind is so concentrated in his own love-reverie,
that he sees none but the Master.... In one of his hymns, Bhai
Gurdas says: "Pour into my heart a drop of thy life-giving wine
of light, break our principles of piety and erase our names from
the list of the 'moralists' that drink not the nectar of life."[100]

In the inimitable words of Bhai Nand Lal, poet-devotee of
Guru Gobind Singh, the master has been depicted thus:

The sight of the perfect master
Is vision of the Lord Himself,
And from thy master's tongue
Thou hearest the Lord's secrets.
The form of the Lord is manifest
In the form of the master;

> Keep thou ever the master's form
> Impressed within thy heart.
> When his form findeth a place
> In someone's heart,
> The Word of God findeth its abode
> In that heart.[101]

The necessity of the master

What is love for the master? This implies first the question: 'What is the master?' If the master is an ordinary mortal, then why not love the Lord directly, who is pervading all creation and every atom? The real object of human love must be the Perfect, the Absolute. And it is through such love that salvation can be attained. Love of the finite will keep us entangled in delusion and will not give us deliverance from the cycle of eighty-four.

But – and it is a crucial *but* – the all-pervasive, formless entity of God cannot be the object on which our feelings can be fixed or attached. And what cannot be within the range of 'feeling' cannot be within the scope of love. Indeed, for such an entity we cannot be sure even of His existence, let alone His love or worship. It is an axiomatic truth that for love to be enkindled, the beloved must exist.

Now the supreme Lord is not unaware of this human predicament. He therefore initiated the system of masters, who would come into the world at all times, in all ages, to give guidance to stumbling mankind. To the seekers groping in the dark, they would show light by initiating them into the mystery of *Shabd* or *Nam*, the practice of which would release them from the cycle of birth and death:

> Without the guru's Word
> One is not emancipated;
> Reflect and realize this.

One may perform as many deeds as he likes;
Without the guru there is all darkness.
What shall we say to those
Who are blind of mind
And devoid of wisdom?

Without the guru the way cannot be seen;
How is one then to get along?

Gauri, M.1, p.229

The true melody bringeth forth true honour,
Without *Nam* none attaineth salvation.
Without the true master, none obtaineth *Nam*;
Such is the eternal arrangement
Devised by the Lord Himself.

Maru, M.3, p.1046

Thus, the system of incarnation of the Lord in the form of true masters is the arrangement designed by the Almighty Himself.

The master is the manifest form of the Lord, and it is the manifest form that can be the object of love. And if God can only be realized through love, the master is an indispensable link for God-realization. In *Dakhani Onkar*, Guru Nanak says:

Everyone prays, 'Give, O God, give',
But He gives to whomsoever He pleases
Through the guru's door,
Who quenches our thirst.

Ramkali, Dakhani Onkar, M.1, p.933:30

The necessity of a master is clearly brought out by Guru Nanak. The question, however, may be raised: Can a past master not serve our purpose? Can he not give us spiritual aid and guidance? Why should a living master be indispensable? The answers to these questions may be gleaned from an analogy. Let us suppose that there is an electric bulb, which is connected to a generator or a powerhouse. It gives brilliant light and enables us to see clearly and also to do our work. We take a photograph of the lighted bulb and keep it in front of us. Now it so happens that the filament of the bulb snaps or burns out and it stops giving light. We are engulfed by the surrounding darkness. Although the photograph of the illumined bulb is right before us, it does not help us in dispelling the darkness. Likewise, past masters cannot give us the light of spiritual knowledge. It is true that their writings have immense influence on us and inspire us to follow in their footsteps. It is also true that they turned those ordinary people into realized souls, who came in contact with them during their lifetime. But they cannot take us to the transcendent regions *now*, nor can they give us any guidance in our spiritual journey within. Without a living master, we would be lost, groping in darkness, notwithstanding the voluminous scriptures previous masters have written for our guidance.

The living master

In fact, the term 'master' cannot but mean the living master. The difference between a perfect mystic and God is that while the former exists in the human body and on the physical plane, the latter exists in His absolute, transcendent state. When the mystic leaves his body, he goes to the absolute Lord and merges in Him. He then ceases to have his distinctive identity. No difference remains between God and that mystic. Now, if we have to depend on a past mystic for our spiritual transport, we might as well depend directly on God, for the two are now one. There should be no need for an intermediary. And, if we depend on God, it would mean that we deny the need for a mystic adept altogether. In that case we have to answer the question why perfect masters have come to the world at all.

The mystic has two forms: his human form in this gross world, when he is living; and his 'Shabd form' or his form as God, which he retains at the absolute level even while alive and into which he merges after death. Guru Arjan says:

> The Lord's servant
> Is like the Lord Himself;
> Take him not to be different
> Due to his human form.
>
> *Maru, M.5, p.1076*

Now, if we say that a mystic adept is essential for union with God, we do not mean that God is essential for union with God. For that is what a dead mystic is. Obviously, therefore, we can mean nothing but the *human form* of the adept when we talk about him. And the human form exists only so long as he lives in this world. Only the mystic of the time is manifest in the human form. Thus, if we need a guru – as the scriptures constantly remind us that we do – we need a living, a contemporary guru, a guru of our own time and not one of the past mystics who has left his physical body forever and merged in the Lord for good. He should be present now to initiate us and to take us to the higher spiritual regions. Guru Nanak says:

> He who *sees* the true guru
> And gets *initiated* by him,
> Surrenders his mind and body
> And goes within.
> He examines his self and finds
> The reach of his soul.
>
> *Gauri, M.1, p.227*

If we think about it objectively, our faith in past masters is based on sheer imagination. Such faith is entirely subjective in nature. No relationship can be established between a past mystic and a present disciple. We, in our own mind, adopt a past mystic as our master, but he does not tell us whether he has accepted us as his disciple. And if we leave one past master for another, neither the one nor the other tells us if we have been rejected or accepted. We must remember that the relationship between the master and the disciple depends on the master and not on the disciple. It is the prerogative of the master to accept or reject a disciple; the disciple cannot force someone to become his master. Thus, there is no relation whatever between the two. It is our own mind that makes us believe that we are the followers of such-and-such a master. It is our own mind that determines all our actions.

Again, once we have made up our mind that there is going to be no true master after a particular one has left the world, we are being quite unfair to those born before and after that master came to the world. God, who is just and all-merciful, would not dispense His mercy in so capricious a manner. He would not confine His saints to a brief period and debar those born earlier or later from attaining salvation and union with Him. In particular, those who are born prior to a certain saint or master would be singularly unfortunate in the matter. For they would not even be able to have an imaginary picture of the master who is supposed by succeeding generations to be the sole saviour of the world.

The Lord, in fact, has been all-merciful in His grace. He has so ordained that the world will never be without saints. This is a divine law, which, unlike social or political laws, cannot be changed. Those who seek union with Him will always have a master to help and guide them. If they have true longing and a sincere urge in their heart, the master will appear. Guru

Nanak says: "Blessed are Thy saints *in every age*, O God. For they ever praise Thee, sweetening their tongue with Thy love" (*Maru*, M.1, p.1025).

The indispensability of the master is again and again emphasized in the writings of the house of Nanak:

> Let no one remain
> In delusion in the world;
> Without the guru
> No one shall ever go across
> The ocean of phenomena.
>
> *Gaund, M.5, p.864*

> Without serving the true guru,
> None finds the Name;
> One may tire oneself with reading,
> He will not get peace.
>
> *Maru, M.3, p.1046*

> God hath revealed this to me,
> O Nanak: Without a guru
> No one can attain salvation,
> O brother.
>
> *Gaund, M.5, p.864*

> Without a gracious guru,
> None can find the Lord,
> Even if one were to perform
> Millions of practices.
>
> *Maru, M.3, p.1057*

> If one meets the true guru, the seer,
> He finds God, the treasure of excellence.
>
> *Sri, M.1, p.21*

He alone realizes the Lord
Who finds the true guru;
He conquers his ego
And realizes the Word.

Gauri, M.1, p.228

This love and reverence for the master is no less intense in the mystics of Persia. This is what Shams-i-Tabriz writes about masters:

If thou seekest the sight of God, apply thou the collyrium of the dust of their feet, for even to the one born blind do they give eyes.[102]

The true guru

Having quoted from various scriptures to show how indispensable the spiritual teacher is for God-realization, we may now try to arrive at the definition of a true guru. A true guru is one who has in his spiritual transport realized the ultimate Reality, and who enables others to attain that Reality. He is thus a necessary instrument for mystic realization, and serves as the key that opens the locks of mystic transport in the seeker. Guru Angad brings out the role of the guru thus:

Guru is the key, man the lock,
Mind the chamber, and body the roof.
Without the guru,
The mind's door cannot be opened,
O Nanak, and none else hath the key.

Sarang-ki-Var, M.4, Shalok M.2, p.1237

Through his mystic experience, the guru has become one with God and has, as it were, merged in Him. This union and identification of the two, as has been stated earlier, is the definition of the highest mystic consciousness. On this, Guru Nanak writes, "God hath put Himself in the guru" (*Maru, M.1,* p.1024). Guru Arjan adds:

> God and His mystics are one,
> Take them not as different
> Due to their human form;
> As the wave riseth above the water
> And mergeth into it again,
> So do saints merge into the Lord.
>
> *Maru Solhe, M.5, p.1076*

This merging of the master in the Lord has been beautifully expressed by Shams-i-Tabriz in the following lines:

> The almighty Lord had put Himself behind strongly fastened locks; He then put on the garb of man to come and open the door Himself.[103]

Finally, as a criterion of a perfect master, Guru Nanak says that such a one not only enables a seeker to realize God within himself, but that he does so through the instrument of five *shabds* or divine melodies.

The five melodies
In the monistic philosophy of Guru Nanak, which teaches the all-pervading *Shabd* as the source of all creation and as the one Reality behind all appearances, a reference to five *shabds* seems to need an explanation. The only way this contradiction can be resolved is that although in the last analysis, *Shabd* is one all-pervading power, yet in mystic transport it passes through five stages and takes on differing forms. It is like the course of

a river, which has a different character at its source, in the high mountains, in the valley below, in the vast plains, at the delta, and ultimately in the ocean into which it merges. Just as the same water assumes different forms and sounds at the various stages of its course, so also the *Shabd*, which passes through various spiritual realms, assumes different forms. However, one who has to know the entire course of a river must know all the changes it undergoes in the geographical terrain through which it passes. So also, the perfect master must be familiar with all the changes that *Shabd* undergoes in the spiritual realms through which it passes. Thus Guru Nanak, in elaborating the definition of a true guru, writes:

> Who showeth us our home within us
> Is a true guru.
> And the ringing and resounding
> Of the five melodies
> Is the sign of the reverberating *Shabd*.
>> *Malar-ki-Var, Shalok* M.1, *pp.1290–1291*

This reference to five melodies is not confined to Guru Nanak, or even to Indian mystics. A Persian mystic writes about it thus:

> In silence listen thou to the five melodies coming from the firmament, for they emanate from beyond the seven skies and the six centres in the body.[104]

Honest living

A pure moral life is a necessary prelude to, as well as an inevitable consequence of, a truly spiritual life. Without the precondition of a virtuous life, no spiritual attainment is possible. It is equally true that after attaining spiritual realization, virtue flows from the realized soul just as fragrance emanates from a flower.

A true mystic is not one who has mere faith in the theory of mysticism, but one who has attained the mystic experience. In other words, the emphasis in God-realization is not on theory, but on practice. Not till one has been able to vacate his body up to the eye centre and has had the experience of light and sound within, can he be called a mystic. Now in order to have such an experience, a virtuous life is an essential prerequisite. The aspirant must have clear dealings with all those he comes across. Among other things, he must earn his living through honest means. Guru Nanak says:

> That alone is accepted hereafter, O Nanak,
> Which is earned through one's own hard labour.
>
> *Asa-di-Var,* M.1, *p.472*

Not only should the aspirant work conscientiously for his livelihood, but he should also willingly part with some of his earnings by sharing with others. That is the way which will help him gain the spiritual wealth he seeks. Says the Guru:

> One who earns with the sweat of his brow
> And gives a part of his earnings to others
> Is the one who knows the way
> To God-realization.
>
> *Sarang-ki-Var,* M.1, *p.1245*

Even the food that one eats, earned through righteous means, will affect one's mind in a positive way. It will be conducive to spiritual progress. The same food, earned through evil means or without being earned at all, will have a negative effect. One who aspires to spiritual realization has to be careful not only about what he eats, but also about how the food has been acquired.

Guru Nanak is unambiguous in his condemnation of those who lead a hypocritical life. In the true seeker there should be conformity between his speech and his thoughts, and between his thoughts and his deeds. His conduct must manifest his cogitations. In regard to people who manage to acquire fame in the world, who appear paragons of virtue before others but are full of evil designs in their hearts, Guru Nanak writes:

> False within,
> Famous without,
> If such be thy way of life
> The filth will not go,
> Even if thou bathest
> In all the holy waters.
>
> *Asa-di-Var,* M.1, *p.473*

Guru Nanak was particularly severe on those qazis, pundits and religious preachers of his time who led a double life, who posed as holy to the world, but were subject to all the failings that the human flesh is heir to. He says, for example:

> The qazi occupies the chair of justice;
> He tells the rosary
> And invokes the name of God.
> Yet he takes bribes
> And deprives the rightful owner of his due;
> If one asks why,
> He quotes verses from the Quran.
>
> *Ramkali-ki-Var,* M.1, *p.951*

Again:

> Fie on them who trade in the Lord's Name,
> They destroy their farm
> And nothing will grow on it.
> Without true practice of the Word
> They will receive no honour in the hereafter.
>
> *Sarang-ki-Var, M.1, p.124*

One great obstacle in the spiritual path is the desire for material wealth. Man, in his quest for it, loses all sense of perspective. The more he gets, the more greedy he becomes. His greed grows the more it is fed. In the words of Guru Nanak:

> Thy appetite will never be appeased,
> Even if thou collect
> The wealth of the world.
>
> *Japji, M.1, p.1*

Man, in his ceaseless pursuit of wealth, employs all kinds of corrupt methods to gather it:

> Myriads of thefts,
> Myriads of illicit loves,
> Myriads of deceits and abuses,
> And myriads of secret frauds,
> Day and night he perpetrates.
>
> *Asa-di-Var, M.1, p.471*

Guru Nanak adds that without unfair means, wealth can never be accumulated. And tragically enough, what one gains through much cunning and many a disgrace remains behind when he dies. He says:

Many a one hath suffered disgrace,
Many a one hath been brought to ruin,
And all for accumulation of wealth.
Without sins wealth is not gathered,
And it goes not with one at the time of death.

Asa, M.1, p.417

In his denunciation of dishonest living, Guru Nanak was equally critical of Hindus and Muslims. The eating of beef by Hindus and pork by Muslims is taboo for them; Guru Nanak says that depriving one of his due is as bad as eating beef or pork:

To deprive one of his due
Is to eat beef for the one
And pork for the other;
The guru will stand by him
Who doth not take what belongs to others.

Var Majh, M.1, p.141

On vegetarianism

Guru Nanak was a staunch believer in vegetarianism. This belief was rooted in the ancient Indian tradition of non-violence and respect for life. Right from the time of Mahavir and Gautam Buddha, down to the present age, there has been a stress on non-violence in Indian culture.

Zulfiqar Adistani Azur Sasani, author of *Dabistan-i-Mazahib*, an authentic book on Guru Nanak, writes that meat and intoxicants were prohibited among Guru Nanak's disciples. In the author's own words:

Holding wine and pork unlawful, [Nanak] abstained from animal food and enjoined against cruelty to animals. After his death, meat-eating became common among his disciples. And when Arjan Mal, who is one of the prophetic order of Nanak, found that evil, he prohibited people from meat-eating and said, "This practice is not in accordance with the wishes of Nanak."[105]

In some sections of the Adi Granth, where Guru Nanak denounces the hypocritical mode of life led by Hindu and Muslim priests of his time, he specifically condemns the practice of meat-eating. He says:

> Countless are the cutthroats
> Who trade in violence;
> Countless are the sinners,
> Who thrive on sin and evil;
> Countless are the impious,
> Who live on unwholesome food.
>
> *Japji, M.1, p.4:18*

> He kills and cooks a goat,
> And eating it says to all:
> "Oh wear thou the sacred thread."
> …The man-eaters say their *namaz*,
> And those who wield the knife
> Wear the sacred thread.
> In their homes the Brahmins
> Blow the conch, but they too
> Relish the same taste of meat.…
> False is their speech,
> False their repast.…
> In their hands is a knife
> And they are the butchers
> Of the world.
>
> *Asa-di-Var, M.1, pp.471–472*

The institution of *langar*, the free community kitchen which the Gurus started, never permitted meat to be served. This tradition of keeping gurdwaras and other holy places free from the sacrilege of meat and intoxicants still continues. Their sanctity has not been allowed to be violated, despite various other changes that have occurred in the management of gurdwaras.

The *sakhis* of Mecca and Medina, and the *janamsakhi* of Bala[106] confirm the view that vegetarianism was practiced at the time of Guru Nanak.

At the root of the tradition of vegetarianism in India is a firm belief in the law of karma. No one can escape the effect of his actions. The result might come in this life or in one of the future ones. As one sows, so must one reap. If someone takes another's life in this birth, he has to pay back in the same coin in some future birth. So, if one kills an animal, he will have to be killed to pay off the debt. There is hardly any school of thought in India that does not believe in the law of karma, that is, the law of cause and effect. And this law extends to lives other than the present one. On the results of one's actions, Guru Nanak says:

> In the web of its own actions
> Is the whole world caught,
> And it does not realize it.
>
> *Maru, M.1, p.1009*

> Our good and bad deeds
> Are judged in the presence of the lord of law.
> Our actions keep us far from Him
> Or draw us near Him.
>
> *Japji, M.1, p.8*

A secondary but important factor behind vegetarianism in the Indian spiritual tradition is the firm belief that food has a profound effect on the character and mental make-up of the individual. There are foods that make one calm and serene, and there are foods that arouse passions and desires. There are foods that are conducive to solitude and meditation, and there are foods that direct human energies outwards and make one an extrovert. The saints stress that one must confine himself to those foods that are conducive to spiritual realization. For the kind of food one eats determines the kind of mind one has. Therefore they strongly enjoin upon their disciples not to eat stimulants of any kind – which include alcohol, hallucinatory drugs, meat, fish and eggs – and they prescribe instead a simple but nourishing diet of vegetables, fruit, milk, nuts and cereals.

Conclusion

Aristotle once said of his great master: "Plato is too high for the mean to praise him." Can this verdict not apply to our estimate of Guru Nanak? We often praise him as a great social reformer. We give him credit for producing communal harmony. We attribute to him the abolition of caste distinctions. Guru Nanak no doubt achieved all these to a great extent, but these were incidental results which flowed from his great teachings. He was much greater than we credit him as having been. Those who came into contact with him imbibed his teachings and followed his instructions. He gave them insight into the nature of the ultimate Reality. He gave them vision of the Supreme Being. He made them realize, not merely intellectually, but in personal experience of the Divine, that the all-pervading One resides within all men, and that differences among them are of appearance only, and superficial. He gave them that depth of knowledge through their mystic consciousness that the feeling of separateness itself became an illusion. After such an insight, what scope remains for conflict and aggressiveness? What room is left for malice, hatred and selfishness?

After the departure of a great master from this world, there is always the lurking fear that with the passage of time, his message will become diluted, polluted or even altogether forgotten. I cherish the hope that this will not happen in the case of Guru Nanak, and that the torch of his light will never be extinguished. Let me end with this humble prayer: Give us, O Lord, the wisdom to understand his teachings correctly, and the strength to put them into practice.

SECTION THREE

Hymns

Selected Hymns of Guru Nanak

Japji

Shalok

Sodar

Asa-di-Var

Rehiras

Arti

Sohila

Sidh Gosht

Paihre

Patti

Barah Maha

Japji

THE *JAPJI* IS GENERALLY REGARDED as the epitome of Guru Nanak's teachings. It was given the first place in the Adi Granth, when the fifth Guru, Arjan, compiled it. Some disciples are said to have remarked at the time that the *Japji* was too intricate and involved and needed elucidation and elaboration. Guru Arjan replied that the entire Adi Granth was an elucidation of the *Japji*.

Differing views are held regarding the circumstances and the date of its composition. According to most of the *janam-sakhis*,* the opening lines were uttered by Guru Nanak soon after his mystical experience at Sultanpur, when he disappeared into the river Bein. This would fix the date some time between 1500 and 1507. Most scholars, however, do not accept this view. They believe that the *Japji* as also *Asa-di-Var* and *Sidh Gosht* display a maturity of style and richness of content which would place the composition some time in the later part of the Guru's life, when he had finished his travels and had settled down at Kartarpur. This gives the probable date of the composition as 1532.

Japji follows the traditional pattern of contemporary compositions, beginning with an invocation to God and ending with thanksgiving on the successful completion of the work.

---

* For explanation of terms, see Glossary.

Japji commences with a statement on the nature of God: His omnipotence, uniqueness, immortality and the like. He is both Truth and Reality. It ends with the statement that the knowledge of God is obtained only through the grace of a master.

Japji is considered by the Sikhs as their most important prayer. They are supposed to recite it every morning before they start their day's work.

These excerpts have been selected as they illustrate important aspects of the *Japji*, as indeed of the entire teachings of Guru Nanak.

God the Absolute

In this extract, Guru Nanak pays tribute to the absolute nature of God. He is One. He is self-existent and self-sufficient. He is the Truth and the creator of all. He fears nothing, nor does He strike fear in anyone. Through the grace of the guru, one comes to know Him.

*Ik onkaar satnaam karta purakh**

He is one, He is the first.
He is all that is.
Eternal Truth is His Name.
He is the creator of all.
Fearing naught,
Striking fear in naught;
Timeless is His image.
Not begotten, He is self-existent.
Through the grace of the guru,
He is made known to men.

Japji, p.1†

---

* Punjabi and Hindi poetry is usually identified by its first line. The Punjabi first lines are given at the beginning of each poem in Section Three.
† Page numbers throughout refer to the pagination of the Adi Granth comprising 1,430 pages; the name of the section of the scripture precedes the page number.

God the Eternal

He is primordial. He was, He is and He ever will be. He is beyond time. He is beyond thought. He is beyond the silence of meditation. He cannot be known by the conquest of the worlds, for man's desire is insatiable.

Futile are the attempts of man to know Him. How then to find Him? How to get rid of the dark pall? Guru Nanak says that one way to do so is to merge our will in His, to make it our own.

> *Aadi sach jugaadi sach*
>
> He was in the beginning; He is through all ages;
> He shall be the One who lives forever.
> Beyond thought, no thinking can conceive Him,
> Not even if the minds of men
> Should think for ages and ages.
> Nor silence can see Him,
> Even if the minds of men
> Meditate on Him for ages and ages.
> Nor can He be known by gaining the worlds;
> For man's desire is never satiated,
> Even though all the worlds laden with gold
> Fall to his share.
> Nor can human thoughts carry man far;
> The movements of his mind,
> The thousand acts of wisdom of the world,
> Leave him dark; nothing avails.
> Vain are the ways of men.
> How then to find Him?
> How then to get rid of the dark pall?
> One way there is – to make His will our own.
> No other way, naught else.
>
> *Japji, p.1*

God's Supreme Will

God's will is sovereign. All things are the manifestation of His will. By His will all sentient life comes into being. It is His will that some are great, some small. Nothing is outside the range of His will. To seek His will is to live. One who has realized it never says, "'Tis I."

Hukamee hovan aakaar

Great is His will!
All manifest things are forms of His will.
His will is indefinable!
Of His will is made all sentient life;
It is His will that some are great,
Some are small.
All existence is bound by His supreme will.
Nothing is outside the sphere of His will;
Such is Truth!
Seek His will – this is to live.
If one sees the universal will at work,
Then one can never say, "'Tis I."

Japji, p.1

God the Infinite

The Lord is immeasurable. Human intellect is incapable of comprehending Him. Man can neither know His beginning, nor end.

Guru Nanak pays homage to the Lord, whom he calls the beginningless beginning, the colourless purity, the immortal truth and the performance behind all change.

Dharati hor parai hor hor

Endless is Thy creation,
We see nor Thy near nor Thy far,
Thou hast nor this nor that shore,
We cannot touch Thy limit at any point.

Japji, p.3

Aades tisai aades

Salute the beginningless beginning,
The colourless purity,
The deathless verity,
The changing permanence
That changeth not through ages and ages.

Japji, p.6

God the Creator

In this beautiful excerpt, nature is described as a miracle of God. There are countless forms of life found in the cosmos. They signify the Lord's writing. No one can write or even count what He has 'written'.

How beautiful are the forms which He has created! By the sheer grace and numbers of what the Lord has created, His power is hard to imagine. How great is the kingdom of nature which He has bequeathed to man! And He created just by one Word this many-splendoured nature. It is beyond the power of man to praise it adequately, much less to understand it.

Jeea ajat ranaga ke naav

Ah! who can count
The countless forms of life
With which this world teems
Below and above,
Their names or species or hues?
They are the letters
Writ by His flowing pen;
Who now can write, count or reckon
That which the Maker has made?
How fair are the forms
Made by the Creator!
How mighty Thou, O Lord!
How enchantingly sweet
Is Thy emanation!
How great is the kingdom of nature
That Thou hast given to man!
Thou didst create all this
But by one Word.

From one Word of Thy lips
Is made this thousand-revered nature!
How shall I praise Thy miracle of nature?
At its altar,
I fain would lay myself as a sacrifice,
But too poor am I
To gain my heart's desire,
Ah, even but once!
Thy will, O Beautiful, is good.
Thy pleasure is all!

Japji, p.3

Beyond the Theologians

The pundits do not know when the world was created. The Puranas throw no light on this subject. The qazis, too, have failed to give the date of creation in the Quran. Nor do the yogis know of the hour, the day or even the season when creation came. He alone knows the 'beautiful hour' when He made this world.

The Lord, the 'beautiful maker', is beyond human speech, praise and description. Still everyone speaks of Him according to his limited intellect. Each of them thinks himself wiser than the other.

He is infinite and great, and great is His *Nam*. Whatever He wills comes to pass. He knows whatever exists.

If anyone claims that he knows Him, he is little better than a fool in the eyes of those who live in the higher regions. There are skies above skies and earths below earths which human intellect can never grasp.

All knowledge of man and all the holy books written by him proclaim but one truth: He is the substance behind all phenomena. He is the one metal of which all utensils are made. There is none other. Since the infinite cannot be reduced to the finite, all attempts to describe Him are failures. Only the infinite can know the infinite.

All that we finite beings can do is lose ourselves in His worship and in His adoration. We need not attempt to fathom the unfathomable. Let us merge ourselves with the infinite, just as rivers flow to the sea with a song. They do not know, nor do they care, how wide is the ocean's flood.

Vel na paaeeyaa pandati

The pundits know naught
Of the dawn of Thy creation
To record it in the Puranas,
Nor have the qazis seen that time
To put it down in the Quran,
Nor do the yogis know
Of that season, hour, date nor day.

That beautiful hour
When He made this world,
He alone doth know;
Beyond our speech, our praise,
Our description and knowledge
Is the beautiful Maker!

Still they speak of Him,
Each and all according to their mite,
As one is wiser than another.
He is the great and the infinite One,
And great is His *Nam*;
What He wills comes to pass.
He knows whatever is.

If anyone else says he knows Him,
He is but a fool
In the eyes of the dwellers
Of higher regions.

There are skies above skies
And earths below earths,
And man's mind is tired
Of this great search,
It cannot reach the end of His vastness.

All knowledge of man
And his thousand books proclaim
But one substance of which
All this is made.
There is but one metal in all.
None else! None else!

How can the infinite
Be reduced to the finite?
All attempts to describe Him are lost.
The infinite knows the infinite.

Ours is to lose ourselves
In worship and adoration,
Nor need we ask, Why?
No need to fathom the unfathomable:
As the rivers flow to the sea with their song,
Let us flow on to the infinite,
Not knowing how wide is the ocean's flood.

Japji, p.4

Beyond the Scriptures

The Vedas have spoken of Him, as also the Puranas. The learned have discoursed on Him. Indra and Brahma have expounded His law. Krishna and his *gopis*, Shiva and the adepts tell about God. The Buddha proclaimed Him. Millions have spoken thus, and millions more will come, yet He will forever remain undescribed.

The Lord is beyond our comprehension. He is as great as only He is. He is the one Truth. He is the one Reality. He alone knows Himself.

Dharam khand kaa eho dharam

Though the Vedas and the Puranas
Speak of Him,
Though the learned discourse on Him,
And Indra and Brahma expound His law,
Krishna and his *gopis* speak of Him,
Shiva and the adepts tell about God
And all the Buddhas proclaim Him,
Though millions have spoken thus;
Though millions came and sat
And left their seats and have gone,
And if there came as many more creations
That speak of Him,
Yet He shall forever remain the Undescribed!
Thou, O Lord,
Art more than our minds can comprehend.
Thou art as great as Thou canst be!
Thou art the Verity,
Thou art the one Reality;
Thou alone knowest Thyself.

Japji, p.7

The Power of the Master

The guru's Word is the divine melody; the guru's Word is the holy writ, the guru's Word is all-pervading. The guru is higher than the three gods, Brahma, Vishnu and Shiva, and the mother goddess Shakti.

It is through the guru that one knows God truly. The guru reveals the mystery that there is only one Truth and one bestower of life, and that one should never forget Him.

Gurmukh naadang gurmukh vedang

The Word of the guru
Is the inner music;
The Word of the guru
Is the highest scripture;
The Word of the guru
Is all-pervading.
The guru is Shiva,
The guru is Vishnu and Brahma,
The guru is the mother goddess.
If I knew him as he truly is,
What words could utter my knowledge?
Enlightened by God,
The guru has unraveled one mystery:
There is but one Truth,
One bestower of life;
May I never forget Him.

Japji, p.2

The Authority of the Master

They whom the Lord appoints and to whom He gives authority are the true teachers of men. They guide and lay down for
man the true path. They are the honoured ones in the court
of the Lord. They are the stars that illumine this earth. The
chosen of God come under their protection. They themselves
are absorbed in the contemplation of God.

> *Panch parvaan panch pardhaan*
>
> Those whom He appoints
> And to whom He gives authority
> Are the true teachers of man;
> They guide and lay down for man the path.
> They are the honoured of the kingdom of God.
> They are the stars that illumine this earth.
> The chosen of God live in the guru;
> Their one fixed *dhyan* is his person.
> (Their breath is his breath,
> Their life is his life.
> Their mind wanders not,
> Nor their heart strays
> From the sphere of the sphere
> Of the love of the Lord!)
>
> *Japji, p.3*

Nam as Reality

Nam pervades as the vital principle in all living beings. It is the substance, the inner core of things. It makes the heart vibrant.

The Lord is the sustainer of all life. He is the giver of all things to men. Nothing belongs to us, not even our life. What then can we offer Him in return for His bounty?

The early morning hours are considered by saints as invaluable for meditation. Our sins will then be washed away and we shall reach His presence with honour. We shall be released from bondage by His glance.

The light of divine knowledge comes from within and God is seen as the inner resplendence.

Saacha saahib saach naaee

His *Nam* is the substance
Of which all life is made.
His *Nam* enlarges the heart
And makes it limitless.
His creatures beg
Their daily needs from Him,
He gives all things to men.
Naught is our own,
All is His that we possess,
This life and all is His!
With what offerings
Could we enter His temple?
With what virtue, His presence?
What words have we on our lips
To win His delight?
Meditate on His *Nam* at morn
Wet with the ambrosia of the daybreak!

Our doings make this vesture of our body;
The heaven shall cover our shame with honour,
And by the light of His glance
We shall go free.
The dawn of divine knowledge
Comes from within,
And man sees God as the light revealing.
High above all things is the revealed Infinite,
In Himself self-resplendent, glorious!

Japji, p.2

By Hearing the Word

In the following four stanzas Guru Nanak expands upon the fruit of communion with the Word, whose secret is revealed by a master.

One who has attained such communion gains knowledge of the earth and other heavenly bodies and the power that supports them. To him the mystery of creation stands revealed. He is purged of all sins and suffering. He triumphs over death and can pass through its portals – the tenth door – unscathed.

Communion with the Word enables one to gain supernatural powers and yogic insight into the mystery of the self. He also comes to understand the true import of scriptures and gains various other achievements, leading ultimately to God-realization.

Suniai sidh peer sur naath

By hearing the Word
Men become perfected, spiritual adepts,
God-like and true yogis.
By hearing the Word
Men learn of the earth,
The power that supports it and the firmament.
By hearing the Word
Men learn of the upper and nether regions,
Of islands and continents.
By hearing the Word
Men triumph over the Lord of Death.
O Nanak,
His devotees ever live in a state of bliss;
By hearing the Word
They are absolved of all sins and sorrows.

Suniai eesar barma ind

By hearing the Word
Mortals are to godliness raised.
By hearing the Word
The foul-mouthed are filled with pious praise.
By hearing the Word
Are revealed the path of yoga
And the secrets of the body.
By hearing the Word
Is acquired the wisdom of all scriptures.
O Nanak,
His devotees ever live in a state of bliss;
By hearing the Word
They are absolved of all sins and sorrows.

Suniai sat santokh gyaan

By hearing the Word
One becomes true, contented and wise,
By hearing the Word
The merit of bathing in all holy places
Is achieved.
By hearing the Word
Men achieve scholastic honour.
By hearing the Word
Men attain to the blissful state of *sahaj*.
O Nanak,
His devotees ever live in a state of bliss;
By hearing the Word
They are absolved of all sins and sorrows.

Suniai sara guna ke gaah

By hearing the Word
One plumbs the depth of the ocean of virtue.
By hearing the Word
One becomes learned, holy and the King of kings.
By hearing the Word
The blind are set on the path.
By hearing the Word
The unfathomable becomes fathomable.
O Nanak,
His devotees ever live in a state of bliss;
By hearing the Word
They are absolved of all sins and sorrows.

Japji, pp.2-3

By Practicing the Word

After describing the benefits of communion with the Word, Guru Nanak goes on to give further details of the state of one who through continual practice of the Word has become immersed in it. His state is, in fact, indescribable.

Such a one transcends the ordinary level of consciousness and acquires an enlarged, cosmic awareness. He is now able to envision the whole of creation. Drawn by the power of the divine melody of the Word, he progresses from one spiritual plane to another, till he reaches the final destination, the primal source. In the course of his spiritual journey, his horizon widens. His soul is cleansed of all past sins. He is released from the binding chains of karma. He transcends suffering and escapes the wheel of transmigration. Once he has attained true salvation, he can also help others on the path.

Great indeed is the power of the Word, but unfortunately there are few who know it.

Manne kee gat kahee naa jaae

The state of one who is immersed in the Word
Cannot be described;
Whosoever attempts it will realize his folly.
No paper or pen, nor any scribe
Can ever describe his condition.
Great, indeed, is the power of the Word,
But few there are who know it.

Mannai surat hovai man budh

By practice of the Word
One soars into cosmic consciousness;
By practice of the Word
One envisions the whole creation.
By practice of the Word
One is released from sorrow and suffering.
By practice of the Word
One goes not with Yama after death.
Great, indeed, is the power of the Word,
But few there are who know it.

Mannai maarag thak naa pae

By practice of the Word
One rises to higher spiritual realms unhindered;
By practice of the Word
One is received with honour in His court.
By practice of the Word
One does not lose oneself on the false path;
By practice of the Word
One gets connected to the righteous way.
Great, indeed, is power of the Word,
But few there are who know it.

Mannai paavai mokh duaar

By practice of the Word
One attains emancipation;
By practice of the Word
One also saves his kith and kin.

By practice of the Word
One redeems many others through guidance;*
By practice of the Word
One wanders not, nor goes abegging.
Great, indeed, is the power of the Word,
But few there are who know it.

Japji, p.3

---

* After he becomes an adept himself.

Words and the Word

Countless names have been given to the Lord and countless are the places with which He is associated. Countless are the heavenly bodies that owe their existence to Him. Even the word 'countless' is quite inadequate to depict Him.

We use words in speech and in writing. Words give us sensory knowledge and they enable us to sing His praises. It is by them that our destiny gets 'written', based on our past deeds. For we are within the realm of time and space and its consequent karmic law. But He who ordains everything is above such limitations. He manifests Himself through His creative and all-pervading Word. Such power of the Lord, who is everlasting, is beyond human comprehension.

Asankh naav asankh thaav

Myriad are Thy names
And myriad Thy places;
Inaccessible are Thy countless
Heavenly planes;
Even the word 'myriad'
Fails to describe Thee.
By words we describe Thee
And by words we praise Thee.
By words we acquire knowledge
And in words we sing Thy hymns.
We use words in speech and writing;
In words our fate is ordained,
But He who ordains is above such writ.
As Thou ordainest, so do we receive.
Thou pervadest all,
And nothing is where Thy Word is not.

How can I ever conceive
Of Thy creative power?
Too poor am I
To sacrifice myself for Thee.
Whatever pleases Thee is good;
Thou art forevermore,
O formless One.

Japji, p.4

Nam the Cleanser of Sins

When our hands and feet get soiled with mud, we can clean them with water. When our body becomes dirty, we can wash it. But when the dirt of sins sullies our mind, only His *Nam* can restore it to its original transparent purity.

Men are ruled by the law of karma. They reap as they sow. They go through the wheel of birth and death, as He wills.

The merit earned by making pilgrimages and penances or being kind and philanthropic is nothing compared to 'going within oneself' and bathing in the ambrosial lake within. If holy inspiration has not blossomed within, if the seed of faith has not sprouted in the heart, if the plant of love has not taken root, all external activities and ritual observances have been in vain.

Bhareeai hath pair tan deh

Thy hands and feet and skin
When mud besmeared
Are washed free of dirt by water,
Our clothes when soiled
Are cleaned by washing;
But when the dirt of sins
Makes dark our mind,
Naught else but Thy *Nam*,
Can restore to it
Its fair transparency;
It needs be washed
With the love of Thy *Nam*, O Lord!
Man reaps as he sows.
It is His will, men come and go
In the wheel of birth and death.

Small indeed is the honour
Won outside of self
By making pilgrimage and penance,
Or being kind and giving charity to others,
If one has not been within himself
And bathed in the ambrosial river within –
If one has not felt holy inspiration within,
If the seed of faith
Is not put in the soil of the heart,
If love has yet not sprung!

Japji, p.4

The Finitude of Man

Man is an ignoramus, but he thinks much of himself. His ideas, his resolves, his efforts will come to nothing if they are not already in his destiny. He does not realize that his past deeds are his own undoing. He cannot escape the wheel of birth and death except through the grace of God.

Guru Nanak prays to the Lord not to leave him to himself. Of his own will, he can neither speak nor keep silent. Let him not be thrown on his own strength, for by himself he cannot even pray or offer himself to the Lord. He has no power either over life or over death. Nor can he be a beggar or a king by his own choice. By himself he can neither know his soul nor the Lord. Nor can he ever cross the ocean of change, this phenomenal world. Guru Nanak ends by saying that let anyone who thinks otherwise, try. All men are the same. All men are weak, when viewed from the height of the Eternal.

Aakhan jor chupai na jor

Man plays the fool
In thinking so much of himself.
What are his resolves,
His ideas and efforts, labour and pain?
Are not his deeds
As fates combined against him?
Is not his past self his own undoer?
No way of escape
From the wheel of birth and death
But His saving mercy,
His grace and glance!

O Lord, throw me not on myself,
Of my will I can nor speak
Nor observe silence.
Throw me not on my strength;
Of my will I can nor pray
Nor give myself to Thee!
I can follow nor life nor even death!
Not by my own power
Can I a beggar be, or a king;
Throw me not on myself,
For by myself I can nor gain my soul
Nor the knowledge of Thyself.
Throw me not on myself,
For I am unable to cross the sea of change.
I cannot, O Lord!
Let him who has strength in his arms try,
But man is weak man for all that.
All men are the same, nor more nor less,
When seen from the Eternal.

Japji, p.7

Sach Khand

In the highest realm lives the Lord. In this absolute realm reigns the formless One. His glance is the soul's beatitude. This realm contains all the other regions. Out of the formless Infinite came the forms and finite beings.

Sach khand wasai nirankaar

Higher than all
Is the realm of my Lord –
The realm absolute!
Here reigns the formless One.
Here His glance is my soul's beatitude.
In this realm are contained all regions,
And all the starry heavens without end.
Out of the formless Infinite
Came the forms and finite beings,
Never hasting, never resting.

Japji, p.8

Shalok

Born of Air, Water and Earth

In the epilogue of the *Japji* Guru Nanak concludes that the human body is the joint product of air, water and earth. He has compared air to the guru, because air is as indispensable to the life of the body as the guru is to the life of the soul.* Water has been called the father as water nourishes plants and makes nature verdant. The earth produces living beings from inanimate nature and is vast in extent, qualities which characterize the mother. Night and day rock us in their lap and nurse us with love, while the winds fan us with a gentle breeze.

Guru Nanak then emphasizes the importance of human actions, which will be judged after our death according to their merit before Dharam Rai, the dispenser of justice. Our actions will determine whether we are near or far from Him. Whosoever meditates on *Nam* will escape the fatigue of ceaseless transmigration. He will then enjoy everlasting bliss in union with the Lord. And not only will he himself be liberated; he will bring freedom to countless others.

---

* "Air is called 'guru' because, just as without a guru man's soul remains dead, so without air the physical body cannot breathe" (*Shabdarath*, 1:8, fn.14).

Pavan guroo paanee pita

Born of the waters,
We children of great earth
Learn our lessons from the winds,[*]
And we spin in the arms
Of day and night;
They nurse us well.
Before the great judge
Will be read out our actions,
Good or bad;
By our own actions
We shall be nearer Him or farther off.
Those who fix their *dhyan* on *Nam*
Will pass above the pain of labour.
Their task is done.
Bright are their faces!
And in the joy of one liberated soul
Shall many more be,
Through His great love, made free!

Japji, Shalok, p.8

---

[*] Literally, 'air the guru'.

Sodar

The Door

There is a door* through which one can enter the inner spiritual regions. The spiritual journey will ultimately end in the highest realm, where union with the Lord will be attained. This door, in esoteric terms, signifies for the mystic the third eye, which in Hindu scriptures has been mentioned as *shiv netra* or 'Shiva's eye'. In Muslim scriptures it has been called *nuqta-i-suvaida* or the 'black spot'. In the Bible it has been named the 'single eye'.†

This has been called 'the door' by Guru Nanak because the spiritual journey really commences from this point. It is, as it were, the threshold through which one enters the great mansion.

It is from this entrance that one can hear the music of the world below. From here also is obtained a panoramic view of all that one surveys. Even gods and goddesses are seen engaged in adoration of the Lord.

At this stage the ability to be a seer, the ability to prophesy, is acquired. One's vision is enlarged and events which at the lower level are to happen in the future acquire the character of the present.

---

* *Sodar*, literally, 'that door'.
† "If thine eye be single, thy whole body shall be full of light" (Matt. 6:22).

The entire activity of the universe, with the movements of its stars, planets and satellites, seems like a symphony or an orchestra. All move according to His will. He controls all that happens in the cosmos. He is seen as the King of kings, the absolute Lord.

Sodar keha so ghar keha

Where art Thou, O Lord?
Where is Thy door?
Where is Thy tower-house
From where Thou carest for all,
On whose walls breaks the music of the universe
In its endless song?
How many are the instruments!
How countless are the times and chants
Of this world-music!
How countless are the voices that sing,
Countless are their undulations!
O Lord,
The winds and waters and fires sing Thee;
The king of right and wrong, and his angels;
Ishwar and Brahma
And the goddesses Thou hast clothed
With Thy beauty,
Sing Thee;
Indra, the owner of the three worlds
With his court of gods,
Sings the same chorus!
The silence of the adepts and saints sings!

The heroes of self-control,
Of patience, of celibacy, of learning,
Are a song to Thee!
The seers pass with prophecy along the ages,
Singing;
And the goddesses that invest the air,
The sky and earth
With the music of their limbs and eyes,
Their robes and gems, their life and joy,
Are a song.
The holy lands and rivers roll in music,
The crystal jewels of men roll in Thy song.
The mighty and all-heroic are made of song.
Thy kingdoms four sing Thee!
And Thy vast solar systems,
Thy planets and their satellites
Whom Thou art holding in Thy hands
Raise the music of Thy praise!
Only those whom Thou admittest
Can enter into this song;
Thy poets, divinely led,
Whose souls are dyed
With the red dye of Thy lips,
Are in Thy song eternal!
There is music in music,
Aye, music beyond music!
Transcendental is Thy song!
The same and the same and the eternally True
Is my Lord!
He forever subsists, His *Nam* is True.

He is, He shall be;
He cannot be thought away,
Nor doth He depart.
He made this world
Of diverse shapes and colours,
Fold on fold, embryo within embryo,
That new to newer grows
And watches my Lord and His, in glory!
All moves by His will.
He wills as He wills.
None can undo His will.
My Lord is the King of kings,
The Absolute!

Japji, p.6

Asa-di-Var

ASA-DI-VAR IS A COLLECTION of hymns meant to be sung in the early hours of the morning like the *Japji*. But it is generally sung in a group, whereas the *Japji* is recited by the individual. It is composed in the form of a heroic ballad *(var)* and is set to the musical mode of *Rag Asa*, associated with the mood of devotion. It is divided into *shaloks* (staves or couplets) and *pauris* (stanzas). They follow each other as a statement and a commentary thereon.

Asa-di-Var is not restricted to a single theme, nor is it a logical development of a particular thesis. Nevertheless there is one idea that seems to underlie the whole work: how can man elevate himself from his present low state to the divine, and thus be ready for union with God?

The *Var* opens with praise of the master. It is he who can raise man to the level of the Lord. Anyone who thinks he can by himself accomplish it without the master, is doomed to failure.

God created the cosmos and the laws which govern it. These laws are all true and just. Guru Nanak suggests that we should glorify the Lord and His Name, because He alone is immortal and bountiful. We cannot comprehend the ways of the Lord. All that we can do is marvel, and shower praise on Him.

All that exists in the world abides in His 'fear', that is, it works according to His will. He alone is completely fearless, for He alone is totally free. He alone is beyond time. Even the great incarnations of Lord Vishnu, Rama and Krishna performed like jugglers under the Lord's command and then left, unliberated victims of the karmic law and of the cycle of transmigration.

Guru Nanak says that God-realization is not attained by wandering about. It comes through a true teacher, a *Satguru*, whom one meets through the grace of God. The true master imparts the method for practicing the Word, *Shabd*, which enables the disciple to transcend his mind and ego, and attain liberation from the wheel of birth and death.

God created both reality and illusion, and He can help us to distinguish between the two. We cannot rise above illusion and merge in reality by performing rituals, which are a futile activity.

Without the intercession of a perfect master, a *Satguru*, no one has or ever will realize God, because God manifests Himself in the *Satguru*. He is the spokesman for God, and he is our only link with the Word or *Shabd* that takes us back to God.

Ego is the root of all ignorance, all evil. To overcome ego and purify the mind, one has to lead a pure life, abstain from meat and wine, and practice the Word imparted by his master.

No amount of book-learning can teach us how to find God. No book can ever be a substitute for a master. In fact, book-learning without spiritual practice often boosts the ego. Likewise, going on a pilgrimage usually makes a man sanctimonious. Nor can asceticism do any good, for the sense of selfhood can be eradicated only by practice of the Word.

When a man becomes pure, he sees the light of God pervading everything. He then becomes compassionate to all living beings.

Ours is a dark age *(kaliyuga)*. Evil passions like lust and greed have complete sway over people. Our scholars have no real learning; our soldiers have no real valour. God knows our innermost secrets and we shall get what we deserve.

Pain is often a blessing, and comfort a curse. Pain can be the panacea for our ills because it directs our attention towards God; an easy life, on the other hand, may cause us to forget the Lord. The only way to escape from the evils of *kaliyuga* is to find a true master, whose teaching and spiritual guidance is like balm.

One should not be deceived by appearance. Guru Nanak gives the example of the silk-cotton tree, which is graceful to look at – huge and straight with an enormous spread – but neither its leaves, nor its flowers, nor its fruit are of any use. Greatness lies in humility, like the fruit-laden tree that bows down to the earth.

Exhibitionism, such as daubing the forehead with saffron and parrot-like repetition of scriptures, is of no avail. The sacred thread of the Hindus may become soiled, burned or broken. Why not make a sacred thread of mercy, contentment, discipline and truth?

Guru Nanak points out that the people who earn their wealth by dishonest means and then offer a part of it on behalf of their dead forefathers will be charged with theft. Even the priest who performs the obsequial ceremony will be punished.

Cleanliness and purity consist in what lies in our heart, the motives with which we see, we hear and we act.

Guru Nanak says that one should not denigrate women. They are conceived and born even as men are conceived and born. Why slander the sex that gives birth to kings and great men? And is there anyone living who is not born of woman?

Indeed, we should not slander anyone. A slanderer's arrow poisons his own body and mind. Everyone shuns a slanderer. People take him to be a knave and spit on him. One who is false from within but manages to earn respect and fame through cunning is an imposter. Even a beggar in rags who is rich at heart is better than he.

Praise the perfect master, the *Satguru*, as the greatest of mortals, because it is he who teaches the path of righteousness. He exorcizes the evil within men and prepares them for union with God.

The following excerpts have been selected as representative of the *Asa-di-Var*.[*]

---

[*] See also pp.346–351.

Who Dwell Not on the Guru

Those who consider themselves all-wise and do not seek the
guidance of a guru are like spurious sesame seeds, which are
discarded and left behind in the fields. They who have no master are forlorn. They are forsaken and yet they have a hundred
'masters' to please – their desires, cravings and fears. Even when
they seem to prosper materially, they are wretched within.

Naanak guroo na chetni

Nanak, they who dwell not on the guru
And are wise in themselves,
Like the spurious sesame
Are abandoned on the farm;
Abandoned and alone,
They have a hundred masters to please,
And though they seem to flourish,
Within the body of the wretches
There is nothing but ashes.

Asa-di-Var, p.463

The Deluded World

Countless good deeds and countless virtuous acts will not bring deliverance from suffering and the cycle of birth and death. Nor will austerities or visits to holy places, heroism on the battlefield or reading scriptures lead to salvation.

The Creator regards all these devices as false. It is only His grace that blesses the one He wills with Truth. His grace manifests itself in the form of the true guru. The unwise one does not know it, and being self-willed takes himself to be self-sufficient.

The scholar, equally deluded, inflates his ego by book knowledge. Even if he were to read cartloads of books and were to read ceaselessly, month upon month and year after year, with every breath of his life, it would all go to waste. There is only one thing that will count on the day of his death: love for his master and practice of the Word imparted by him.

As for worldly knowledge, the more one writes and reads, the more he is consumed by ego. The more one visits pilgrimage places, the more he boasts of his piety. The more one takes to a hermit's way of life, the more he suffers. All these ritualistic observances and external acts are futile.

In ascetic practices one starves and loses the taste of the tongue. In love for worldly people, one comes to grief. In keeping silence, he is wasted away. How can deluded man ever wake from slumber except through the help of his master?

The ascetic walks barefooted and suffers the pain of bruised feet. He eats unhygienic food and smears ash on his head. He lives in jungles or in a cremation ground and bears discomfort. Guru Nanak calls him a purblind fool because he does not know that all these austerities are futile without the practice of the Lord's Name. If he had been fortunate enough to meet a true master, he would have learned this truth and would have attained peace.

Guru Nanak concludes with the words: He on whom falls God's grace, realizes the Lord. Through practice of the Word he is emancipated both from hope and fear, as he has been able to overcome his ego.

Lakh nekeeya changiyaaia

Shalok
Myriads of good actions,
Myriads of approved virtues,
Myriads of austerities at holy places,
Or the practice of *sahaj yoga*
In the wilderness;*
Myriads of heroic deeds
And giving up one's life on the battlefield,
Myriads of scriptures
And knowledge of them,
Concentration
And the reading of the Puranas
Are vain.
For the Creator who created all,
And wrote the coming and going of all,
Before Him, all devices are false;
His grace alone is the true standard
Of our being approved.

2

---

* The reference is to *sahaj yog* of the yogis, which is different from that of the saints.

Pauri

True, O Lord, art Thou alone,
Who hast manifested Thyself in all as Truth.
He whom Thou dost bless with Truth,
Alone practices Truth.
It is through the true guru
That one receives the Truth,
And within our hearts is embedded
Nothing but the Truth.
The *manmukh* knows not the Truth;
Being self-willed, his life is lost.
Why did such a one come into the world,
Oh why?   8

Shalok

If we have cartloads of knowledge,
If our whole caravan
Carries nothing but loads of books;
Yea, if we have boatloads of them,
And fill up with them
All hollows and caverns too;
And read them all month upon month
And year after year,
And life after life, breath upon breath:
To God, one thing alone is of account –
Practice of the Word –
The rest is all the vain prattle of ego.   1

The more one writes and reads
The more is one burned,
The more pilgrim-places one visits
The more one prates;

The more one takes to garbs
The more his body suffers.
Now endure, my dear,
The results of thine own deeds.
And as one starves,
One loses the taste of the tongue;
And in love with the other,
One immensely grieves.
One wears not clothes
And shivers night and day.
Sunk in silence, one is wasted away:
Oh, how can one wake from slumber
Without the guru?
Barefooted he goes,
But whose is the fault?
He eats dirt
And throws ashes upon his head;
The purblind fool
Has himself lost his honour,
For without the Name,
He finds no place.
He lives in the wilderness
Or the cremation ground,
For the blind one knows not the Lord,
And regrets in the end.
If one meets the true guru
One attains peace
And imbibes the Lord's Name in the mind.
Nanak, he on whom is His grace,
Realizes the Lord,
And free from hope and fear,
He burns his ego with the Word.   9

Asa-di-Var, p.467

False Is the World

All things and relationships of the world are false. Guru Nanak gives a long list of them in this extract from *Asa-di-Var*.

The ruler of a state, as also his subjects, is transient and so are his palaces and other valuable possessions. The body and its beauty, no less than the garments which adorn it, are ephemeral.

All worldly relationships, too, are illusory. Even the one between the bride and the bridegroom is deceptive as well as temporary.

What a pity that the false ones love the false ones and forsake their Lord!

If the whole world is false, then whom shall we befriend? Guru Nanak answers that the Lord is True and His Name is True. So the only one worthy of our love is the Lord. Since the Lord is not visible to us, His manifest form in this world, that is, the master, merits our love. Whereas worldly relatives may forsake us during our life, the master does not leave us even after death. Guru Nanak prays that he be given the dust of his Master's feet to be applied to his forehead*. But this boon can only be granted if it be so written in his destiny. For man, otherwise, loses through his petty mind even the little merit he might have earned through service.

Kur raaja koor parja koor sab sansaar

False is the king,
False are the subjects,
False is the whole world.

---

* In esoteric terms the reference is to the effulgent light within, of the astral form of the master.

False is the palace,
False are the skyscrapers,
False the indwellers.
False is gold, false is silver,
False is the wearer of them.
False is the body,
False the garments,
False the infinite beauty,
False is the groom,
False the bride,
For they all come to ruin.
The false ones love the false
And forsake their creator Lord:
Then whom shall I befriend
When the whole world will pass away?
False are the sweets,
False the honey;
Yea, through falsehood have drowned
Boatloads of men.
Prays Nanak:
O Lord, without Thee, all is false.   *1*

We know the Truth
When the heart is True,
And we cleanse our body
Of falsehood
And make it pure.
We know the Truth
When we love the Truth,
And if hearing the Name
Our mind is pleased,
We attain to the door of deliverance.

We know the Truth,
When our soul knows the Way:
And 'cultivating' our bodies,
We sow the seed of God.
We know the Truth
If we receive the true instruction;
We are compassionate to all living beings
And give something by way of charity.
We know the Truth,
If we dwell on the pilgrim station
Of the soul.
As is the guru's will, so abide we.
Truth is the cure-all,
It washes one clean of sin.
But Nanak's prayerful call
Is to those whose only possession
Is the Lord's Truth.   2

I seek but the gift of the dust
(Of the guru's feet)
That I apply it to my forehead.
Forsaking false greed,
I dwell with a single mind
Upon the one unknowable Lord.
We reap the fruit as we plant the deeds.
Yea, if it be so writ in one's destiny,
One receives the dust of the guru's feet.
But through the ego of our little minds,
We lose even the merit of service.

Asa-di-Var, p.468

What Is God's Grace?

'Grace' is often identified with pleasure, health and prosperity. Guru Nanak, in this excerpt, defines grace as that which leads one to the remembrance of and union with the Lord. It is in this sense that he calls pleasure a malady, for it makes one forget the Lord. On the other hand, pain is a cure, for it is in adversity that we remember God.

Guru Nanak pays homage to the Lord by calling Him the Creator, Infinite, the True and the One whose light is in all beings.

Further, he gives tribute to his guru, for without his master he would never have gathered wisdom.

The distinction between the literate and the illiterate can be misleading. Guru Nanak says that a literate sinner is not to be preferred to an illiterate saint. A man is to be judged in terms of the actions he performs. As are the man's deeds, so is he known. We should, then, refrain from playing a part that will bring disgrace to us in the eyes of God. If we follow our mind's design, we shall come to grief.

Dukh daaroo sukh rog bhaya

Pain is the cure,
Pleasure the malady;
For where there is pleasure,
There Thou art not.
Thou art the Creator;
Who am I to create?
For if I try to create, I cannot.   *1*

A sacrifice am I to Thee,
O Thou who dwellest in Thy nature.

Limitless art Thou,
Whose end no one knows.   1:P*

In Thy creatures is Thy light
And in Thy light are Thy creatures;
In an artless art dost Thou pervade all,
Thou art the true Lord:
Beautiful is Thy praise.
Yea, he who praises Thee is ferried across.
Says Nanak: All wonder is the Lord's;
And whatever He has to do,
He does that indeed.   3

The pitcher holds the water,
But without water can the pitcher be shaped?
The mind is held by wisdom,
But how can one gather wisdom
Without the guru?   8

If a literate man be the sinner,
An illiterate saint is not punished in his stead.
For as are the deeds of a man,
So is he known.
Why play then such a play
Through which one loses in the true court?
Who is literate, who the illiterate,
Is to be considered in the life to come,
And he who follows his mind's will
Shall suffer hereafter.   12

Asa-di-Var, p.469

---

*P or 'pause' is the refrain, a couplet that is emphasized by placing the
word *rahau* ('pause') after it.

Impurity

Guru Nanak disillusions us about the idea of impurity. We find impurity in many things. Once the idea of impurity is accepted, one sees impurity in everything. There are worms in cow dung and in wood. There is life in every grain of corn. There is life in water, which gives the green colour to every plant and tree. If we were to conceive of impurity in this way, it would be impossible to avoid it. Guru Nanak says that impurity can be washed away only by the practice of the Word or by acquiring divine knowledge.

Impurity of the mind is of various kinds. Impurity of the heart is greed and that of the tongue is falsehood. Impurity of the eyes is gazing on another's wealth and his wife, and impurity of the ears is listening to slander. People who indulge in all these impure practices will surely go to hell, even if in appearance they are pure as swans. The source of all impurities is ignorance, which leads to worldly attachments.

One who wishes to become free from all impurities should seek the guidance of a master. He is the one worthy of all praise, for in him lies all greatness. Placing his hand on our foreheads he can remove all our evils. He can make the Lord Himself dwell within us. And with God manifest within us, we possess the greatest possible treasure.

Jekar sootak manneeyai sabtai sootak hoe

Shalok
If the idea of impurity be admitted,
There is impurity in everything:
There are worms in cow dung and in wood;
There is no grain of corn without life.

In the first place, there is life in water
By which everything is made green.
How shall we avoid impurity?
It falleth on our kitchens.
Saith Nanak,
Impurity is not thus washed away:
It is washed away by divine knowledge.   *1*

Impurity of the heart is greed,
Impurity of the tongue is falsehood;
Impurity of the eyes
Is gazing on another's wealth,
His wife and her beauty;
Impurity of the ears
Is listening to slander,
Nanak, the swanlike man
Who indulges in such practices
Shall go bound to hell.   *2*

All impurities consist in superstition
And attachment to worldly things.
Birth and death are ordained;
As it pleaseth God, we come and go.
Food and drink
Earned through honest means
Are pure.
Nanak, those who realize God
Through the guru
Are free of all impurity.   *3*

Pauri
Shower praises on the true guru
In whom lies all greatness.
If He wills, we meet the guru.
If it pleases the guru,
God dwells in our heart.
Placing his hand on our foreheads
He removes all evil from within us.
When God is pleased
The nine treasures are obtained.   *18*
Asa-di-Var, p.472

Evil Speech and Wicked Deeds

One who speaks evil of others, his own mind and body become evil. He acquires the reputation of an evil man. He is rejected in this world as also in the hereafter. People spit on his face and the Lord declines to admit him in His court.

If a person is wicked from within, but poses as virtuous and struts with pride, his filth will not be washed away, even if he were to bathe at all the holy places of pilgrimage. On the other hand, those who wear rags but are pure within are the good people of this world. Their mind is fixed on God and they are ever desirous of beholding Him. They live in this world as they like without fearing anyone except the Lord. They beg only at His door and are grateful for whatever He gives them.

Evil-doers will have to suffer the consequences of their evil deeds. In Guru Nanak's words, they will be pressed like oil in a mill.

The latter part of the hymn has a pantheistic strain. The Lord Himself created the world and He Himself infused power into it. He is the creator as well as the spectator. At the end, Guru Nanak entreats us not to forget the Lord, who has given us life and breath.

Naanak phikai boliyai tan man phika hoe

Shalok
Nanak, the mind and body
Of him who talketh evil
Are evil;
He is called most evil,
And most evil is his reputation.

The evil person
Is rejected in God's court,
His face is spat upon;
The evil person is known as a fool,
And he receiveth shoe-beatings
As punishment.   *1*

If a man,
Foul within and fair without,
Puff himself up in the world,
His filth will not depart
Even though he bathe
At the sixty-eight places of pilgrimage.
They who wear silk within
And rags without,
Are the good ones of this world;
They have set their heart on God
And ever seek to behold Him.
They laugh, they weep,
They keep silence, as they will;
They care not for anyone
Except for the true Lord.
They beg for food at God's door,
And only eat
When He giveth it to them.
For them there is but one court
As there is but one pen;
We and you are alike in that court.
The accounts of the wicked
Shall be examined
By the Lord of Justice
And they shall be pressed, O Nanak,
Like oil in a mill.   *2*

Pauri

Thou Thyself didst create the world,
And Thou Thyself didst infuse power into it.
Thou beholdest Thine own work,
Putting the chess pieces each in its place.
Whoever hath come shall depart;
The turn of each will come.
Why forget the Lord
Who awardeth life and breath?
With thine own hands
Arrange thine own affairs.   20

Asa-di-Var, p.473

Rehiras

REHIRAS IS A PART of the evening prayer of the Sikhs. It consists of hymns by Guru Ram Das and Guru Arjan, as well as two by Guru Nanak. Only those composed by Guru Nanak appear in this section. In the first hymn, he says that although all men speak of God's greatness, only he who speaks from personal experience knows how great He is. One who has seen Him, alone knows His greatness. For all others, He remains inconceivable and indescribable. Even theologians and preachers have been unable to grasp one jot of His greatness.

Guru Nanak further says that good deeds of men and their sublime achievements are His gifts. And when His grace is there, nothing can stand in the way of one seeking perfection. Guru Nanak concludes that perfection springs only from God, the true One.

In the second hymn, Guru Nanak begins with a highly charged devotional note. In remembering Him there is life, and in forgetting Him there is death. He is the essence of the devotee's life. And yet it is very hard to contemplate on His Name. In the strong desire for the Lord's Name all suffering is dissolved.

His Name can never be adequately praised. Men who have tried their best to do so grew tired but could not weigh His true worth. If all men with their joint effort were to exalt Him, He would neither grow greater nor lesser by their praise.

He is beyond birth and death. He is beyond suffering. He has an inexhaustible store of gifts, which never becomes empty. The greatest of all wonders is that there never was nor ever will be one like Him.

How Great He Is

Sun vada aakhai sabh koi

On hearsay
All speak of His greatness;
How great He truly is,
Only the one who hath seen Him can say.
None can assess His worth,
None can describe Him.
They who seek to describe Thee,
Have first to merge in Thee.   *1*

O my great Lord,
Thou art of depth unfathomable,
Thou art of virtues boundless.
None knoweth
How vast is Thy expanse.   *1:P*

All men of intuition
Have exercised their intuitive power;
All valuators have sought
To weigh Thy worth;
All the learned, the seers,
The men of piety
Have not been able to mouth
One jot of Thy greatness.   *2*

All charities, all austerities, all virtues,
The great achievements of men of miracles,
Without Thee no one attained.
Nothing can ever stand in the way of one
On whom Thou hast bestowed Thy grace.   *3*

Vain are their words
Who seek to praise Thee;
Thy treasuries are already full
Of Thy praises.
He to whom Thou givest,
What can ail him?
Says Nanak: The true One alone
Straightens out our problems.   4:2

Asa, p.9

Thy Name

Aakha jiva visrai mar jaau

I practice Thy Name and live;
I forget Thee and die.
How hard it is to practice Thy Name,
O true One!
If I long for Thy true Name, O Lord,
My woes shall wither away.   *1*

O mother, why should I forsake Him
Who is True, whose Name is Truth divine?   *1:P*

Many have tired themselves with praising Thee,
But not a whit of Thy true worth
Have they appraised.
Even if the whole universe
Rings with Thy praises,
Thou becomest neither greater nor lesser.   *2*
He neither dies,
Nor is there any grief over Him.
He gives and His giving knows no bounds.
His virtue is unique that He alone is;
None else ever was,
Nor ever will there be.   *3*

Thou art as great as Thy beneficence,
Thou who created the day as also the night;
He who forgets Thee is a low-caste wretch.
Says Nanak: Without Thy Name,
One is nothing but a worm.   *4:2*

Asa, p.9

Arti

THIS IS THE BEDTIME PRAYER of the Sikhs, which they recite just before going to bed.* It is traditionally believed that it was composed at Jagannath Puri, when Guru Nanak met Chaitanya Mahaprabhu.

Using the analogy of the *arti* or lamp-waving ceremony, Guru Nanak describes the beauty of nature, the handwork of God. In it the sky is compared to the salver, the sun and the moon to the bright lamps and the stars to the pearls scattered in the salver. The fragrance of the sandalwood forest is the incense, and the breezes blow the royal fan in service to the Lord. The flowers of the forests lie as offerings at His feet. What a wonderful worship of the Lord this is!

Above all, the melody of the unstruck sound is reverberating everywhere.

Although the Lord has no eyes, no ears, no shape, yet He sees and hears everything and pervades everyone. The cosmos is His play and Guru Nanak is bewitched by it. The light that illumines every heart is His light. But this light becomes manifest only through the guru's teachings.

The best *arti* is that which pleases the Lord.

---

*Like *Asa-di-Var* it is generally sung collectively, unless it is recited as a part of *Sohila-Arti*.

Guru Nanak ends by saying that he yearns for the lotus feet of the Lord, like the honeybee that thirsts for the nectar of flowers or the rainbird that drinks only raindrops, even if the vast ocean be spread before him.

Bedtime Prayer

Gagan mai thaal ravi chand deepak banei

The firmament is Thy salver,
The sun and the moon Thy lamps;
The galaxy of stars are as pearls scattered,
The fragrance of the sandal forest is Thine incense
That comes from the Malai Mountain;[*]
The breezes blow Thy royal fan,
The flowers of the forests
Lie as offerings at Thy feet.   *1*

And the unstruck melody reverberates
From within the drum.
What wonderful worship with lamps is this,
O Thou destroyer of birth and death!   *1:P*

Thousands are Thine eyes,
And yet Thou hast no eyes;
Thousands are Thy shapes,
And yet Thou hast no shape;

---

[*] A mountain in Madras, on which sandalwood is grown.

Thousands are Thy lotus feet,
And yet Thou hast not one foot;
Thousands are Thy noses,
And yet Thou hast no nose.
All this wonder of Thine bewitches me.   2

In every heart there is the same light;
By that light is every soul illumined.
But this divine light becomes manifest
Only by the guru's teachings.
What is pleasing to Thee, O Lord,
Is Thine *arti*, Thy worship with the lamps.   3

O Lord, my mind yearns for Thy lotus feet,
As the honeybee for the nectar of flowers.
Night and day, Lord, I am athirst for Thee,
Give the ambrosia of Thy mercy to Nanak:
He is like the rainbird
That drinks only raindrops,
So that he may ever dwell in Thy Name.

Dhanasari, p.13

Sohila

SOHILA,[*] 'SONG OF PRAISE', is the last prayer of the day recited at bedtime, just as *Japji* is the first prayer sung in the early morning.

The *Sohila* contains two of Guru Nanak's hymns. In the first hymn, it is enjoined upon man to meditate on the Lord while living. That way alone everlasting bliss will be attained. For the Lord resides within man and there He has to be searched for and found.

The bountiful Lord ever watches and looks after His creatures. No one can assess His greatness or set a price on His gifts.

The moment of death is the happiest time of one's life, according to Guru Nanak. It has been compared to the wedding day, when the bride (the soul) is united with the bridegroom (the Lord). The call for death comes to everyone, and Guru Nanak reminds us that the day of our summons is not far.

In the second hymn the truth is brought out that although the systems of philosophy may be varied, the Lord who rules over them all is One. There is a mention here of the six schools of thought in Indian philosophy, each of which gives its own viewpoint. Yet, they are aspects of one reality. Guru Nanak has compared divine knowledge to the sun, and the six schools to the seasons, which are all the products of the sun.

---

[*]The word *Sohila* is derived from *sowan wela* meaning in the Punjabi language "the time for sleep" (M.A. Macauliffe, *The Sikh Religion*, 1:258, footnote).

The House of the Lord

Jai ghar keerat aakheeai karte kaa hoe beechaaro

The house* in which dwells the Lord,
Seek Him in that house;
Sing His praises there,
And meditate in it on His Name.   *1*

Sing the praises of my fearless Lord,
I am a sacrifice unto that *Sohila*
Which brings bliss everlasting.   *1:P*

He who protects us every day,
Who watcheth His living creatures,
Whose gifts are beyond measure –
None can set a price on His gifts,
Or say how great He is.   *2*

The year and the day for my wedding is fixed;
Gather ye all to pour oil at the door
To welcome the bride;†
Offer your thanks to my true friend,‡
Through whom I shall meet my Lord.   *3*

To every house is sent the wedding call;
To everyone, every day, it is issued,
Remember Him, O Nanak,
Who sends the summons;
The day is not far when your turn will come.   *4:1*

Gauri Dipaki, p.12

---

* The body.
† According to Hindu custom, when the bride arrives at her in-laws' house
after marriage, oil is poured at the door as an auspicious omen.
‡ The guru.

The Lord Is One

Chhia ghar chhia gur chhia updes

Six the systems,* six their exponents,
And six are their different teachings.
But the Lord of them all is One,
Though various are His manifestations.   *1*

O brother, the house† in which
Abides the Creator-Lord,
Keep ye undefiled, unsoiled
The sanctity of that house.   *1:P*

Seconds, minutes, hours, watches of a day;
Lunar and solar days make up a month;
And though there are various
Periods and seasons,
One single sun runs through them all.
Likewise, O Nanak, the Lord is One,
However various His manifestations.

Asa, p.12

---

* The six schools of Indian philosophy.
† The body.

Sidh Gosht

Nanak and the Yogis

These are excerpts from the *Sidh Gosht*, a dialogue in which the yogis ask some basic questions on Guru Nanak's spiritual philosophy. The Guru answers all of them in detail.

Charpat Yogi asks how the sea of life, which is beset with grave dangers, can be crossed. Guru Nanak replies that one should live in this world like the lotus flower or like the duck. The roots of the lotus flower or water-lily are in water, but the blossom itself is always above the water level. The duck lives in water, but always flies with dry wings. So also our mind should be detached from worldly objects and persons, and attached only to the Lord. It should be fixed on the Word under the guidance of a master. We should be in the world but not of the world. It is in this way that we can cross the great ocean of life.

Then, Loharipa Yogi gives his own views on yoga and how human life should be led. He argues that one should shun towns and highways and retreat to forests and jungles. For sustenance one should eat roots and wild fruit. Also, for purification one should visit places of pilgrimage.

Guru Nanak replies that there is nothing wrong in living near highways and in towns, provided one is careful. One should not hanker after others' goods; he should remain attached only to the Lord's Name. What is required is not physical distance from the allurements of city life, but freedom from temptations in his mind. A practicing yogi should eat and sleep little.

Loharipa remonstrates that yoga has specific symbols, which a yogi must adopt. He should put on a patched coat, wear earrings and carry a beggar's bowl. His system, Loharipa says, is the best of the six systems of philosophy and his sect the best of the twelve yogic sects.[*]

Guru Nanak answers that his system lies in constant meditation on the Word. For him, the Word within is the wearing of earrings; seeing God in all things and in all men is putting on a patched coat and carrying a beggar's bowl. What can make man free is the Lord. The Lord is the Truth, as is His Name.

Another yogi questions why Guru Nanak left his home and wandered like a hermit. What does he seek to buy and how does he set free his disciples?

Guru Nanak answers that he left his home to look for a master. It was his intense longing to see the Lord that made him wander like a hermit. He trades in Truth, and sets free his companions through the grace of God.

Still another yogi asks Guru Nanak what the source of life is. To which period does his system belong and who is his guru? Who are his disciples? What teaching keeps him in detachment?

Guru Nanak answers that from air originated life. His system is the path of the true guru. And the real form of the true guru is the Word, while the true form of the disciple is the soul. What keeps him detached is meditation on the Lord. God becomes manifest to him through the Word. The flames of desire are extinguished by saints.

----

[*] Het; Pav; Ai; Gamya; Pagal; Gopal; Kanthri; Ban; Puj; Choli; Rawal; Das.

A yogi then asks more questions. How can steel be chewed with teeth of wax? What food can cure the ego? In what cave can peace be found for the mind? What is pervading everywhere, with which the mind should be united? What is that form on which the mind should contemplate?

Guru Nanak answers: Eliminate your ego from within yourself. Realize that there is none other than God. The world is, no doubt, hard as steel for the stubborn and self-willed people of the world, but through the power of the Word it can be digested. Both outside and within yourself seek the knowledge of God. By the grace of the perfect master, you will die no more. You will die only once to live forever.

The yogis then ask where the Word abides. Guru Nanak answers that the Word abides within man and one has to attune oneself to it. Once the attunement is attained, one becomes all-wise and all-seeing and eventually merges into the Lord Himself.

When the Word has been realized within, it is seen pervading the entire universe, like air. In other words, the Lord abides in all, without any artifice, 'in an artless art'.

It is through the perfect master that the Word is realized within. After this realization, God is seen to exist everywhere and in everyone. The God-realized man transcends the world of multiplicity and duality into that of unity. The One, he perceives, is without colour or form. Whatever the God-realized man utters is of the quintessence, for he has realized the infinite Lord. He has risen above the three attributes and has stilled his mind. He has known the paths of *sukhmana, ira* and *pingula* and knows that the Lord is beyond all these paths.

CHARPAT YOGI QUESTIONS:

Dunya saagar dutar kahiai

The sea of life is hard to cross,
How can we safely reach the other shore?

NANAK ANSWERS:

Aape aakhai aape samjhai

How can one instruct him who says he knows,
Who says he has crossed the ocean of life?
What answer then, need I give thee?   4

As the lotus flower
Does not drown in the pool,
As the duck
Is not made wet by the pond,
As the flower thrusts upwards,
As the duck swims,
So is the soul
Intent upon practice of the Word.
One can safely cross
The great sea of life
Living in solitude,
Utterly intent
Upon the One;
In the midst of worldly desires,
Become free from them.
Nanak is the slave
Of the one who beholds
The Inaccessible
And maketh others behold Him.   5

LOHARIPA YOGI ARGUES:

Haatee baatee rahai niraale

Know this to be the way of yoga:
Shun towns and highways,
Live in the forests under the trees,
On roots and wild fruit.
This is the wisdom
The yogis impart.
Also for purification,
One must bathe
At the places of pilgrimages.   *7*

NANAK ANSWERS LOHARIPA:

Haatee baatee need na aavai

Even while living
In towns and near highways
Remain alert; do not covet
Your neighbour's goods.
Without the Name
The mind is stilled not,
Nor are our appetites assuaged.
As the guru has shown shops and cities
Within the home of this body,
We trade in Truth,
Reposed in the trance of *sahaj*.
We eat but little,
We sleep but little,
This, saith Nanak,
Is the quintessence of yoga I've found.   *8*

Let the Lord's vision be thy coat,
Thy earrings and thy wallet, O yogi.
The One alone pervades
The twelve yogas;
There are six systems of philosophy,
But the Path is one.
It is through this knowledge
That thy mind is tamed
And it suffers no more blows.
Nanak speaks,
But only through the guru
Will you understand;
In this lies the true way of yoga.   9

Let the Word within thee be thine earrings,
Rid thyself of ego and attachment,
As also of lust and anger;
The Word of the guru
Will give thee this realization.
Behold thou the Lord
Pervading everywhere;
Make this thy wallet, thy coat.
The Lord is True and True is His Name;
He testifies to the Truth of the guru's Word.   10

A YOGI QUESTIONS:

Kis kaaran grih tajio udaasi

Why hast thou forsaken thy home
And become a recluse?
Why hast thou donned the garb
Of a mendicant?
What is it that you seek to buy?
How settest thou free thy disciples?   17

NANAK ANSWERS:

Gurmukh khojat bhae udaasi

I left my home to look for a master;
The desire to see the Lord
Hath made me a hermit.
I am out to buy Truth.
Through the grace of the guru
I shall set free my companions.   *18*

A YOGI QUESTIONS:

Kavan mool kavan mat vela

What is the source of life?
To what period belongeth thy system?
Who is thy guru of whom thou art the disciple?
What gospel keepeth thee detached?
Tell us all this, my child.   *43*

NANAK ANSWERS:

Pavan arambh satgur mat vela

From the air originated life;
My system belongs to the time of the true guru.
The true guru is the Word,
And the soul is its disciple.
What keepeth me in my detachment
Is meditating on the unutterable gospel;*
My master is the cherisher of the world
Age after age.

---

* *Anahad Shabd*, the unstruck melody, is often referred to in the Adi Granth as *Akath Katha*, the unutterable 'utterance' or 'gospel'.

It is through the Word
That one realizes the gospel,
And the *gurmukh* quenches the fire of ego.   44

A YOGI FURTHER QUESTIONS:

Main ke dant kiu khaaiai saar

How can steel be chewed with waxen teeth?
What food to eat to curb the ego?
Our house is of snow, our robes are of fire;
In what cave can the mind rest in peace?
Who is it that is everywhere,
And into whom everyone should merge?
Whose is the form
That the mind should contemplate on?   45

NANAK ANSWERS:

Hau hau mai mai vichoh khovai

Extinguish the ego from within thee,
Erase the other, let the One remain.
True, the world is as hard as steel
For the worldling,
For he is stubborn and unwise in his folly;
But through the practice of the Word
This steel can be digested by him.
Within and without, he then beholds
The one Lord pervading all.
By the grace of the true guru
He dieth not again, O Nanak.   46

SOME OTHER YOGIS QUESTION:

So sabad kaa kaha vaas katheeale

Where does that Word abide
Through which one is ferried
Across the ocean of life?
What supports the air that travels
The distance of ten fingers
In exhaling?*
How is the invisible One to be seen,
Who sports, speaks and is dynamic
Within us?

NANAK ANSWERS:

Sun suaamee sach naanak pranvai

O Swami, hear thou:
This is how I've tamed
My own mind.
I attached myself to the Word
Given by my master,
And through his grace
The Lord united me with Himself.
I then became all-wise, all-seeing,
And through perfect good fortune,
I merged in the Lord.   58

That Word abides within us all,
And wherever one sees,
It is there.

---

*The yogis believe that the breathed-out air from the nostrils spans the distance of ten fingers.

The Lord is omnipresent as is the air;
He is everywhere in an artless art.
When He is merciful,
He makes one realize the Word within
And rids one of doubt;
His body and mind
Become pure as the Word,
In whose mind the Name
Has taken abode.
One swims across the ocean of life
Through the Word and the guru,
And he knows the One alone,
Both here and hereafter.
O Nanak,
He is known through the Word,
Who hath neither colour nor sign,
Neither shadow nor type.   *59*

The true God is the support
Of the air that one outbreathes.
The *gurmukh* utters the Truth,
Which he churns within him,
For he has realized
The invisible, infinite Lord.
He eradicates the three attributes,
Enshrines the Word within
And rids his mind of ego.
He beholds the One,
Both within and without,
And endears the Lord's Name
To himself.
He knows of the path
Of *sukhmana, ira* and *pingula*,

For he has seen the invisible One.
O Nanak,
The true One is above all the three,*
The true guru
Makes one merge in the Word.   60
                    Ramkali, pp.938–944

Then the yogis ask more questions: Where does mind abide? Where does the vital breath abide? And where does the Word abide, which can end the ramblings of mind?

Guru Nanak answers: When the grace of the Lord is there, He leads one to a true guru. It is the guru who enables the mind to reach its home. One's ego is brought under control and the mind becomes motionless.

The yogis further ask how one can know the Lord and his own self, and how the sun can enter the house of the moon; that is, how can the dark, 'cold' mind be turned into an illumined or 'warm' one?

Guru Nanak answers that when through the grace of his master he is able to rid himself of his ego, he attains the perfect equipoise of *sahaj*. The mind then becomes motionless, the Lord is realized, and the light and 'warmth' of the Word permeates mind and soul.

The breath is located in the navel region. One realizes this through the master's help.

The Word abides in its own home, which is within oneself. When the power of the Word has been awakened, knowledge of the three worlds is gained. When longing for the Lord in one's heart is aroused, the anguish of the world is extinguished, because the heart is filled with love for the Lord. Guru Nanak further states that the true meaning of '*Anahad Shabd*' or the

---

*The practice of traversing these three paths.

'unstruck melody' is known only by rare individuals. And the few who know, come to acquire this knowledge through their master.

Continuing, the yogis question: Where would mind have been, if body and heart had not existed to contain it? If there had been no navel, where would the breath have rested? If there had been no form of man, where would the Word have resided? If there had been no physical body, how would one have known the Lord? And how can God be perceived, if He has no form, colour or garb?

Guru Nanak begins his answer by saying that those who become absorbed in the Lord's Name get detached from the world. They see the Lord pervading everywhere and at all times. Then answering the questions in detail, he continues: had there been no body and no heart, mind would have abided in Sunn (the Void) in a detached state; had there been no navel lotus, the breath would have remained in its own home, absorbed in the Lord's love; had there been no form or shape, the Word would have abided in the Absolute; and had there been no earth or sky, the Lord's light would still have permeated the three worlds. All colours, garbs and distinctions would have subsisted in that one Word. The Lord alone is perfect and He is beyond description.

The yogis ask further how the world came into existence and how suffering can be ended.

Guru Nanak answers that the world comes into being through the ego, the false sense of individuation. Suffering is born when the Word is forsaken. The *gurmukh* practices the Word and the Word destroys his ego. It is the Word that makes his body and mind pure, and enables him to unite with the Lord. Again, it is the Word that detaches him from the world and attaches him to the Lord. It is the Word through which yoga or union with Him can be attained.

But it is a rare one who practices the Word. For such practice a master is essential, who alone can make the Word manifest. Through the master one's mind is dyed in divine love, and attains access to its true home. Through the master the true method of yoga is learned.

Guru Nanak then recounts the calamities that befall one who is devoid of help from a true master. Such a one can never get release from transmigration and attain union with the Lord. Without the true master one remains a captive of his ego and continues to suffer, thus losing the game of life.

The *gurmukh*, on the other hand, subdues his mind and conquers his ego. He enshrines the Lord in his heart. He is master of the world, and has no fear of the Messenger of Death. He is received in the Lord's court with honour. Guru Nanak ends with a tribute to the master, without whom one cannot attain the Word or the Name, nor emancipation from suffering, nor union with the Lord.

THE YOGIS QUESTION:

Eh man maigal kaha baseeale

Where abides
This elephant of the mind?
Where abides
The vital breath?
Where does the Word abide,
Which should end the mind's wandering?

NANAK ANSWERS:

Nadar kare taa satgur mele

When He is merciful,
The Lord leads one
To the true guru;

Then the mind reaches its own home.
When one eliminates one's ego,
One becomes pure
And controls one's restive mind.

THE YOGIS QUESTION:

Kio mool pachhaanai aatam jaanai

How is one to know the primal Being?
How can he realize his self?
How is the sun to enter
The house of the moon?[*]

NANAK ANSWERS:

Gurmukh haumai vichoh khovai

When by the grace of his master,
One rids himself of his ego,
Then, O Nanak,
He attains to the state of *sahaj*.   64

Eh man nihchal hirdai vaseeale

When the mind becomes motionless,
Then, through the master
The primal Being is known.
The breath resides in the navel region;
By the master's help
One realizes this truth.

---

[*]The moon in its natural state is cold and dark; it owes its light to the sun. Likewise, mind in its original state is cold and dark. It will become illumined and warm when the Word enters it with all its splendour.

The Word abides within,
In its own home;
Through the Word
The light of the three worlds is seen.
The longing for the true Lord

Rids one of one's anguish,
And one remains satiated
With the love of the true Lord.
The unstruck melody is known
Only through the master;
It is only a rare one
Who knows its true meaning.
Nanak says and speaks
Nothing but the truth:
He who is dyed in the true One
Never loses his colour.   65

THE YOGIS QUESTION:

Jaa eh hirda deh na hotee

Had the body and the heart not existed,
Where would the mind have abided?
Had there not been support of the 'navel lotus',
Where would the breath have rested?
Had there been no form, no shape,
On what would the Word have been fixed?
Had there been no body – tomb formed
By ovum and sperm,
How would one have known His true worth?
If God's colour, form or garb could not be seen,
How could one then perceive Him?

NANAK ANSWERS:

Naanak naam rate bairaagi

Nanak, they who are imbued with the Name
Are detached from the world;
They see the Lord pervading now,
Then and for all time.   66

Hirda deh na hotee audhoo

Had there been no body and heart, O yogi,
The mind would have abided in Sunn
In a detached state.
Had there been no support of the navel lotus,
The breath would have stayed in its own home,
Imbued with the Lord's love.
Had there been no form,
No shape, no individuation,
Then the Word, in its native state,
Would have abided in the Absolute.
Had there been no earth, no sky,
The light of the Lord
Would still have permeated the three worlds.
Then all colours, all garbs, all distinctions
Would have abided
In the one wondrous Word.
Without the true One
None can become immaculate;
Ineffable is the Lord's story, O Nanak.   67

THE YOGIS QUESTION:

Kit kit bidh yog upjai purkha

How does the world come into being?
How does suffering come to end?

NANAK ANSWERS:

Haumai vich jag upjai purkha

The world comes into being, O man,
Through a sense of individuation.
Suffering comes by forsaking the Name.
The *gurmukh* practices
On the quintessence of divine knowledge.
The Word burns up his ego.
Purity of the Word
Makes his body and mind pure,
So he merges in the true One.
Through the Name
He remains detached
And he enshrines the Lord
Within him.
Without the Name, O Nanak,
Yoga can never be attained.
Deliberate in thy mind on this and see.   *68*

Gurmukh saach sabad beechaarai

Rare is the one
Who through the master
Practices the true Word.

It is through the master
That the true Word
Becomes manifest.
It is through the master
That the mind gets imbued
With divine love;
But rare is the one
Who realizes this.
It is through the master
That one abides in his true home.
It is through the master
That the yogi
Knows the way of yoga.
It is through the master, O Nanak,
That one knows the One alone.   69

Bin satigur seve jog na hoi

Without serving the true master,
Yoga is not achieved.
Without meeting the true master,
There is no release.
Without meeting the true master,
The Name cannot be attained.
Without meeting the true master,
There is immense suffering.
Without meeting the true master,
Great is the eddy of ego.
O Nanak, without the master,
One is dead
And has lost the game of life.   70

Gurmukh man jeeta haumai maar

The *gurmukh*
Conquers his mind
And eliminates his ego.
The *gurmukh*
Enshrines the true One
In his heart.
The *gurmukh*
Conquers the world
And slays the Courier of Death.
The *gurmukh* loses not
In the court of the Lord.
He alone meets the Lord,
Whom the master gives this boon.
O Nanak, through the master,
One realizes the Word.   *71*

Sabdai ka nibera sun too

Hear ye, O yogis,
The quintessence of the Word:
Without practice of the Name
There is no yoga.
Imbued with the Name
One is intoxicated day and night.
With the Name
One is perpetually
In a state of bliss.
From the Name
Is all manifestation;
From the Name
Comes all understanding.

Without the Name
One goes astray,
Despite the many religious garbs
One may wear.
Such is the Lord's will.
From the true master
The Name is attained, O yogis;
It is thus
That the way of yoga is known.
Says Nanak:
Deliberate in your mind and see,
Without the Name
There is no emancipation.   72

Ramkali, pp.945–946

Paihre

The Four Stages of Life

According to Indian tradition, human life is divided into four parts: childhood, youth, middle age and old age. In the following two hymns, Guru Nanak has compared these four stages in man's life to the four *paihre* or watches into which night can be divided. Into the description of each of these watches, the Guru has infused a spiritual significance. Human life has been compared to a night. Man is expected to wake up to the light of day, which should bring to an end all his suffering in life. He has, however, to work hard to attain this goal. Guru Nanak has forcefully brought out in these two hymns that childhood is spent in play, youth in sense pleasures, middle age in worldly acquisition and old age in disease, when mere existence becomes a task. Thus the rare gift of human life is wasted away in futile pursuits. And this is despite the fact that in the mother's womb he had resolved that he would not fritter away his energy, and would spend his time in devotion to the Lord.

The main theme of the hymns is that the real purpose of human life is lost in useless and frivolous activities. The true goal of man's life is to meet the Lord through meditation and escape the cycle of birth and death once and for all. The method and techniques of proper meditation can be learned only from a master, who himself has achieved the aim and is in a position to give practical guidance.

Pahilai paharai rain kai wanjaariya

In the first watch of the night,
O my trader* friend,
You were ordained
To be cast into the womb.
With your head upside down
You did penance
And prayed to the Lord,
O my trader friend;
Yea, you prayed to the Lord
With your head inverted
And your mind fixed on Him.
Contrary to the customary rules,
Naked you came to the world,
And naked you will pass out of it;
And as is writ on your forehead,
So will you live in this world.
Says Nanak, in the first watch,
One is cast into the womb
By His command.   *1*

In the second watch of the night,
O my trader friend,
You became oblivious of the Lord.
You were tossed about
From hand to hand,
O my trader friend,
Even as Yashodha did to Krishna;[†]

---

* One who had come to this world to trade in spiritual wealth, but has wasted his time in the acquisition of worthless worldly goods.
† Lord Krishna, as a child, used to be tossed from hand to hand, out of love, by Yashodha, his mother.

Yea, you were tossed about
From hand to hand,
And the mother said, "He is my son."
O my ignorant foolish mind,
Remember that in the end
None is your own.
The One who has created you,
You know Him not;
Gather knowledge within your mind.
Says Nanak, in the second watch,
You forsook your Lord. 2

In the third watch of the night,
O my trader friend,
Your mind was fixed
On the beauty of youth
And the lure of wealth.
You remembered not the Name of God,
O my trader friend,
Which would have led you
To deliverance from bondage;
You remembered not
The Lord's Name, friend,
And suffered anguish
In the web of Maya.
Revelling in pelf
And intoxicated with youth,
You wasted away your life for nothing.
You bargained not for righteousness
And befriended not good deeds.
Says Nanak, in the third watch,
You got yourself caught
In the bait of wealth
And the lure of beauty. 3

In the fourth watch of the night,
O my trader friend,
Your crop is sheared
When the Messenger of Death
Pounces upon you,
O my trader friend,
And drives you no one knows
The mystery where.
No one has yet solved
The mystery of God,
When the Angel of Death
Catches him unawares.
Around his corpse are shed
Crocodile tears,
And in a trice he becomes a stranger.
That object alone you obtain,
On which you set your desire.
Says Nanak, the fourth watch
Is all being spent
In harvesting your crop.   4:1

                            Sri, pp.74-75

Pahilai paharai rain kai wanajariya

In the first watch of the night,
O my trader friend,
You were ignorant as a child.
You sucked milk
And your parents fondled you,
O my trader friend,
For you were a son to your father and mother.

Your father and mother loved you, their son,
Immensely,
But all attachment is born of delusion.
You came into this world
Through good fortune,
Reaping the reward
Of your past actions;
But without the Lord's Name
You attain not salvation
And are drowned in duality.
Says Nanak,
Man gets deliverance in the first watch
By meditating on the Lord.   *1*

In the second watch of the night,
O my trader friend,
You were intoxicated
With wine and youth.
Day and night
You were immersed in lust,
O my trader friend,
And were blind to the Name of the Lord.
The Lord's Name dwelt not within you,
But you indulged in all other tastes.
You gathered not knowledge,
Nor practiced contemplation,
Nor the virtue of continence,
And wasted away your life.
Pilgrimages, fasting,
Truthfulness and repression
Bring not salvation,
Nor do acts of piety,
Virtue and worship.

Release from birth and death, O Nanak,
Comes through love and devotion
To the master;
All else leads to duality. 2

In the third watch of the night,
O my trader friend,
Swans of white hair
Descended on the lake of your head;
Your beauty waned and age triumphed,
O my trader friend,
And your days diminished.
At the close of your life you repented,
O blind one,
When the Messenger of Death had come
To lead you by the nose.
You called all your acquisitions as your own,
But in a moment they became alien.
You bade farewell to sense
And took leave of wisdom,
And perpetrating sinful acts you grieved.
Says Nanak,
Contemplate on the Lord, O friend,
In the third watch of the night. 3

In the fourth watch of the night,
O my trader friend,
Your body grows old and weak,
You cannot see with your eyes,
O my trader friend,
And you cannot hear with your ears.
Your eyes become blind
And your tongue cannot taste;

Gone are your activity and power.
Devoid of all virtue
How can one get peace?
Being a slave of your mind,
You keep on coming and going
In transmigration.
When the body 'crop' is ripe,
It bends, breaks and perishes;
What pride, then,
For that which merely comes and goes?
Says Nanak,
In the fourth watch,
Know you the Word
Through the grace of the master.   *4*

Your breath has come to an end,
O my trader friend,
And your shoulders are laden
With cruel old age.
You gathered not an iota of merit,
O my trader friend,
Your vices will bind you
And drive you along.
He who lives the life
Of virtue and continence
Suffers not the blows of Fortune,
Nor is he born nor dies.
The snare of doom
And the Messenger of Death
Can touch him not,
For he swims across the ocean of fear
With love and devotion.

With honour he goes,
Merges in *sahaj*
And banishes all his woes.
Says Nanak,
Such a one is saved
Through his master's grace
And attains honour
In the court of the true One.   5:2

Sri, p.75

Patti

Acrostic

The *Patti* or 'tablet' is an acrostic in which the thirty-five letters of the *Gurmukhi* (Punjabi) alphabet are taken consecutively. It is said that Guru Nanak wrote it at an early age, when he went to school. It was written on the wooden tablet or *patti*, which was generally used for the purpose of learning the alphabet.

The *Patti* brings out many of the essential teachings of Guru Nanak, such as the nature of God, the need for a guru, the law of karma and transmigration, and the way to escape from birth and death. The following couplets are representative selections from the acrostic.

> The One who hath created the universe
> Is the Lord of all;
> His advent into this world is blessed,
> Whose mind is attached
> To the Lord in His service.   *sa:1*

> Why hast thou forgotten Him,
> O foolish mind?
> When thou hast adjusted
> Thine account, brother,
> Then alone shalt thou be deemed wise.   *1:P*

He who hath realized divine knowledge
Is the learned pundit;
He knoweth the one Lord in all beings,
And doth not say 'I exist by myself'.   *ma:4*

The disciple who serves the master
And is attached to the Word,
Who treats good and bad alike,
Will in this way be merged in the Lord.   *gha:8*

Thou createst doubt and ignorance in all;
It is all Thy doing, O Lord.
By creating doubt
Thou Thyself leadest them astray.
Then in Thy grace,
On whom Thou art merciful,
Thou makest them meet the guru.   *chha:10*

Man, why dost thou die of toil and worry?
What He hath to give thee, He gives.
He gives and beholds and sustains thee,
As is in thy writ.   *jha:12*

When I see with the inner eye,
I see not another.
The One pervades in all places
And in all minds.   *na:13*

He Himself destroys and creates;
As He wills, so He does.
Having created, He beholds His creation
And issues commands;
He emancipates those
On whom is His grace.   *dha:17*

I blame not another,
I blame my own karmas.
Whatever I sowed, so did I reap.
Why then put the blame on others?   *da:21*

Whose power sustains the universe,
And who imparts His dye to everything,
Whose gifts are received by everyone,
He works His will according to our karmas.   *dha:22*

The whole world is caught in a noose:
It is bound with the chain of death.
He alone is saved by the guru's grace,
Who has taken shelter of the Lord.   *pha:25*

Asa, p.432

Barah Maha

The Twelve Months

It was once a common practice among Indian poets to compose poem cycles on the twelve months, called *Barah Maha*. They described nature and human moods and drew moral lessons to be conveyed to their readers with images drawn from the different seasons of the year.

There is a special significance that the gurus have infused into their *Barah Maha* compositions. Each month has been compared to a human birth, which is too valuable to be wasted in futile activity. The spiritual meaning of each month has been related to the nature of the weather with which the month is characterized.

The *Barah Maha* of Guru Nanak has been composed in *Tukhari Rag* and is most highly rated as poetry. In the present collection four months have been selected, corresponding to the four different seasons.

CHET
March – April

Chet is the month of spring. Nature is resplendent in all its glory. Flowers are in full bloom. The bumblebee is buoyant with life and hope. And yet in this all-pervading atmosphere of joy and cheer, the wife whose husband is away feels melancholy and life seems a burden for her. Guru Nanak conveys that a seemingly successful man of the world with all amenities and comforts at his disposal lacks real happiness and inner peace if he has not realized the Lord within himself.

Chet basant bhala bhavar suahavde

It is the month of *Chet*,
It is spring. All is vibrant.
The beauteous bumblebees can be seen
In the flower-bedecked woodlands,
The home of my childhood days.
But there is sorrow of separation in my soul;
Longingly I wait for the Lord.
If the husband comes not home,
How can a wife find peace of mind?
The sorrow of separation wastes away her body.
The *koel* calls in the mango grove,
Her notes are full of joy,
But there is sorrow in my soul.
The bumblebee hovers about
The blossoming bough,
A messenger of life and hope.
But, O mother of mine, 'tis like death to me,
For there is sorrow in my soul.
How shall I find peace and blessedness?
Sayeth Nanak: Blessed peace is attained in *Chet*,
If the Lord comes and meets the wife.   5

ASAR
June – July

In contrast to *Chet*, *Asar* signifies the most inhospitable weather. It is the hottest month of the scorching Indian summer. The earth burns like an oven. It becomes parched under the blazing sun. Still it continues to perform its duty patiently.

The housewife seeks the cool evening shade for comfort. If the comfort she seeks is rooted in sin and evil, she will suffer sorrow in the hereafter; if founded on truth, she will be rewarded with unceasing joy.

Asaar bhala sooraj gagan tapai

In *Asar* the sun scorches,
Skies are hot,
The earth burns like an oven,
Waters give up their vapors.
It burns and scorches relentlessly,
In anguish the parched earth suffers,
Yet it fails not in its patient duty.
The sun's chariot passes the mountain tops,
Long shadows stretch across the land;
The housewife
Seeks the cool shades of the evening,
And the cicadas
Give a shrill call from the glades.
If the comfort she seeks
Be rooted in falsehood,
There will be sorrow in store for her;
If it be in truth,
Hers will be a joy everlasting.
My life and death are at the Lord's will;
To Him, says Nanak,
I have surrendered my mind.   *8*

SAWAN
July – August

The month of *Sawan* brings a welcome change from the scorching heat of summer. It is the advent of the rainy season, when the parched earth quenches its thirst with the rains. It is the season of rejoicing, when nimbus clouds bring joy to the heart. But the bride who is without her spouse feels all the more sad, because the poignancy of her pain is brought out in sharp contrast to the atmosphere of mirth and gaiety all around her. She is frightened by the dazzle of the monsoon lightning. She has lost sleep and appetite and even her clothes feel a burden on her body.

> *Saawan saras mana ghan varsai*
>
> O my mind, rejoice! It is *Sawan*,
> The season of nimbus clouds and rain.
> My body and mind yearn for the Lord,
> But my Lord is away in distant lands.
> If He return not,
> I shall die pining for Him.
> The lightning frightens me by its dazzle.
> My bed is empty;
> I am lonely and sad.
> O mother of mine,
> I am on the verge of death:
> How can I have sleep or hunger
> Without my Lord?
> My very clothes
> Are a burden on my body.
> Says Nanak: Blessed is the bride
> Who is enveloped
> In the embrace of her Lord.   9

POKH

December – January

Pokh is the severest month of winter. Just as in the bitter cold of winter, trees and bushes wither and die, so also the Lord's absence saps the energy of the body and mind of the bride without her spouse. The unhappy wife pines for her husband, without whom existence is meaningless.

Infusing a clear spiritual content in the latter part of the stanza, Guru Nanak says that the Lord who gives life to the whole world is realized through practice of the Word imparted by the guru. At the end, Guru Nanak stresses the presence of the Lord in all forms of life, those derived from egg, womb, sweat and earth. It is His vision which will give deliverance from suffering.

> *Pokh tukhaar parai van trin ras sokhai*
>
> As in the month of *Pokh*
> Snow freezes the sap in tree and bush,
> So does Thy absence kill my body and mind.
> O Lord, why comest Thou not?
> Thou abidest in my body, mind and mouth.
> He that gives life to all the world,
> Him I have realized
> Through the guru's Word.
> His light shines in all life
> Born of egg or womb or sweat or seed.
> O merciful Lord, give me Thy vision,
> That I may attain salvation.
> Says Nanak:
> She who is in love with the Lord,
> Alone revels in bliss with Him.   *14*
>
> *Tukhari, pp.1108–1109*

Topics from Guru Nanak's Teachings

God

Guru

Word

Rituals

Mind

Love

God

Thy Greatness Is Immeasurable

It is said that this beautiful hymn, written in a spirit of gratitude and humility, came as an outburst after Guru Nanak's crucial mystic experience of the Lord at the Kali Bein. After three days of continuous ecstasy he realized that he could not pay adequate homage to his Lord, even if he lived for millions of years and meditated in a cave without interruption. He said God, the formless One, is indescribable and cannot be known by hearsay. He can be known only by His own grace, if He chooses to reveal Himself.

Nor can He be known by going through penances and ascetic practices. Even the ability to fly like a bird to great heights and to be able to live without food and drink are of no avail in gaining knowledge of Him.

Guru Nanak ends the hymn by saying that even if he had tons and tons of paper and possessed the wisdom of great books, and even if he had an inexhaustible amount of ink and the ability to write with the speed of wind, he would still fail to measure the greatness of the Lord and to signify the glory of His Name.

Koti kotee meree aarja pavan piaan apiaau

Were I to live for millions of years
And could make air my food and drink,
Were I to seal myself in a cave,
Ceaselessly to meditate
Without seeing the sun or the moon
And without a wink of sleep,
I would still not be able
To measure Thy greatness,
Nor signify the glory of Thy Name!   *1*

The formless One is the eternal
Irreplaceable Truth;
Attempt not to describe Him
By hearsay knowledge;
If it pleases Him,
He in His grace will reveal Himself.   *1:P*

Were I to be shredded and ground
Like grain in a mill,
Were I to be burned in a fire
And dissolved with ashes,
I would still not be able
To measure Thy greatness,
Nor signify the glory of Thy Name!   *2*

Were I to fly like a bird
To a hundred heaven,
Were I to vanish from human gaze at will
And could live without food and drink,
I would still not be able
To measure Thy greatness,
Nor signify the glory of Thy Name!   *3*

Were there ton upon ton of paper,
Saith Nanak,
And had I absorbed the wisdom
Of volumes without count,
Had I a supply of ink inexhaustible
And could write
With the speed of the wind,
I would still not be able
To measure Thy greatness,
Nor signify the glory of Thy Name!   4:2

Sri, p.14

The Ocean and the Fish

The Lord is like a mighty ocean and men are like small fish. How can the small fish fathom the depth of the ocean? How can they know its expanse?

The Lord is all-pervading. One who does not see Him everywhere gets suffocated and perishes. Man does not know when death will come. But when he is confronted by the Messenger of Death, it is to the Lord that he turns.

Man believes, in his ignorance, that God is far away. He does not realize that He is right within him and sees everything that he does. How can he then deny his actions?

Guru Nanak, in humility, proclaims that he is not worthy of the Lord because he has not realized His Name. He says he will gratefully accept whatever He gives. There is no other place where he can go.

At the end, Guru Nanak offers his body and mind to the Lord, who ever sees, who ever hears and who is present everywhere. He has created the whole world and whatever He wills comes to pass.

Too dareeaaoo daana bina

Thou art the mighty ocean, O Lord,
Thou knowest and seest all things.
How can I, a small fish,
Know Thy depth
And Thy expanse?
Wherever I look,
There Thou art;
Separated from Thee,
I suffocate and perish.   *1*

I know not the fisherman,
I know not his net;
But when I am caught in suffering,
It is to Thee I turn.   *1:P*

Thou art present everywhere, O Lord;
I believed Thou wert far from me.
Whatever I do, it is in Thy presence.
When Thou seest all,
How can I deny my deeds?
I am of no use to Thee,
I have not realized Thy Name.   2

Whatever Thou givest,
That shall I eat;
There is no other door but Thine –
Where else, then, shall I go?
Nanak hath but one prayer;
Let his body and his mind be Thine.   3

Thou art near, Thou art far,
Thou art in between the two.
Thou seest by Thyself,
Thou hearest by Thyself,
And Thou createst the whole world.
Whatever pleases Thy will,
That comes to pass.   4

Sri, p.25

The Lord Provides

Man, in his ignorance, believes that he earns his livelihood by his own efforts. In fact, the Lord provides for all whom He brings into this world. Beasts and birds are sustained by Him. They need not build treasuries and granaries. God gives them sustenance and shelter through forest trees and natural pools. The Lord alone endures, while all else is perishable.

Na rijak dast aa kase

It is in no one's power
To give livelihood to another;
The Lord alone
Is the sustainer of all.
The One endureth,
Naught else is there –
Thou alone art!
Thou alone art!   5

Parandae na giraah jar

Behold the birds of the air:
They build themselves no treasuries,
They construct no tanks of water;
They depend on the forest trees
And on the natural pools –
The Lord provideth them with all.
Thou alone art!
Thou alone art!   6

Majh-ki-Var, p.144

The Microcosm and the Macrocosm

Great spiritual truths are revealed in this hymn. Just as a drop of water exists in the ocean and the ocean is potentially in the drop, so also man resides in God and God abides in man. Every human being is divine by nature and is capable of rising to the level of the Lord. Every man is potentially God. God created the entire universe and then hid Himself in every atom of it. This knowledge is attained through a master, and the one who attains it is freed from human bondage.

With paradoxes and riddles, Guru Nanak hints at various spiritual truths. He says there can be utter darkness at noon; and at midnight, the blaze of the midday sun. The reference is to beholding the sun in the inner spiritual regions. This sun does not suffer decline or extinction. One who sees the light of this sun, will see it even when there is utter darkness of night outside. And the one who does not see it, is spiritually in darkness even when the noon sun is shining.[*]

This experience is acquired only through the guidance of a master. No one else, however astute, can impart this knowledge.

The master says that through the practice of the Word one attains true knowledge and understanding. All riddles are thus solved. Such practice leads to concentration and concentration leads to knowledge. This has been called the miraculous tale of the guru's Word.

Guru Nanak ends with the prayer: "May I be a sacrifice to those who are entirely absorbed in the Word."

---

[*] "When thou becomest a confidant of the divine secret and beholdest the midnight sun, then shall I open my lips to thee" (Jalal-ud-din Rumi: *Masnavi*).

Saagar mahi boond boond mahi saagar

The drop is in the sea,
And the sea is in the drop;
Who will solve this riddle?
Who knows the secret?
He from whom all creation came,
He who surveys that which He has created,
He, the Lord,
Is the one knower of the secret.   *1*

The man who understands this in his heart
Is freed from human bondage,
Is made one with the Lord Himself.   *1:P*

At noon there is the darkness of night,
At night there is the blaze of day;
At the centre of burning heat
There is freezing cold.
His being, His state none knows;
Without the master,
No one can understand.   *2*

In man is woman,
In woman is man;*
Only the God-realized will know.

---

* Scholars usually interpret this to mean that man is born of woman and
vice versa; esoterically it may be interpreted that God is in the soul and
the soul is in God.

In the sound is concentration,
In concentration is knowledge;
This is the tale of the master
That cannot be told.   *3*

In the mind is the light
And in the light is the mind,
And the five* mingle like fellow disciples;
Nanak, may I be a sacrifice to those
Who are entirely absorbed in the Word.   *4:9*

Ramkali, p.878

---

*Scholars variously interpret 'the five' to refer to the five senses, the five elements, or the five passions.

The Absolute Lord

The Lord is beyond the comprehension of human mind. He is infinite. He is immortal. He is not subject to the law of causation, nor does He recognize the distinction of caste. He is self-existent, all by Himself. He need not go through the cycle of birth and death. He has no form, no colour, no line.

He manifests Himself through the Word. That is the only way to know Him. The method to contact the Word is imparted by a living master. He breaks open the granite doors to understanding and reveals the almighty Lord sitting in profound meditation within.

He created life, but spread the pall of death over it. To be saved from it, Guru Nanak enjoins upon the seeker to find a true master, who will impart to him the secret of listening to the divine melody.

If the vessel of the body has been cleansed of cravings and desires, the Lord will enter it and stay in it. But those whose vessels are quite pure are rarely found. So it is a rare one in whom the Lord dwells.

> *Alakh apaar agam agochar*
>
> Unknowable is my Lord, without end;
> Unfathomable is He, beyond description;
> Immortal, beyond cause and effect,
> Beyond the pale of caste and castelessness,
> Beyond the cycle of life, death and rebirth;
> Self-existent and alone,
> Without desire, without delusion.   *1*
>
> He is the truest of the true.
> To Him I sacrifice my life.
> He has no form, no colour, no line;

He manifests Himself
Through His Word divine.   1:P

He has no mother, no father, no son,
Nor any other kin.
He has no woman nor lusts for one;
He has no ancestors, nothing defiles Him,
He is endless, He is infinite.
Thou art the light of all light.   2

In every heart Thou art hidden;
In every heart burns Thy light.
The guru's message bursts open
The granite doors to salvation,
Revealing the fearless One
Entranced in profound meditation.   3

He created life,
And over it spread the pall of death;
He keeps it all under His control.
Serve the true guru,
A priceless treasure will be thine.
To gain release, practice thou the Word divine.   4

If thy vessel be clean,*
The true One will enter it and there remain;
But rare are those
Whose vessel is without stain.
As essences merge in the quintessence,
So doth man's soul blend in the primal soul.
Sayeth Nanak: Lord, Thou art my refuge.   5:6
                                          Sorath, p.597

---

* That is, if the body is purified of cravings and desires.

Creation, God, Guru and Salvation

The long poem called *Dakhani Onkar* is said to have been composed by Guru Nanak at Benares during his first *udasi*.[*] It comprises 54 stanzas and its main theme is the enunciation and praise of God and His creation.

The present selection consists of four stanzas, and the central point of each of them is given below.

God created the universe spontaneously and permeated the three worlds with His light. This knowledge can be attained through the guidance of the master, in the pursuit of spiritual realization. One who has attained the Lord within also realizes that the world, as it appears, is illusory.

> *Sassai sabh jag sahaj upaaiya*
>
> God created the cosmos spontaneously,
> And permeated the three worlds
> With His light.
> Through the guru
> Is the goal achieved,
> And one picks up pearls and rubies.
> If one but comprehends with penetration
> And reads with understanding,
> One would know that the true Lord
> Abides in the innermost recesses within;
> But it is through the guru's grace
> That he would experience and hold Him,
> And realize that without Him
> The world is an illusion.   2

---

[*] *Puratan Janamsakhi.*

The light of God illumines the earth and the seas. The writ of the master prevails in all the three worlds. He manifests Himself through the master. And it is through the master's grace that one returns to one's original home. Then one's mind is incessantly drunk with nectar. Such a one gets adorned with the jewel of the Word. One who has identified himself with God has verily become the Creator-Lord Himself.

Uram dhooram jot ujaala

The light of God
Illumines lands and seas,
In the three worlds pervade
The guru and the Lord.
The Lord manifests Himself
In the form of the guru,
And in His mercy
Brings one back
To one's home.
Then the stream of nectar
Rains from above incessantly;
It comes as the sublime Word
In glorious splendour.
He who has unravelled
The mystery of the One,
Verily becomes
The Creator-Lord Himself.   8

When a man attains wisdom, he is able to control the five passions. His attention is then directed upwards, for he practices the Word. He sees the Lord pervading all space and time. He is seen everywhere, and in the past, the present and the future. He showers His blessings on everyone and endows man with a body, in which He can be realized. It is the duty of man to always keep Him in his mind and on his tongue. He is the essence behind all existence, and the one who is imbued with His Name, is honoured here and in the hereafter.

Ugvai soor asur sanghaarai

When the sun of *Nam* rises,
One slays the demons
Of the five passions.
With practice of the Word
When he looks from above,
He sees the Lord pervade
The three worlds
From beginning to end.
Yea, the Lord Himself is the doer,
The speaker and the listener.
He, the Creator-Lord,
Bestows on us mind and body,
And the same Lord abides
In our mind and mouth:
He indeed is the life of the world;
Without Him there is not another.
Nanak, dyed in the Lord's Name,
One is received with honour.   9

He works through all ages, for He is timeless. He neither comes nor goes. Nor does He hate anyone, nor is He involved in strife. Whatever exists, exists because of Him, for He reflects all. He is beyond the comprehension of sensory knowledge. It is through yogic practice that He is seen as the life of all life.

Guru Nanak concludes by saying that one can never be emancipated without the practice of *Nam*.

Jug jug thaap sada nirvair

For ages and ages
He hath existed,
With hatred for none;
Nor is He involved
In the predicament
Of birth and death.
Whatever is seen
Is verily His reflection.
He Himself creates,
Himself establishes;
And Himself being transcendent,
The world He hath involved
In complexities.
Through mystic knowledge is He seen
As the very life of the world.
By spiritual practice
Thou attainest true bliss:
Devoid of the Name,
How canst thou attain true honour?   15
      Ramkali, Dakhani Onkar, pp.930–931

When Nothing Existed except God

For countless ages utter darkness prevailed. There was a complete vacuum when no worlds had yet come into being. The Lord alone existed and His will was pervasive. He was in His ceaseless trance.

Since there was no sun, no earth, no moon, there was neither night nor day. There was no air, no water, nor any other source of life. There were neither oceans, nor rivers, neither continents, nor regions under the earth. There was neither beginning, nor end, neither growth, nor decay.

There was neither heaven nor hell, because the cycle of birth and death had not yet begun. Nor were there any upper regions of bliss. There were no gods to inhabit the high heavens. Even Brahma, Vishnu and Shiva did not exist. There was only the eternal One and none besides.

There had come into being neither male nor female. Nor were there pleasure and pain to experience.

There were no ascetics and no voluptuaries, no monks and no hermits. Indeed, there were no religions or creeds of any kind. Except God to think of Himself there was no one to think of anyone. He was His own emanation. He judged His own worth and rejoiced in His own glory.

Krishna did not exist, nor did his consorts. There was no tantric creed, nor any *mantra shaktis*. There were no churches, nor any of their ritual observances. Maya, the veil of illusion, which creates darkness and defiles all, had not yet come into being.

Since there was no birth, there were no castes. Man was not under the sway of his destiny karmas, which would drag him into the mire of worldly attachments and the worship of various gods.

There was no subject for contemplation, nor any object of knowledge. There was nothing to trace the genesis of and nothing to sit in judgement on.

There were no sectarian antagonisms, no parochial approaches. There were no idols, no temples, no clashing forms of prayer and worship, nor indeed anyone to worship or pray. Mullahs and qazis did not exist, nor did *hajis* go on pilgrimage. There were no sheikhs, no kings and their subjects, no masters and their slaves.

The Vedas had not yet come into existence; nor had the Semitic scriptures. None read a gospel at dawn or an epistle at sunset. Only the Unspeakable spoke of Himself to Himself.

And then, with His will He created the universe and spread the sky without anything to support it. He also created the gods, Brahma, Vishnu and Shiva. He also brought into being Maya, the goddess of illusion, who spread the darkness of ignorance and increased worldly attachment.

And then, to a select few, through the grace of the Lord, the Word was revealed by the guru. To them He made Himself manifest. He has ordained this system to continue. The world does not know the extent of the Lord, but the true guru reveals this secret to a fortunate few, and through the Word makes them united with the Lord. It is they who attain the state of everlasting bliss.

Arbad narbad dhundookaara

Through uncountable ages
Complete darkness prevailed
Over utter vacancy;
There were no worlds, no firmaments,
The will of the Lord was alone pervasive.
There was neither night nor day,
Nor sun nor moon,
But only God in ceaseless trance.   *1*

No air and no water,
No utterance, no source of life,
No beginning or ending, no growth or decay,
No continents, no regions under the earth,
No swelling oceans or winding rivers existed.   2

The higher, the middle and the lower planes
Existed not,
Neither was there heaven or hell,
Nor did Kal, the destroyer, exist;
The cycle of birth and death had not begun,
And so there were no comings and goings.   3

There was no Brahma,
No Vishnu, no Shiva;
There was only the One,
The eternal Lord;
There was neither male nor female,
Neither caste nor station;
There was no pain or pleasure
For one to experience.   4

There were no celibates,
No men of charity,
Nor the forest-dwellers;
There were no ascetics and no voluptuaries,
No monks and no hermits,
No religious communities nor their heads,
No liturgies, no creeds.   5

There were no repetitions of scriptures,
No austerities, no abstinence,
Nor were there any fastings and prayers;

There was no one to think of anyone,
Except God to think of Himself.
God emanated Himself and rejoiced,
And He Himself judged His own worth.   6

There was no holy bathing,
No counting of basil beads,
Nor any pious forbearance.
Krishna was not,
Nor were his consorts,
Neither the cows,
Nor the herdsman.
Neither were tantras and *mantra shaktis*
And all their humbug,
Nor did anyone play on the flute.   7

There were no rituals and no creeds,
Nor the ever-buzzing fly of Maya,
Nor could one see caste or birth.
There was no net of attachment,
Nor death writ in one's destiny,
Nor did anyone contemplate on anyone.   8

There was no slander, nor rejection,
There was no living being nor life;
The great Gorakh and Machindera
Did not exist.
There was then no knowledge,
Nor was there any contemplation.
There was no beginning of clans,
Nor any reckoning of accounts.   9

There were no divisions
Of caste or garb,
Of Brahmins and Kshatriyas;
No gods nor temples,
Nor the sanctity of the cow,
Nor was there any recitation
Of the *gayatri*.
There were no sacrificial fires,
No *yajnas*,
No baths in holy waters,
Nor any to worship or pray.   10

There was no recitation
Of the gospel of Puranas,
Neither at dawn nor at sunset.
Only the Unspeakable spoke of Himself
To Himself;
Only the Unknowable of Himself
Had knowledge of Himself.   11

There were no mullahs,
No qazis,
Nor sheikhs, nor hajis,
Nor kings, nor subjects,
Nor the world of ego;
There was none to be proud of self.   12

There was no love and devotion,
There were no Shiva and Shakti,
There was neither friend nor mate,
Neither sperm nor ovary.
God was both merchant and peddler then,
Such being His pleasure.   13

There were no Vedas,
Nor other Hindu scriptures,
Nor the holy texts of the Semites;
When He so willed,
He shaped the Universe;
The firmament He spread
Without a prop to support it.
He created the high gods,
Brahma, Vishnu and Shiva,
And increased the sway of illusion
And attachment.   *14*

To a select few
The guru reveals the Word.
The Lord decrees His creation
And He watches His decree operate.
He made the heavenly bodies,
Our universe with all its regions
Above, below and around it.
And out of the unmanifested ground
Of His Being,
To us and in us,
He made Himself manifest.   *15*

None knows the extent of the Lord,
The true guru alone reveals Him to us.
Says Nanak:
They who are imbued with the true One
Are intoxicated with wonder,
And in blissful amazement
They ever sing His praises.   *16:3:15*

Maru, pp.1035–1036

God Is All-Pervading

This hymn brings out the all-pervading nature of God. He is not only the creator of all that exists; He is also to be found in every one of His creatures. In fact, a pantheistic strain runs through most of the stanzas of this poem. He has not only created all things, but is also present in them. Indeed, He is the reality behind them all. He is not only the maker of things, but also comes as the purchaser, and puts the price on His wares Himself.

There is also a stress on the special significance of the human body. Unlike the bodies of the lower animals, the human body is not confined to the nine outlets.* It has a secret tenth door, which is the gateway to the Lord. This can be opened only through instruction from a living master, who imparts the technique of achieving it. The company of such a teacher is not merely advisable on the spiritual journey within, but indispensable. For the guru has himself traversed the path and is a necessary guide for saving the disciple from many dangerous pitfalls.

Aape aap upaai niraala

The detached God of Himself creates Himself,
And the compassionate One creates also
His true abode;
He binds air, water and fire together,
And out of them creates
The fortress of the body.   *1*

---

* Two eyes, two ears, two nostrils, the mouth and the two lower orifices of elimination.

To it the Creator-Lord
Has fixed the nine doors,
And within the tenth, lives He,
The unfathomable and infinite Lord;
The seven seas* of the God-conscious being
Are brimful with the Lord's nectar
And he is stained no more.   2

The lamps of the sun and the moon
And all their light
Emanate from Him:
Yea, He it is who creates them
And witnesses His own glory.
For He is the embodiment of light,
Our bliss-giving God,
And He blesses the true ones with glory.   3

Within the fortress of the body
Are townships and shops and trade;
And lo, the merchant, our Lord,
Weighs His wares to perfection,
And He Himself buys the jewel,
And He Himself puts the price on it.   4

Himself He puts the price tag,
And unconcerned is He,
For His treasure is inexhaustible.
He holds all powers in His hands;
Rare is the one
Whom He makes to realize Himself
Through the guru.   5

---

* The five sense organs, mind and intellect.

When He is full of mercy,
He leads us to the perfect guru,
And then the cruel Angel of Death
Hurts us not.
And as the lotus blossoms in water,
So doth He flower within us
Through contemplation on the guru.   6

The Lord of Himself
Rains His nectar upon us,
And His jewels and rubies and pearls
Of infinite worth;
Yea, when the true guru has been found,
One attains unto the perfect Lord
And is blessed with divine love.   7

Priceless is the blessing of true love,
For it weighs not less
Whenever it is weighed;
But he alone who deals in Truth,
Attains unto the commodity of Truth.   8

Rare is the one
Who gathers the commodity of Truth,
For it is only
When the perfect guru has been found
That one meets with the Lord;
And he alone,
Who lives in the will of his guru,
Knows the Lord's will and merges in it.   9

It is through the Lord's will
That one comes into the world
And then merges back into Him;
Yea, it is through His will
That the world came into being,
And the heaven and the earth
And the underworld;
And He upholds His creation too
Through His will.   *10*

It is the bull of the Lord's will
That carries the load of the earth
On its head;
It is through the Lord's will
That air, water and space came into being;
It is through the Lord's will
That the soul comes to abide
In the house of Maya,
And in His will one plays one's part.   *11*

In the Lord's will is the sky vaulted over all;
In His will abide creatures in water, on land
And in the three worlds;
In His will do we breathe
And gather our sustenance;
And in His will do our eyes see.   *12*

In His will He created the ten incarnations,
And countless angels and numberless demons:
Yea, whosoever submits to His will
Is honoured at the Lord's court,
And privileged to merge into him.   *13*

In His will the Lord sat in trance
The thirty-six *yugas* through.
And in His will He created His seekers
And adepts and men of wisdom:
Yea, the Lord has yoked man to Himself,
And forgiving him, gives him deliverance.   *14*

In the fortress of the body,
Abides the king, our mind,
With his special assistants,[*]
Courtiers[†] and with a beauteous door;[‡]
And within the inner home,
There's neither greed nor illusion;
For avarice and sin have no place in it.   *15*

This township of the body
Is manned by truth and contentment,
And by chastity, charity and self-control.
If one seeks His refuge,
Then with ease one meets the Lord.
This honour one attains
Through the guru's Word.   *16:4:16*

                                        Maru, pp.1036–1037

---

[*] Organs of action.
[†] Sense organs.
[‡] The tenth door, the third eye.

The Omnipresent Lord

God is present everywhere. He is compassionate. He is timeless. And although pervading everything, He remains detached
from His creation. He has no father, no mother, no brother,
no sister, nor indeed any relatives. He has no clan or class. He
does not die, nor is He born. He is all-powerful and even the
ruthless Kal is only a morsel of His.

He can be known only through the Word and in the state
of *sahaj*. Only saints can disclose the technique of attaining
such a state and hearing the unstruck melody within. They are
the beloveds of God and are imbued with His love.

The human body, which is composed of five elements, can
find peace and bliss only when God has been realized within
it. Such a realized one is contented forever and is not affected
by desire. He has not only realized the Lord within himself,
but also sees Him in everyone else. He is intoxicated with the
nectar of the Lord's Name, and sweetness flows from his lips.
But such persons are rarely to be found in this world. They are
not only themselves emancipated, but they also emancipate
their associates. Guru Nanak says at the end of the hymn that
he alone finds his true home, who is fortunate to meet and
come under the shelter of a master.

Jah dekha tah deen dayaala

Wherever I look,
I see the one compassionate Lord:
He, our merciful God,
Neither comes nor goes.
All life He pervades in a mysterious way,
But He Himself, our king, keeps detached.   *1*

The world is the reflection of Him
Who has neither father, nor mother,
Nor has He earned a sister or brother,
Nor is He born nor dies He,
Nor belongs to any class or clan;
O, that ageless One is pleasing to my mind.   2

O God, immortal art Thou, the Purusha;
Over Thy head, death is not.
Unfathomable, infinite, and detached art Thou,
Compassionate, content and cool art Thou,
Known through the Word;
And one is attuned to Thee in *sahaj*.   3

The world moves and has its being
Within the three attributes,
While Thou abidest in the fourth state of bliss,
Yea, the ruthless Kal
Is but one morsel of Thine.
Thou art the life of all life, pure light;
And one realizes Thee
Through the unstruck melody of the Word,
By the guru's grace.   4

Blessed are the saints, beloved of God,
For they are ever imbued with the Lord's love
And emancipate others.
Nanak seeks to be the dust
Trodden on by the saints:
Yea, it is through the guru-saint
That one attains unto God.   5

O God, the inner-knower of all hearts,
All life belongs to Thee.
Yea, Thou art my compassionate Lord,
I am but Thy slave;
Bless me in Thy mercy
With Thy nectar-Name,
And let the guru's jewel of knowledge
Illumine my mind.   6

Of five elements was this body created,
But only when it attains
Unto the all-pervading God,
Is it in bliss;
The deeds of such a one
Yield the nectar-fruit of God,
And his mind treasures the jewel
Of the Lord's Name.   7

His mind is content:
Yea, he hungers not, nor thirsts,
And he sees the detached Lord
In all hearts;
And becoming detached,
He is imbued with the Lord's nectar,
Steeped in the love of the guru's Word.   8

He does deeds, night and day,
That awaken the soul,
And deep within him burns
Ever the pure light of God;
Inebriated with the nectar-essence
Of the Word,
His tongue plays the sweet notes
Of the bin.   9

Yea, he alone plays the sweet notes of the *bin*
Who knows the mystery of the three worlds.
Says Nanak: Know this state, O ye men,
Through the guru's Word,
And be attuned to the Lord's Name.   *10*

All too rare are such men in the world
Who, practicing on the guru's Word,
Remain detached;
Emancipating themselves,
They emancipate their associates too;
Fruitful is their birth in the world.   *11*

He alone knows his true home
And the tenth door
Within the temple of the body,
Whose mind is awakened
Through the perfect guru;
Within the fortress of the body
Is the castle of the true Lord,
And the Lord sits therein
On the true throne.   *12*

The fourteen regions
And the two lights,
The sun and the moon,
Are the witnesses
That the servants of God, yea, the elite,
Taste not the poison of Maya.
Within us are priceless things
Of incomparable beauty;
Meeting with the guru,
One attains to them,
The wealth of the Lord.   *13*

He alone sits on the throne of the Lord
Who is worthy of it,
Who practices the guru's Word,
And merges in the five melodies.
He realizes that God
Is since the beginning of the beginning
And will also ever be,
And purges himself of all doubt.   *14*

To this throne of the immaculate Lord
Everyone pays his obeisance
Night and day.
This is the true glory that one earns,
Attuned to the guru's Word.
Says Nanak:
Contemplate ye the Lord's Name
And thus swim across,
And attain unto God
Who will guide thee to the end.   *15:1:18*

Maru, pp.1038–1093

Omnipotent and Omnipresent

God is infinite. He is all-powerful and through His power manifests Himself everywhere. He feeds all and His will prevails over everyone.

When He wishes to unite one with Himself, He makes him meet a master. The master removes all his doubts. He turns him into an embodiment of bliss. Such a state can never be attained without the master.

The master connects the disciple with the Word. The Lord and the master work on the same plane. God loves the saints. Neither reading scriptures nor besmearing the body with ashes enables one to conquer wrath and ego. These passions can be tamed through the help of the master. Mere stratagems do not lead to the attainment of true union.

Likewise, going to places of pilgrimage, keeping fasts and living in forests do not bring peace and salvation.

Pranayam and awakening the coiled energy above the rectal centre are also futile for spiritual realization.

It is only through practice of the Word given by the master that the mind gets tamed. God is realized within and is also seen pervading everywhere.

> *Kudarat karaniahaar apaara*
>
> Infinite is God, the Creator-Lord,
> Who manifests Himself
> Through His power.
> The created one is helpless before Him.
> He creates all beings and feeds all,
> And His writ is over the heads of all.   *1*

The Lord pervades all
And He drives all
As is His will.
Whom shall I call near Him,
Whom far?
Yea, find the Lord in every being,
Both manifest and unmanifest,
For He works in all.   2

He whom the Lord unites with Himself,
In his soul abides He,
And he, through the guru's Word,
Contemplates on the Lord's Name.
And, meeting with the guru,
He is rid of his doubts:
He becomes the embodiment of bliss,
Of unparalleled beauty and incomprehensible.   3

The Lord's Name is dearer to me
Than my body, mind and wealth.
It goes along with me to the beyond;
It is my only friend in the end.
Oh, who has ever attained peace
Without the guru,
In the world of desire,
Where no one owns anyone?   4

He on whom is the mercy
Of the perfect guru,
Him the chivalrous guru
Yokes to the Word.
Says Nanak: Serve ye at the guru's feet,
Who brings the strayers back to the path.   5

The saints are in love
With the Lord's riches,
Yea, the Lord's praise;
And through the guru's wisdom
Are blessed with the Lord's Name.
The seeker serves at the Lord's door,
And sings His praise ever in His presence.   6

Whosoever meets the true guru,
He is called into the Lord's palace.
And he is blessed
With honour and emancipation
At the true court;
But the worldling gets no refuge
In the temple of God
And he comes and goes
And grieves forever.   7

O man, serve the true guru,
The unfathomable sea of wisdom,
And be blessed with the Lord's riches,
Yea, the jewel of the Lord's Name.
And the soil of Maya is washed off,
Bathing at the guru's pool
Of the nectar-Name,
And you are blessed with contentment.   8

Tarry not, and serve the true guru,
And remain detached
Even in the midst of the world of hope;
Serve him who rids you of doubt and woes,
And you are gripped not by pain again.   9

He whom the true One likes,
Him He blesses with glory,
And there is not another
Who may instruct him in any other way.
The guru and God work as one,
For God loves the guru.   *10*

One reads the Vedas and Puranas
And other sacred texts,
And another sits and hears with the ears,
But how can the inner door be opened?
Without the true guru
One finds not the quintessence.   *11*

One smears one's body with ashes,
But within him are the demons
Of wrath and ego:
Yea, through stratagems
One attains not yoga:
Without the true guru,
One attains not the unfathomable God.   *12*

One goes on pilgrimages and fasts
And observes a set code
Of religious conduct,
And lives in the woods,
And discourses on wisdom and charity,
And self-control;
But without the Lord's Name,
One attains not bliss,
And without the true guru,
One is not rid of doubt.   *13*

Cleaning one's insides and passing breath
Through the furnace of the *bhuyangma* vein,
And inhaling and exhaling
And holding the breath by forcing one's will,
He practices only a fake religion
And has no love for God;
It is only the guru's Word
That is found as the great nectar.   14

Seeing the Lord's powers
My mind is tamed;
I recognized the Lord in all,
Through the guru's Word.
Lord of the soul, He pervades all;
Nanak, the true guru has made Him,
The invisible One, visible.   15:5:22

Maru, pp.1042–1043

The Self and God

Unless the finite self is transcended, God cannot be realized. The two cannot coexist. This truth cannot be known except through the grace of the master.

When we have the good fortune to meet a perfect master, he teaches us the technique to rise above the empirical and finite self. When the self dies, doubt and fear also die, as also the pain of transmigration.

The highest wisdom comes from the master, since he is able to show and take us to our Liberator.

Guru Nanak ends this short hymn by disclosing that he has merged into the Lord and the two have become one.

Haumai karee taa too naahee

Where self exists, God is not;
Where God exists, there is no self.
Sage, probe this mystery.
Of the immanence of the Lord in all that is,
Without the grace of the guru
We could not know this essence of truth.

When we encounter the true teacher,
And when the little self dies,
Doubt and fear die with it,
As also the pains of birth, death and rebirth.
The guru's teaching is the highest wisdom
Since it shows us where our Liberator is.
Nanak repeats: "I am that. That is I."
The three worlds are included in that formula.

Maru, Var, p.1092

God and Soul

God resides in soul and soul abides in God. This wisdom is imparted by the master. And this realization comes through the practice of the Word.

The main obstacle in the way of this realization is the ego, the false sense of individuation from the universal Reality. Guru Nanak says that he finds this malady rampant among mankind. In fact, not only man with all his learning and scholarship, but even gods and goddesses suffer from this chronic disease. Only those who practice the Word are fortunate enough to be rid of it.

This disease of the ego manifests itself as duality and love of the impermanent. Guru Nanak recounts various things and objects which suffer from the disease of impermanence. All the elements of nature, such as air and water, are perishable; none of them is lasting. Amongst living beings, even our closest relatives, like father and mother, are bound to us only through a karmic account. When that account has been settled, they leave us. Other things apart, even our body is not really our own, for one day it will be consigned to the earth or to fire. All that belongs to the phenomenal world or *maya* – known through the senses – is illusory and passing and suffers from duality.

Even gods and goddesses, including the Hindu trinity of Brahma the creator, Vishnu the preserver, and Shiva the destroyer, are not free from the disease of duality.

No path other than the path of *Surat Shabd Yoga* or the practice of the Word can cure one of this malady. No amount of pedantic knowledge or profound study of the various philosophical systems can give deliverance. Nor can visits to pilgrim places, reading of scriptures, the practice of external observances or asceticism give inner spiritual experience, leading to salvation and escape from the cycle of birth and rebirth.

Unless the grace of God is there, this malady can never be cured and God-realization can never be attained. The grace of God descends on man in the form of a master. For it is the master who gives the method of establishing contact with the Word.

Aatam mahi raam, raam mahi aatam

> God abides in soul,
> Soul in God;
> One realizes this
> From the guru's teaching.
> When the Word* is realized,
> One's sorrows end,
> One's ego is eliminated.   *1*

> Says Nanak:
> Cursed are the maladies
> Born of the ego.
> Wherever I look,
> There is the same affliction;
> It is through His primal grace,
> In the form of the Word,
> That one is saved.   *1:P*

> God Himself tests, approves and accepts one;
> Thereafter he is no more rejected.

---

* The words *Amrit*, *Bani* and *Shabd* are used interchangeably in the Adi Granth.

The one on whom falls God's grace
Meets the guru,
For what He wills, that alone is true.[*]   2

Air, water and fire are diseased,
Diseased is the earth with all its excesses.
Diseased are father and mother, body and *maya*;
Diseased are our kinsmen
Who are bound to us through destiny.[†]   3

Diseased are Brahma, Vishnu and Shiva;
Yea, diseased is the whole world;
But they who meditate on the Lord
Through practice of the guru's Word
Attain to deliverance.   4

Diseased are the seven seas,
With all their rivers;
With disease are filled the worlds
And the underworlds;
But the men of God abide in truth and bliss,
For the Lord showers His grace on them
Wherever they are.   5

---

[*] A coin is first tested and approved before it is accepted in the treasury. Those coins which fail to pass the test are marked with a cut and rejected. Using this as a metaphor, Guru Nanak says that the Lord Himself tests one and if approved unites one with Himself. Those that are rejected are thrown into the wheel of eighty-four. In other words, they continue to revolve in the cycle of birth and death. But it is the Lord Himself who makes one worthy of acceptance. It is He who pervades all. The same pantheistic idea is expressed by a Persian mystic thus: "He Himself is the pot, Himself the potter and Himself the clay of the pot; He Himself then comes as the customer."

[†] The disease of transience.

Diseased are the six systems of philosophy;
Diseased are those who wear specific garbs;*
Diseased are they who practice rituals
And asceticism.
Oh, how can the Vedas and other scriptures
Be of avail to them
When they know not the One?   6

By eating dainties to appease the palate
The disease becomes worse;
Nor doth one attain peace
Through sustenance on roots.
For whosoever forsakes the path of Name,
And takes to another,
Regrets it at the end of his life.   7

One is rid not of this disease
By wandering to pilgrim places;
And the reading of scriptures
Leads one to futile debate.
Indeed, suffering from the disease of duality
Is aggravated,
For the victim becomes a slave to *maya*.   8

The *gurmukh* is true,†
For he is attached to the Word.
His mind is pure, rid of ego.
He is all-immaculate, O Nanak,
As he is stamped with God's grace.   9:1

Bhairo Ashtpadi, p.1153

---

* The original word used in the text is *bhekh*, which is a corrupted form of
the Sanskrit word *vesh*, meaning 'dress, manner or guise'. Various orders
of faqirs, such as *jogis*, *sannyasis*, *bairagis* and *udasis*, have their own
respective *bhekhs*.
† Imperishable; free from the bondage of birth and death.

The Lord's Mansion

When Guru Nanak went to Mecca, there a qazi by the name of Rukn-ud-Din met him. A long discussion took place between the two on spiritual subjects. The following excerpt is a selection from that dialogue.

Qazi Rukn-ud-Din asked the Guru the nature of the abode where God resides. To make it explicit to the *qazi* that God resides within the human body and nowhere outside such as in a temple, mosque or church, Guru Nanak gives a detailed description of the mansion where the Lord resides.

This mansion is described as a grand palace which is characterized by specific features. It has twelve towers (joints of the arms and the legs), nine doors (the nine orifices), fifty-two turrets (teeth and nails), and two windows (the eyes). Five watchmen (the five sense organs) and twenty-five deputies (the *prakritis*) serve as its security officers. So wonderful is this palace that even gods and goddesses desire to live in it. According to Kabir:

> Even the gods pine for the human body;
> Put this body to the service of the Lord.
>
> *Bhairo, Kabir, p.1159*

There are countless treasures and powers lying hidden in this body. They have only to be awakened to be acquired.

The only way to awaken these latent powers and to hear the divine melody within is to find a mystic adept and to work under his guidance. Such a master will instruct and help one to pass through an extremely narrow tunnel *(bunk nal)* to the Lord's mansion, eventually uniting the disciple with the Lord Himself.

QAZI RUKN-UD-DIN QUESTIONS:

Rukn aakhe naanaka dargaah di suna

Tell me of the abode where resides the Lord.
What is the colour of the palace He abides in?
What are its roofs, balconies,
Towers and chambers?
Of what type are its doors
And window frames?
What constitutes its mortar?
What makes it majestic?
What does it look like?
How can it be seen?
What is inscribed at its gate?
Who is His friend?
What circumcision to adopt,
What *namaz* to say to attain it?
What prophet will take us there?
What preparation to make for it?
Give me the clues for all these,
That I may call you the first among saints,
You will then be the master of masters,
The chief among chiefs.

GURU NANAK ANSWERS:

Naanak aakhe rukn deen dargaah di sudh lai

Know ye this, O Rukn-ud-Din,
Of the abode of the Lord:
The colour of His palace is wondrous
And it is adorned with gems and rubies.

Myriads of suns and moons
Burn like torches
To give it light.

There are twelve towers and nine doors
In the palace,*
The five senses are its watchmen
And twenty-five are its deputies.†
Its roofs and balconies are priceless,
Adorned with enamelling.
Its mortar is saffron,
Its door frames are of sandalwood.
Its thresholds are made of 'philosopher's stones',
Its doors of granite.

Myriads of *kamadhen* and goddesses of wealth
Serve as maids there,
The miraculous powers and the nine treasures
Ever wait at its door.
Fifty-two are the turrets of the castle,‡
Above it is the palace of light.
Seven oceans and moats
Contain within them
Tranquil lotus flowers.

---

* The twelve joints of the arms and the legs (three joints in each); the nine orifices of the body (two eyes, two ears, two nostrils, one mouth and the two organs of excretion).

† The five external sense organs (eye, ear, nose, tongue and skin); the twenty-five *prakritis*.

‡ Thirty-two teeth plus twenty nails of hands and feet.

There is one palace and two windows;*
Shiva and Shakti rule over them.
The all-wise Being of light
Sits on the throne eternal;
Secret instruments play their divine tunes
Of countless kinds;

They recite wondrous notes
Of ragas and raginis.
He alone beholds this splendour
For whom the door is opened
By the master.

From on high the Lord gives the call;
Those who are steeped in slumber
Hear it not.
God's repeated calls all go to waste.
The whole world is unfortunate,
For they hear not the calls.
Fie upon them
That are sunk in deep slumber!
The one who wakes will hear the call
And will unite with Him.

The path leading to the Lord
Is extremely narrow;
It is thinner than the tenth of a hair.
The elephant of the mind
Cannot be contained in it;
Its ego does not let it pass through
The straight path.

Bala Janamsakhi, pp.125–126

---

* Two eyes.

Guru

Be One with the Master

The devotee merges his being into that of his master, even as pieces of metal of the same kind melt into one another. He who with single-minded attention meditates on the Lord becomes one with Him.

Guru Nanak advises the aspirant to become dust at the feet of his master and attain deliverance. Good deeds of earlier lives give one the gift of human birth. Association with the master and practice of the Word give him access to the Lord's mansion, which lies high in the firmament in a beauteous setting.

Man remains the captive of his three kinds of karmas. How can he escape their noose? He can do so through the guidance of his master and eventually attain the blissful state of *sahaj*. It is from the master that we know that the Lord's mansion is placed in our own body. Were He to shower His grace, we would be cleansed of our sins. We would then find Him with the help of our master.

At the end Guru Nanak enjoins upon the seeker to give up all hopes other than the Word, on which he should fix his mind. He concludes by saying that his life is a sacrifice to the master, who has himself seen the Lord and has also shown Him to others.

Dhaat milai phun dhaat kau sifti sifat samaai

As a metal merges in its kind,
So does a worshipper merge
In the object of his worship.
Like the dark red of the poppy flower
Is he dyed in fast colours of Truth.
He who in repose and single-minded attention
Meditates on the truthful One
Becomes one with the Lord.   1

O brother, be as the dust
Under the feet of the saints.
In the company of the saintly you'll find
Your guru and the gift of salvation;
You will get *kamadhen*,
The celestial cow,
The giver of all things desired.   1:P

High in the firmament,
In a beauteous setting,
Stands the mansion of the Lord.
A truthful life and good deeds done
Earn us the right to human birth;
By love we find our way to the gate
Of the Lord's mansion.
The mind is tamed
By the guru's wisdom,
And the soul through inner knowledge.   2

Within the three kinds of our karmas
We remain victims of hopes and anxieties.
How can one escape the stranglehold
Of this triple noose?
How to find peace
And the blissful state of *sahaj*
Save by the guidance of the guru?
Under the guidance of the guru
We know that in our own home
Stands the mansion of the Lord.
Were He to shower His grace,
We would be cleansed of our sins.   3

Without the guru's help
We cannot wash off
The dirt of the world;
Without the Lord's grace
How can we our haven find?
Abandon all other hopes,
On the divine Word fix your mind.
Sacrificed to his guru
May Nanak's life be,
Who having himself seen the Lord
Shows others how to see.   4:12

Sri, p.18

Seek the True Master

This hymn is a call to the mind to attach itself to the master and meditate on the Word. If it does so, it will triumph over death, and sorrows will leave it.

Just as a separated wife can never be happy, so also the human soul can never be at peace without union with the Lord.

Guru Nanak is beholden to his master for imparting to him the secret of the Name, for the Name is his only treasure, his only haven. Through his master he receives honour at the Court of the Lord and is united with Him. The Lord's Name will henceforth guide his steps.

Guru Nanak warns against being duped by false gurus. Those who are themselves blind, what guidance can they give to others? One has to be cautious, therefore, in adopting a guru; he must be a true master. The true master practices the Word himself and imparts that knowledge to his disciples. He has been able to transcend his ego and lives in a state of *sahaj*. And this is what he teaches his followers.

The one who 'dies' or merges in the Word does not die a second time. Without *Nam* or the Word, people continue to wander in delusion in the cycle of eighty-four. They die only to be reborn and die again, ad infinitum.

Sun man bhoole baavre gur ki charnee laag

Hear, thou, O my deluded mind:
Attach thyself to the feet of the guru;
Repeat thou and meditate
On the Name of the Lord.

The demon of death will then fear thee
And sorrows will depart.

A separated wife suffers much agony,
How can her marriage be happy?   *1*

Brother, I have no sanctuary
Save His Name; it is my only treasure.
My guru gave it to me,
I am forever beholden to him.   *1:P*

Through the guru's teaching
We attain honour.
To the guru be all praise
For uniting me with the Lord.
Without him I would not live
A single moment,
Without the Name I would surely perish.
Blind am I,
Let me not lose sight of the Name;
Let it guide my steps
So that I may reach my home.   *2*

Those whose guru is himself blind,
Pointless is their pursuit of Truth;
Without the guidance of the true guru
We cannot find the Name.
Without the Name life has no purpose.
It is birth and death and regret;
It is like the crow visiting a deserted house.   *3*

Without the Name the body writhes in pain;
It is like a wall of sand.
We cannot reach His palace
So long as Truth does not abide in our hearts.
If we are dyed in the Name
We attain to our home of immortal bliss.   *4*

Ask of thy guru what he commands
To guide thy life.
"Give abode to the Word in thy mind
And let the pain of ego be burned out.
In the state of *sahaj*, unite with the Lord;
And merge in the truest of the true."   5

Those imbued with the Word are pure;
They lust no more,
They conquer anger and ego,
They worship Thy Name
A hundred times and more
And have Thee enshrined in their hearts.
Why forget Him who sustains life?   6

He who dies in the Word
Dies to death;
He dies not a second time.
Only through the Word shall we find Him
And fall in love with the Lord's Name.
Without the Word, people wander in delusion;
They die only to be reborn
Over and over again.   7

Everyone praises himself –
One more than the other.
Without the guru's help
He knows not his real self.
What use is what others say of him?
O Nanak, he who knows the Word
Never thereafter takes to pride.   8

Sri, p.57

Lost without the Master

There is no use for a woman to decorate herself if she is not going to have union with her spouse. Such a woman remains forlorn, notwithstanding her ornaments and jewellery.

Guru Nanak stresses the need for meditation to attain union with the Lord. But for doing proper meditation, instructions and guidance from a master are indispensable. Indeed, without the master, love for the Lord will not awaken. And it is through the company and service of the master that happiness and tranquillity of mind will come.

If woman, the soul, has sincerity in her love for the Lord, it is bound to bear fruit. She will then blossom and be in a state of bliss. If she wishes to win her Lord, she has to give up mind and ego. Soul and God will then be woven into one like pearls on a string.

A man of the world is born, gets worn out and then dies. His is an insipid, purposeless life. But the one who has realized the Word and merged himself into it will remain unaffected by these changes. Time will have no effect on him, for he has transcended it.

The traders, who trade in Truth and deal with Him, reap great profit from their deal. Their true capital is their master, who is free from all evil. All untruth, in the form of worldly desires, hopes and temptations, is eradicated from their lives.

Guru Nanak concludes by saying that mere talk on theology and study of scriptures will not cleanse the mind. It is practice of the Word received from the master that will lead to salvation.

Bin pir dhan sigaariai joban bad khuaar

Without the spouse,
Why bedeck thyself, O woman,
For all thy beauty is in vain.
All thy decoration is like the empty wind
For thou enjoyest not the bed of the spouse.
Thy suffering is profound,
O unfortunate woman,
For thy lord is not at home.   1

O my mind,
Meditate on the Lord and get bliss.
But one attains not love without the guru;
In the Word is found all rapture.   1:P

In the guru's service
One attains happiness;
Adorned with the state of *sahaj*
One finds the Lord;
One truly enjoys the Spouse
And loves Him intensely.
Through the guru is He realized;
Meeting the guru,
One gathers virtuous traits.   2

Through Truth, O woman,
Meet thou thy Lord
And thou wilt be enraptured by His love.
Thy body and mind will flower in Truth,
And thy state will be beyond measure.
Through the true Name
Thou becomest pure,
And findest thy Lord in thy home.   3

If ego dies in the mind,
The groom enjoys the bride;
As pearls on a string,
The two are woven into one.
In *satsang* peace comes to them,
And through the guru
They lean on the Lord's Name.   4

One is born in a moment,
One wears oneself out,
And then one dies.
But he who realizes the Word
And merges in it,
Him Kal torments not.
The Lord is immeasurable,
Nor can He be described.   5

They who trade in the Lord
Have the reward writ in their lot.
They trade in Truth
And reap the profit by His grace,
Their true capital is the guru,
Who is without the blemish
Of avarice and guile.   6

Truth is their balance,
Truth their weights;
By the guru's grace,
Truth is what they weigh.
Desire and hope, which allure all,
Are stilled by the guru
Whose Word is Truth.
He, the Lord Himself,
Weighs and weighs to perfection.   7

By mere talk of Him
We are not saved,
Nor by reading a load of books.
Without loving adoration
One's body is not cleansed.
Forsake not the Name, O Nanak,
Which unites thee with the guru
And the Lord.   8:9

Sri, pp.58–59

If We Find a True Master

This hymn is written in tribute to the perfect master, who bestows countless gifts on us.

If we find a perfect master, we learn the priceless method for concentration of the soul. If we present our mind to the master, we are rewarded with all-embracing love and salvation, despite the innumerable sins we have committed.

Without the master there can be no knowledge. Brahma, Narad and Vyas will testify to it. Without hearing the divine melody within, there can be no knowledge. This melody one hears through the instruction of the master.

The master's treasury is the unsullied Name and pure love. Only the one with a perfect destiny can collect this treasure. The master gives joy and dispels sorrow. He destroys the five evil passions.

The ocean of life is terrifying. One can see neither the land behind, nor the shore ahead. Nor is there a boat or a raft, an oar or even a boatman. Only the true master can ferry us across.

If we forget the Lord, sorrow will afflict us and our joy will depart. The body's earthen vessel will crack and death will grab us. At the moment of death all regrets will be in vain. During our life we called many things 'mine'. We discover at the time of death that even our body is not ours, let alone wealth and wife.

There is only one treasure that goes with us when we die, and that is the wealth of *Nam*. And there is only one relative who will go with us and that is the master. Without these two, man is lost in the maze of *maya*.

Our birth, death and the rest of our destiny are all determined. Not a word can be erased from this writ. We must bear it smilingly with courage and fortitude. However, we must take care not to sow new seeds, for we have to suffer their fruit. By the practice of the Word, under the instructions of the master, we should be able to rise above the stream of karmas and merge into the Lord.

Satiguru poora je milai, paaiyai ratan beechaar

If we meet the true, the perfect guru,
We shall be blessed with the gem
Of concentration;
If we present our minds to the guru
We are rewarded with all-embracing love;
We get the gift of salvation,
The Forgiver forgives us our sins.   *1*

O brother, know that without the guru
There is no knowledge;
Go ask Brahma, Narad and Ved Vyas,
Ask anyone.   *1:P*

Knowledge and contemplation
Come from the melody within,
The melody which is beyond all speech
And description.
The guru is like the tree in full leaf
Casting a vast shade;
The guru's treasury is full of rubies, gems,
And other precious stones.   *2*

In the guru's treasury is found
The unsullied Name and pure love.
With great and perfect fortune
Can we collect this treasure.

The true guru is the giver of joy
And the dispeller of sorrows.
He is the destroyer of the five demons of sin.*   3

The ocean of life is terrifying
And difficult to cross.
We can see neither the land behind us
Nor the opposite shore,
Neither boat nor raft,
Neither oar nor boatman.
The true master is the ship
In this fearsome ocean;
By his grace he will take us across.   4

If for a trice you forget the beloved Lord,
Sorrow will afflict you, joy will depart.
Burn the wretched tongue
Which does not relish practice of the Name.
The body's earthen vessel cracks,
It is wracked with pain;
The demon of death seizes you,
Your regrets are then in vain.   5

All our lives we cry "This is mine,"
And depart crying, "This too is mine."
We discover that neither body, nor wealth,
Nor wife was ours to take away.
There is no wealth except the Name;
Without the Name we are lost
In the maze of *maya*.
Serve the Lord who is Truth;

---

* The five carnal passions: lust, anger, greed, attachment and ego.

The guru will make you realize the One
Who is beyond all description.   6

On the wheel of birth, death and rebirth
Is our nature molded
And the pattern of our lives determined.
What is writ cannot be erased by anyone,
For it is the dictate of His will.
Without the Name of God there is no escape
From the cycle of birth, death and rebirth;
The teaching of the guru shows the way
To union divine.   7

I have no one save the Lord,
My life and soul belong to Him.
I have burned away my ego and attachment;
I have burned my greed and pride.
Says Nanak, follow the path of the Word;
The treasure of all virtues will be yours.   8

Sri, p.59

Love the Master

In this comparatively long hymn a number of analogies have been used to bring out the ideal love between the disciple and his master.

Guru Nanak implores the devotee to love his master as the lotus flower loves water. Although it is constantly buffeted by waves, it does not falter in its love for water. Indeed, the devotee's love should be like that of the fish, which dies when taken out of water; it cannot live without water and the more the water, the greater is its joy. Not till such love is present will release from birth and death be possible.

Another example of such love is that of the rainbird. It will not drink a drop of water from a lake full to the brim, even if it were dying of thirst. It will slake its thirst only from raindrops.

The last analogy given is that of the *chakvi* who yearns for her mate the whole night through and waits anxiously for the sun to rise so that she can find him. She takes her mate to be quite near, when in fact he is far.

For the worldly people God is far; for the godly He is ever-present. The worldly keep on making calculations, but the Creator does whatever He wills. His value is beyond assessment. It is beyond the human power to know. The only way He can be realized is through the guidance of the master. If one is fortunate enough to meet a true master, true love will emanate from him. He will obtain knowledge, and the mystery of the three worlds will be revealed to him.

If one aspires to virtue, he should not abandon *Nam*. *Nam* alone will give release from transmigration and make one immortal. The people of the world are like playful birds who peck at the pool's banks for a while and then depart. Their stay here is all too brief and even this short period is not utilized properly since they do not pursue the goal of spiritual realization.

He who is able to know himself also comes to know the secret of the Word. It is only through the master's instructions that one can know himself. No one else can help him solve the mystery of the self. How marvellous is the state of those who have become one with the Lord! They are consummated, and the Word has become manifest in them. On the other hand, worldly people wallow in ignorance and suffer grievously from separation from the Lord.

Guru Nanak ends by declaring that there is only 'one door' to the Lord's mansion – the tenth door or third eye.

Re man aisi har siu prit

O my mind,
Love thy Lord
As the lotus loves water.
Buffeted by waves,
It falters not in love.
Creatures of water die
When taken out of water.   *1*

O my mind,
How wilt thou get release
Without such love?
Thy dear ones, O Lord,
Are saturated with Thy love.
On them Thou bestowest
The treasure of devotion.   *1:P*

O my mind,
Love the Lord
As the fish loves water.
The more the water,
The greater her delight;
Her body and mind
Revel in peace.
Without water,
She cannot live for a moment;
God alone knows
The anguish of her heart.   2

O my mind,
Love the Lord
As the rainbird loves rain.
The lakes may be full,
The earth may be green;
Of what use are they
If the raindrop is not there?
If His grace is there,
We shall reach our goal;
Or else we shall reap
Whatever we sow.   3

O my mind,
Love the Lord
As water loves milk;
It suffers the heat itself,
But lets not milk suffer.*
He Himself unites the separated;
He Himself bestows true greatness.   4

---

* When milk is boiled, water evaporates but the milk remains.

O my mind,
Love the Lord
As the *chakvi* loves the sun;
She sleeps not for a moment,
Taking what is far
To be at hand.
The worldly people know not;
To the godly He is ever-present.   5

The worldly make calculations;
What the Creator wills comes to pass.
His value cannot be assessed,
Howsoever much one may try.
Through the guidance of the master
Can He be found.
When the true One is met,
Peace descends.   6

True love will not break,
If the true master thou meet.
Thou wilt obtain the gift of knowledge,
The three worlds will be revealed unto thee.
Abandon not the Name that is pure
If thou seekest to be a customer for merit.   7

Gone are those playful birds
That pecked at the pool's edge.
They had a brief exploit;
Their play was for the day
And the morrow.
Whom Thou unitest with Thyself
Win the true victory of life.   8

Without the master, love is not born,
Nor is the dirt of ego rinsed away.
He who knows himself
Comes to know the secret of the Word.
And it is through the grace of the master
That he knows himself;
Who else can be of any help to him?   9
Why speak of those
Who have become one with the Lord?
They have the Word and are consummated.
The worldly know not;
They suffer grievous blows in separation.
O Nanak, there is but one door*
To the Lord's mansion.
There is no other sanctuary.   10:11

Sri, p.59

---

* The third eye.

The God-Realized

The *gurmukh* always utters words of truth and wisdom, for he has completely surrendered himself to the Lord's will. He is quite detached from the world and is unaffected by its desires. Kal cannot touch him as he has taken abode in the eternal home.

In contrast, the *manmukh* is ceaselessly moving in the cycle of birth and death. In every life he suffers the disappointment of worldly love.

Guru Nanak enjoins us to manifest the Word within ourselves and become immortal by drinking the divine nectar. Such a state would be filled with everlasting bliss and rapture.

This state can be realized by meeting a master and receiving initiation from him. If one remains steady on the path shown by the master, the Lord Himself speaks through his mouth.

By surrendering his body and mind to the master, he is able to concentrate his soul and unravel the mystery of the self. Self-realization leads to God-realization, and a realized one sees God pervading everywhere and in everyone.

This is the only way to emancipation, states Guru Nanak, and it is an unfailing way. He ends with a tribute to the master, through whose grace alone he was able to see the invisible Lord and attain deliverance from delusion.

Boleh saach mithya nahi raai

The *gurmukh* speaks truth
Without an iota of falsehood in it.
He takes every step
In accordance with the Lord's will.
He remains detached,
Having surrendered to the Lord.

1

He abides in the true home
And Kal cannot touch him;
The *manmukh* comes and goes,
And suffers the agony of worldly love.   1:P

Drink the divine nectar
And utter the unutterable Word;
Abide in your own home
And attain to the home of bliss.
Drink in the elixir of God,
Be in everlasting rapture.   2

If one walks on the path of the master,
He remains steady and does not flounder.
If one walks on this path,
The true Lord Himself speaks through him.
He drinks ambrosia and churns the essence.   3

He who sees the true guru
And receives initiation from him
Surrenders his mind and body
And goes within;
He examines his self
And finds the reach of his soul.   4

The Lord's Name is excellent food
Which he, swanlike, tastes
And sees God's infinite light;
Wherever he looks, he finds the One,
The absolute Lord.   5

He remains undefiled
And performs only true deeds;
He attained this sublime state
By serving at the guru's feet.
He tamed his mind from within himself,
And his ceaseless wanderings
Through ages ended.   6

Who, oh who, has not been saved thus?
Devotion and adoration of the Lord
Have emancipated His devotees.
I have found my Lord
And now I search not another.   7

The guru has shown me the invisible Lord
In the true palace;
Eternal is this abode
And not a reflection of *maya*.
Through Truth, contentment is attained
And delusion vanishes.   8

Within whose mind dwells
The true Lord Himself,
In their association
A mortal becomes a *gurmukh*;
O Nanak, the true Name
Washes away all dirt.   9:15

Gauri, p.227

The Swan and the Heron

This hymn uses the analogies of an ocean, a swan, a heron and a pond. The ocean is the guru or master. It is full of pearls. The swan signifies a lover of God, a *gurmukh*. The heron symbolizes a man of the world, a *manmukh*, whose interests are centred in earthly desires. The pond, full of muck, denotes the gross material world.

Guru Nanak says that the lovers of God have their sustenance in their master, just as swans feed on the pearls in the ocean. Worldly people, on the other hand, are engaged in the gratification of their carnal desires, just as the herons wallow in the mire of the pond. The men of God have their aim set on spiritual realization, whereas the men of the world have their attention fixed on sensual pleasures. The former get release from the cycle of birth and death, whereas the latter continue to revolve interminably. In the ecstasy of love the devotee merges in the master and the two become one. The drop of the soul, the 'swan', is contained in the ocean, and the ocean in the drop.

Guru Nanak then calls the Lord the 'divine Yogi'. He is indescribable in human terms. The three worlds move according to His will. He is the source of all bliss. Gods and men seek refuge in Him. When the scourge of ego is eradicated, He is realized.

Death is inevitable. No devices, no stratagems can save one from its clutches. The rare gift of human life, therefore, must not be squandered. All effort should be directed towards practice of the Word given by the master, so that the true purpose of human life is achieved.

Gur saagar ratani bharpoore

The guru is an ocean filled with pearls;
The saints peck at them like swans
And are never far from its shore.
They pick up their feed, the nectar of *Nam*;
The Lord loves them and holds them dear.
In this sea the swans find God,
The Lord of life.   *1*

The wretched heron wades in the dirty pond;
It wallows in the mire, it cannot be cleansed.   *1:P*

The wise watch their step before they move;
They reject duality and realize God
As the formless One.
They drink nectar and attain salvation;
The guru rescues them
From the cycle of death and rebirth.   *2*

Swans never leave the sea;
With love and devotion
They attain the state of *sahaj*
Then is the swan* in the sea†
And the sea within the swan;
It knows the unknowable
And pays homage to the guru's words.   *3*
Entranced in profound meditation
Is the divine Yogi.‡

---

* The devotee, soul.
† The guru.
‡ God, meditating in the Void (Sunn).

He is neither male nor female,
How can one describe Him?
The three worlds are attuned
To His divine light.
Gods and men and ascetics
Seek refuge in Him.   4

God is the source of all bliss,
He is the protector of the helpless;
In meditation and in worship
Men of God are engrossed
In the state of *sahaj.*
God cherishes His worshippers
And destroys their fear.
They conquer their ego,
Their steps turn towards the Lord.   5

Despite the countless ways one tries,
Death dogs one's footsteps;
For the one who comes into the world,
Death is destined.
Life is an invaluable gift,
Man squanders it in confusion;
He examines not himself,
He stumbles in doubt and comes to grief.   6

Those who know,
Speak, read, and hear praises
Of the one God,
The God who supports the earth,
Who instills in them faith and fortitude
And becomes their protector;

Their minds become chaste, righteous
And self-controlled.
If they choose,
They attain the fourth estate.*   7

So pure are the truthful,
Nothing can soil them;
The guru's Word dispels doubt and fear.
Nanak seeks the immaculate One,
The primal Lord,
The Being who is the embodiment of Truth.   8

Dhanasari, p.685

---

* Of *sahaj*.

The Rare Opportunity

Human birth is a rare boon. Only the saints know its worth; others waste it, not knowing its value. If one is fortunate enough to meet a perfect master, he becomes dyed in love and becomes aware of his good fortune.

When it is time for them to depart from this world, the *gurmukhs* have with them the accumulated wealth of their good deeds. They are given a place of honour in the court of the Lord.

He who is imbued with love is able to tame his mind. This boon comes from the master.

Guru Nanak prays to the Lord to let him live a life of virtue, for He Himself abides in him.

Those who turn away from the Lord lose their way in a maze of doubt. They die estranged with the stains of sins on their minds and without the experience of divine love in their hearts. The hymn ends with the prayer that one be given the strength to live under the master's instructions, to attain the Word and to get deliverance from the cycle of birth and death.

Maanas janam dulambh gurmukh paaiya

Precious is the human birth,
Only the saints know its worth.
If the guru is gracious
He will grant me the boon.
My mind and body will be dyed
In the bright red colour of love.   *1*

When the time comes for them to go,
The *gurmukhs* take
Their accumulated wealth of Truth.

Through the guru,
They know the fear of God;
They are given a place of honour
In the court of God.   *1:P*

He who with his mind and body
Praises the Truth
Is pleasing to the truthful One.
Imbued with love, the mind is tamed;
This boon comes from the perfect guru.   *2*

Lord, let me live a virtuous life!
For Thou abidest within me.
With Thee ever within my mind
I'll take the gentle path of *sahaj*,
And joy everlasting find.   *3*

Many a time have I told myself,
Admonishing my foolish mind,
"Learn from the guru,
Sing the Lord's praises –
Immerse thyself in His love."   *4*

Treasure thy beloved Lord in thy heart
Every moment.
If thou treadest the path of virtue,
Sorrow will not dog thy footsteps.   *5*

He who turns away from the Lord
Will be lost in a maze of doubt
And will not know the ecstasy of divine love.
Such a one will die estranged,
With his body and soul all stained.   *6*

Abide by the guru's instructions
And bring home thy gains;
Through the guru's teaching
Realize the Word
And attain freedom.   7

Nanak hath but one prayer;
If it please Thee,
Grant me the shelter of the Name,
And I shall sing Thy praises.   8:1:3
                              Suhi, p.751

In Homage to the Master

This is a hymn of gratitude to the guru, in the form of a monologue addressed by a slave to his master. He says that not only is he himself a slave of his master, but also his father and mother were his slaves. Thus, he is an offspring of his slaves.

He then declares that he will serve the master in any capacity that pleases him. He will bring water if he is thirsty, grind corn for him if he is hungry, fan him if he feels hot, and massage his feet if he is tired. He concludes by saying that he is not worthy of the master, but the master showers mercy on him through his grace.

In this hymn, Guru Nanak, in a mood of intense devotion, identifies the guru with the Lord.

Mul khareedee laala gola mera naaun subhaaga

I am a bought servant of thine, O Master:
How fortunate am I that I am thy slave!
In exchange for thy Word,
I've sold myself at thy shop,
And now I go the way thou biddest.   *1*

O Master, how can I, thy slave,
Play clever with thee?
I cannot carry out even thy commands
In good faith.   *1:P*

My mother is thy slave as also my father;
I am an offspring of thy slaves, O Master.
And while one dances to please thee,
The other sings to thee,
And thus do we all worship thee, O King!   *2*

If thou art thirsty,
I bring water for thee;
If hungry,
I grind corn for thee;
I wave a fan over thee
And massage thy feet
And contemplate ever thy Name.   3

O Master, I have betrayed thy salt;
If thou pardon thy slave,
It is to thy glory.
Since the beginning of the ages
Thou hast been the compassionate giver;
Without thee, no one is emancipated.   4:6

Maru, p.991

The Dreadful Ocean

Guru Nanak gives a striking analogy of the world we live in and paints a graphic picture of the plight of the people who inhabit it. The world is compared to a dreadful ocean in which floats rudderless the boat of our mind loaded with the heavy weight of our sins. It is an ocean of which neither this side nor the other one is visible, because no one knows when the world began, nor when it will end. And the boat is neither equipped with oars, nor guided by a boatman. Is there, then, any hope for one to get across the ocean?

Guru Nanak answers that there surely is a way. If the hapless passenger can find a master, then the master will ferry him across. The master will act as the boatman and *Shabd* will serve as the oar. Once the passenger reaches his destination, he will be free from the hazards of the ocean for all time. In other words, he will get deliverance from the cycle of birth and death as well as from the state of finitude. He will attain the state of *sahaj* which will give him unalloyed bliss. Guru Nanak also brings home the truth that mind can be tamed by the nectar of *Nam* and not through repression. Ego, which poisons the mind and is the main obstacle in the way of God-realization, can be eradicated by making *Shabd* abide in the mind. At the end of the hymn, Guru Nanak compares the soul to a parrot and the body to a cage in which the parrot is imprisoned. The parrot could get eternal release from the bondage of the cage if it were to peck at Truth and partake of its nectar.

Bikh bohitha laadya

Having loaded it with the poison
Of our past karmas,
The boat of our mind is set afloat
On the ocean of life.

No shore is in sight,
Neither this side nor across;
No oar is there, nor the boatman,
And dreadful is the sea.   *1*

In an inextricable net
Is the whole world caught.
Only through the guru's grace,
By contacting Name,
Can we swim across.   *1:P*

The true guru is the boatman,
And the Word ferries us across,
Where exists neither wind nor fire
Nor water nor form,
Where the true One
Is dispensing His true Name
Which taketh us across
The ocean of phenomena.   *2*

Those absorbed in devotion to the true One
Are ferried across by the guru.
Emancipated from 'comings and goings',
Their spark merges in the universal flame.
Through the guru's instructions
They attain the state of *sahaj*
And remain merged in the true One.   *3*

Sahaj is to be found in the fourth realm;
The guru bestows this gift on the devotee.
If the snake of the mind
Is confined in a basket,
It sheddeth not its venom
Nor its vicious temper.

One receives what is written
In one's fate:
Whom is one to blame?
Only if he were to listen
To the incantation of the guru's Word,
He would be healed of the poison.   4

Like the crocodile
Which is ensnared by bait,
Are the wicked caught in a net
And they repent ever afterwards.
One comprehends not the wherefore
Of birth and death;
The impressions of past lives
Cannot be erased.   5

Born with the poison of ego,
The world came into being.
This poison dies only if the Word
Abides in the mind.
If one lives in the Truth,
The pain of old age troubles him not.
Emancipated in life is he
Who has rid himself of ego.   6

In the web of its own actions
Is the whole world caught
And it realizes this not.
The egotistic, ignorant man
Has forgotten the fact of birth and death.
He goes across whom the guru saves,
His mind fixed on the true Word.   7

The parrot of the soul,
Caged in the body,
Sings of his love for the world.
If it were to peck at Truth
And partake of nectar,
It would fly out of the cage
Once and for all.
He alone knows the Lord
Who meets a guru, says Nanak,
For then he is at the very gate
Of emancipation.   8

Maru, p.1009

No Salvation without the Master

None of our relatives is our true kinsman, as none will stay with us forever. The only true kinsman we have is God, and He can be realized only through the grace of the master.

Further praising his master, Guru Nanak says that without the help of the master, suffering from recurring births and deaths would never have come to an end.

Guru Nanak compares the soul with the bride and the Lord with the bridegroom, and says that only this relationship is lasting. The 'bride' is ever in bliss in sporting with the Lord; that is, once the soul has attained God-realization it never again separates from God, the 'spouse'.

The master is a boatman, constantly inviting people to go across the sea.

Guru Nanak ends the hymn by saying that no one is bad and one should not consider himself alone as good. One can rise to divine heights by annihilating his ego.

Naa bhainaa bharjaaeea

Neither remain the sisters
Nor the sisters-in-law
Nor the mothers-in-law:
Yea, our only true kinsman is God,
Who is met within
By the guru's grace.   *1*

I am a sacrifice unto the guru
Ever and forevermore.
For without the guru,
My wanderings cease not:
It is through the guru
That I meet with my God.   *1:P*

Neither our paternal
Nor maternal grandmothers remain,
Neither brothers nor sisters-in-law,
For they that come also quit the world;
And boatloads of travellers
Span the seas of existence to and fro.   2

Neither remain maternal uncles nor aunts,
Nor brothers, nor fathers and mothers;
For caravans of our kindred
Have crowded in upon the seashore
To cross into the beyond.   3

My Husband is dyed in the true colour of love;
She who remembers the true Lord with love
Will never again be separated from Him.   4

All seasons are blessed
When one has love for the true One:
Yea, the bride that knows her Lord
Sleeps in peace night and day.   5

Upon the seashore cries the boatman:
"O travellers, cross the sea with haste."
And whosoever boards the guru's boat,
I've seen him being ferried across.   6

Some have departed, others are going too;
Still others are being crushed
Under their load of sin;
Yea, they who've dealt in Truth
Abide ever with the true Lord.   7

Call not thyself good,
Nor see anyone as bad.
Says Nanak,
He who eliminates his ego
Is himself like the true One.   8:2:10

Maru, p.1015

The Lord and the Guru

This hymn starts with a pantheistic concept of God. He is the reality behind all appearance. He Himself is the creator as well as the creation. He Himself is the true guru as also the seeker. In fact, He pervades the entire universe as its essence. God is thus not far. He is nearer than the nearest of things.

This realization can come only through the grace of the guru. The guru imparts the secret of the Word to the disciple, who is able to earn 'eternal merit', that is, ultimate salvation, through the company of his guru.

Every age is blessed by the presence of saints. There is no time when the world is without a saint. The saints are not only themselves free from all taint of sin, but they also purge their initiates of all impurity.

The hymn also warns us that life is short and so the time at our disposal is too valuable to be wasted away in idle gossip and slander.

Guru Nanak emphasizes that God-realization is possible only through practice of His Name, the technique for which is imparted by the guru. Reading and recitation of scriptures are of no avail in getting rid of the five passions. The fire and suffering of hell are the inevitable lot of man unless he is saved through the grace of the guru.

The hymn ends by stating that a saint is not only a realized soul himself, but also redeems his ancestors and followers.

Aape karta purakh vidhaata

Himself, the absolute Lord,
Becomes the creator God;
He is of Himself born,
And He alone knows His Self.

He Himself is the true guru
As also the seeker;
He hath created all that exists.   *1*

Oh, He, our God,
Is near, not far,
And he who knows this
By the guru's grace
Is perfect among beings.
Associating with the guru,
One earns eternal merit;
Such is the glory
Of His beloved sons.   2

O God, blessed are Thy saints in every age,
For they praise Thee ever,
Sweetening their tongue with Thy love;
And praising Thee in this way
Are rid of their woes,
And fear naught but Thee.   3

They are ever awake,
They never go into slumber,
They dispense only truth
And liberate all their associates.
They are purged of the stain of sin,
And immaculately pure are they,
Attuned to the loving adoration of God.   4

O God's men,
Realize the Word of the true guru,
For one's beauty, breath and body
Age and wither away.

Lo, one dies today or tomorrow,
So meditate on the Name of the Lord.   5

O men,
Abandon your idle gossip and false ways,
For the false ones
Are attacked by death with relish.
Yea, the worldlings come to grief
Through ego and duality.   6

Abandon slander and jealousy of one another,
For the study of scriptures
Saves you not from the inner fire
And brings no peace within.
Associating with saints,
Practice the Lord's Name,
And the all-pervading God will befriend you.   7

Abandon lust, wrath and evil deeds,
And abandon also
Your involvements and strife, born of ego.
If you take the guru's refuge, you are saved:
This is the only way to cross
The sea of phenomena.   8

Hereafter you have to cross
The sea of fire with its poisonous flames,
And there no one keeps you company
Save your own self.
Yea, the sea of fire blazes,
Its waves leaping high,
And the worldling is cast into it
And roasted alive.   9

The guru bestows the gift of liberation
At his will;
He alone knows the way
Who has attained it.
Ask of him who has realized the Lord
How the guru's service
Leads to everlasting peace.   *10*

Without the guru one is entangled
In vice leading to death;
The Angel of Death
Strikes him on the head
And puts him to disgrace.
The slanderer is caught in the net
And is released not;
He gets drowned in the sea of slander.   *11*

Practice the Truth
And realize God within yourself.
He is not far from you:
You have only to look within.
With the grace of the guru,
Cross the sea of phenomena,
Overcoming all obstacles.   *12*

Within the body abides the Name of God,
Who Himself is eternal and indestructible.
He neither goes through birth and death,
Nor can He be destroyed.
Yea, through the Word is known His will.   *13*

He is immaculate and all light
Without a trace of darkness,
And He, the true One,
Alone occupies His true throne.
Worldly men keep revolving
Within the bounds of illusion,
And they are born to die again,
Over and over.   *14*

The guru's servants
Are beloved of the guru.
They sit on the throne
Who meditate on the Word,
And they find the quintessence
Of God within.
Oh, such is the true glory
Of the associates of the saints.   *15*

The saint himself crosses over
And also saves his ancestors:
Yea, himself delivered,
He redeems his followers too.
Nanak is but the slave of him
Who, by the guru's grace,
Is attuned to God.   *16:6*

Maru, pp.1025–1026

Prayer to the Master

This is a hymn full of devotion and gratitude for the master. The master is as powerful as the Lord Himself. In fact, Guru Nanak has identified the two in this hymn. It is the master who controls the entire universe, and his will prevails everywhere. And it is he who makes the beautiful inner regions manifest to the disciple. It is he who makes the disciple partake of the divine nectar within. It is he who opens the tenth door – the third eye – to reveal the enchanting flame within, as also the five melodies. Whereas the worldly man is constantly under the domination of the five passions – lust, anger, avarice, attachment and ego – the guru's disciple has triumphed over them all. Thus, the guru alone is our true friend and saviour, both here and hereafter.

Saran pare gurdev tumaari

O my Master, I've sought thy refuge,
For thou art the all-powerful Lord,
Compassionate, the destroyer of demons.
Thy wonders are known to no one,
For thou art the Creator-Lord,
The perfect Being.   *1*

Thou hast sustained this creation
Age after age.
O compassionate one,
Thy form of unparalleled beauty
Illumines all hearts.
Howsoever thou willest,
That way thou leadest thy people;
Yea, everyone doeth as is thy will.   *2*

Within us is the beauteous flame,*
The sustainer of all life,
And there exists the divine nectar
For us all to drink;
And He alone gives and He Himself takes,
For He is the compassionate Father
Of all the three worlds.   3

He created the world
And thus staged His play,
And He made life
To throb in the body of air, water and fire;
And He gave nine gates†
To the township of the body,
While the tenth‡
He kept hidden.   4

The four dreadful streams of fire§
Course through the body,
But rare is the God-conscious being
Who realizes it,
Keeping himself detached
Through the Word.
Worldly men are burned and drowned,
But the guru saves those
Who are attuned to God.   5

---

* This pertains to the first spiritual stage within.
† The nine outlets: two eyes, two ears, two nostrils, one mouth and the two orifices of elimination.
‡ The 'door' above and behind the two eyes, called the third eye.
§ Killing, infatuation, greed and wrath.

In this body of five elements –
Water, fire, air, earth and sky –
Abide the five essences.*
The God-man keeps immersed
In the guru's Word
And gets deliverance
From illusion, ego and doubt.   6

The mind is controlled
And becomes worthy of reliance
Through the Word alone.
For what else other than the Word
Can make it still?
The temple within is being robbed†
But the gross man of the world
Knows not of the demons within.   7

Within us are the five garrulous
And dreadful demons;
They are ever engaged
In the wild dance of strife.
Without the practice of *Surat Shabd Yoga*,
One ceaselessly comes and goes
And is brought to disgrace and dishonour.   8

The body is a lump of dust,
An illusory wall of sand;
Without the practice of *Nam*,
What honour is left for you?

---

* The five divine melodies.
† The five passions – lust, anger, avarice, attachment and ego – are often referred to as robbers or demons.

For you are bound down the four ages through,
And the Couriers of Death
Deal with you mercilessly.   9

At the door of the Angel of Death
Is one bound down and struck,
And there is no one now
To get the sinner released.
He wails and cries as does the fish
Pierced by the rod.   10

Vile man is caught this way,
In the hangman's noose;
Alone, blind and in stark misery,
He is delivered to the Courier of Death.
Yea, without the Lord's Name,
He knows not emancipation,
And today or tomorrow,
Will be consumed by fire.   11

Other than the true guru,
There is no friend.
Yea, he alone is our saviour
Both here and hereafter,
And in his mercy
He blesses us with the Lord's Name,
And makes us merge in Him
As does water mingle with water.   12

The guru makes wise the errant disciple;
If he goes astray,
The guru puts him back on the path.
Serve thou such a guru day and night,
For he destroys thy sorrows
And ever abides with thee.   13
O how can thou ever know to serve the guru?
For even Brahma, Indra and Shiva know it not.
The true guru is infinite, unfathomable,
And he alone realizes it
Whom he grants this boon.   14

With love within,
The true devotee beholds the Lord
Face to face.
Yea, he is in love
And in contact with the divine melody.
Day and night
Shines the immaculate flame
Of the lamp within everyone,
But the *gurmukh* alone sees it.   15

The fare of inner knowledge is sweet,
The quintessence of all essences,
And whosoever tastes it
Sees the vision of God.
Yea, whosoever sees the vision
Attains detachment from the world
And stills the cravings of his mind.   16

He who serves the true guru
Becomes most elevated;
Yea, he realizes the Lord within himself.
Prays Nanak:
O God, bless me with Thy praise
And the society of those
Who have realized God
Through their guru.   *17:5:11*

Maru, pp.1031–1032

Home within Home

Guru Nanak, in this hymn, has defined a perfect master as one
who can reveal to a disciple his true home within his body. The
human body is a wonderful mansion in which resound the five
divine melodies. Not only does it contain within it vast universes,
wondrous in their extent and beauty, but it is blessed with the
sweet unstruck music of *Shabd* also. Above all, sits the majestic
Lord in the midst of all glory emanating from Him. The way to
one's true home and his Lord lies through *sukhmana* and the
region of Sunn. In this final destination, the soul abides as the
unspoken Word in a state of complete equipoise. There, no desires
of the mind exist, and all its outgoings cease. Then the soul merges
in the primeval Lord. Such is the true abode of a *gurmukh*.

This hymn was composed on a historic occasion. Guru
Nanak, during one of his travels, met Sheikh Ibrahim, who
was one of the successors of Sheikh Farid. In the course of their
discussion on spiritual subjects, Sheikh Ibrahim requested the
Guru to enlighten him regarding our real spiritual home. Guru
Nanak in reply recited the following hymn.

> *Ghar mahi ghar dikhaaye de*
>
> It is the true master, the wise one,
> Who shows us our home within this home
> Wherein reverberate the melodies five,*

---

* "There resound the five divine melodies. There the unstruck sound is of
amazing wonder" (*Ramkali*, M.5, p.888).

"The unstruck sound signifies music of the spiritual regions, which
rings without being produced by any instrument. It cannot be heard
with the physical ears, but can only be experienced in the state of inner
concentration" (*Shabdarath*, p.767, footnote).

The ancient Greeks called it, 'music of the spheres'.

The manifestation of the Word.
There continents, islands, underworlds,
Regions vast and universes galore
Evoke wonder.
Amidst the enchanting reverberation
Of melodies deep
Sits the true One on His kingly throne.
One listens to the music in *sukhmana**
Which takes him to the region of Sunn.
There he dwells as the unspoken Word;
There the desires of his mind dissolve.
The lotus of the heart is upturned
To be filled with nectar,
And the outgoings of the mind cease.
One forsakes not the unutterable utterance
And merges in the primeval Lord.
Where the five melodies mingle into one,
That is the true abode of a *gurmukh*.
He who searches the Word, finds that home;
Of him is Nanak a slave.

Malar-ki-Var, Shalok, p.1290

---

* Literally, the 'house of *sukhmana*', i.e., the destination where the *sukhmana* vein leads.

God and the True Guru

This hymn is written primarily in praise of the Lord, to bring out His greatness. The latter part of the hymn brings out the role of a true guru in realizing Him.

At the entrance of the Lord's mansion even the great prophets and incarnations, gods and goddesses wait on Him. Among others there are celibates, anchorites and *jogis*. There are innumerable beings sitting in attitudes of contemplation and supplication. Numberless *sidhs*, with miraculous powers, and their disciples are attending on Him. Even the demons in their thousands are awaiting His command.

Guru Nanak concludes by saying that none of them obtains any peace of mind without instructions from a true guru. None of them can attain admittance to the Lord's mansion without practicing the Word given by the true master.

Jit dar lakh mohammada

At God's gate there dwell
Thousands of Mohammeds,
Thousands of Brahmas, of Vishnus,
And of Shivas;
Thousands upon thousands of exalted Rams,
Thousands of spiritual guides,
Thousands of religious garbs;
Thousands upon thousands of celibates,
True men, and *sannyasis*;
Thousands upon thousands of Gorakhs,
Thousands upon thousands of superiors of *jogis*;
Thousands upon thousands of men
Sitting in attitudes of contemplation;

Gurus, and their disciples
Who make supplications;
Thousands upon thousands
Of goddesses and gods,
Thousands of demons;
Thousands upon thousands
Of Muslim priests,
Prophets, spiritual leaders;
Thousands upon thousands of qazis,
Mullahs, and sheikhs –
None of them obtaineth peace of mind
Without the instructions of the true guru.
How many hundreds of thousands of *sidhs*
And strivers, yea, countless and endless!
All are impure without meditating on the Word
Of the true guru.
There is one Lord over all spiritual lords,
The Creator whose Name is true.
Nanak, His worth cannot be ascertained;
He is endless and incalculable.

Bhai Banno's Adi Granth, p.626

---

* As translated in M.A. Macauliffe, *The Sikh Religion* I:40.

Word

The Glory of the Word

At the time of death, the body is burned to ashes and the mind is rusted with worldly attachments. Our sins pursue us and so falsehood triumphs. In the absence of contact with the Word, we continue to move in the wheel of birth and death. Guru Nanak stresses again and again that if we do not realize the Word through instructions from the master, we shall never cease to revolve in the cycle of transmigration.

A body is pure only if the Word abides and resounds in it. One with such a body is in a blissful state of ecstasy and his body is free from evil passions.

One who is immersed in the Word will be honoured in the court of the Lord.

When the mind is filled with Truth, the grace of God descends upon it. Fear of God is awakened and all the elements of the body become harmonious. Once the light of Truth illumines the mind, all sins are driven out and it shines in its pristine glory.

Tan jal bal maatee bhaia

My body is burned to ashes
And mixes with dust,
My mind is rusted
With attachment to *maya*;

Once again my sins pursue me
And falsehood trumpets its victory.
Without the Word we are caught in the wheel
Of birth, death and rebirth.
Thus has double-minded duality
Been the undoing of multitudes.   *1*

My mind, fix thy attention
On the Word divine;
The Word will take thee
Across the waters of life.
Those who realize not the Word
Through the guru
Will die and be reborn,
Go and come, come and go.   *1:P*

A body is pure
If within it abides the true Name.
The body is imbued with the fear
Of the true One
And its tongue loves the taste of Truth.
Who, by God's grace,
Is in a state of ecstasy,
His body is of passions free.   *2*

The true One made the air,
From air came water,
From the waters He made the three worlds,
And He, the Lord, pervaded all.
The Lord is pure, He cannot be defiled.
He who is immersed in the Word
Will be honoured and remain unsullied.   *3*

When the mind is filled with Truth,
God's grace descends upon it.
The five elements of the body then
Are tempered in the fear of the true One,
And the light of Truth illumines the mind.
O Nanak, one's sins are forgiven
And the guru preserves his honour.   4

Sri, p.19

Dwell on the Lord's Name

Man is born, and after going through his allotted span of life, dies. But he does not know from where he came before his birth and where he is to go after his death. Nor does he know what causes his bondage in this world, what leads to his release and how he can merge his finite being in the infinite being of the Lord.

Guru Nanak answers these points by saying that he who dwells in the Lord's Name becomes like the Lord Himself.

Man is born into this world because of the desires that arise in his mind, and after death he continues to be confined to the realm of mind. *Gurmukhs* are the only emancipated ones and they need not go through the wheel of eighty-four, for they dwell in the Word.

Guru Nanak compares this world to a tree and its inhabitants to the birds that perch on its branches. They aspire to soar in the skies, but lured by the desires of their minds, they end in ruin; that is, the souls have to keep coming back to this world to satisfy the desires of the mind. But those who are merged in *Nam* take this world to be a temporary halting place. Shedding their carnal passions, they break through the veil of ignorance; they acquire spiritual wealth that is boundless. This wealth is acquired by opening the tenth door. The method and technique come from saints. Saints or masters are dear to the Lord and their decisions are never set aside by Him.

Jaato jaai kaha te aavai

Man is born and then he dies;
Where does he come from?
Where does he come from
And where does he go?
Why is he bound down,
How is he released?
How does he merge
In the state of *sahaj* of the eternal Lord?   *1*

He who has the Name in his heart
Has nectar in his mouth,
And dwelling in it,
Becomes detached like the Lord.   *1:P*

He comes and goes in peace,
As is the natural law.
One who is born
Of the desires of the mind
Merges into the mind again.
The *gurmukhs* are emancipated
And go not the round;
They dwell in the Word
And through the Name get deliverance.   *2*

On the tree of life stay many birds overnight;
Of these some are happy, some not;
And lured by the desires of the mind,
They end in ruin.

Night and day,
They look longingly towards the skies
And wander about in all directions,
As is the writ of their karma.   3

But they who are merged in the Name
Take the world to be a pasture-halt,
And shedding their lust and anger,
Break the pitcher of poison.*
Without the treasure of the Word,
Our homes and our stores are empty.
When we meet the guru,
He opens unto us the 'hard door'†.   4

One meets with saints if one is blessed
With perfect good fortune.
They are the Lord's own,
They dwell in the bliss of Truth.
They surrender to the Lord spontaneously
Their mind and body;
Nanak falls at their holy feet.   5:6

                          Gauri, pp.152–153

---

* The body. They vacate the body by practice of the Word.
† The tenth door or the eye centre.

My Mind! Repeat the Lord's Name

The worshippers of the Lord adore Him. With infinite love in their heart they thirst for Him. As a result of their intense longing, they attain bliss and union with Him.

Guru Nanak admonishes the recalcitrant mind to repeat the Name of the Lord and to seek His protection. The Name alone is the boat on which one can cross the waters of life. For proper practice of the Name, the master's guidance is indispensable. Through the master's help the quintessence of knowledge is attained.

Guru Nanak warns against rituals and external observances such as going to pilgrim places and taking holy baths. These acts do not wash away sins or remove doubts. Nor do they end the ever-revolving cycle of birth and death. The state of *sahaj* can be acquired only when the highest spiritual stage has been realized.

Bhagati prem araadhint sach pyaas

Those who adore and love Him,
Whose hearts thirst for the Truth,
With tears in their eyes
They cry out to the Lord
And thus attain peace of mind.   *1*

O my mind!
Repeat the Name of the Lord,
Seek His protection;
His Name is the raft
On which to cross the waters of life.
Make the practice of the Name
Thy rule of life.   *1:P*

My mind!
Repeat the Name of the Lord,
Seek guidance from the guru.
Even death will become thy well-wisher;
The quintessence of knowledge
Will be thine to treasure.
Such will be thy gain
If His Name thou repeat.   2

The world is lured
By ever-shifting wealth;
We are obsessed
With things of the world;
The devotees know
That the Name alone is eternal,
And the guru's guidance
Imbues them with the Word.   3

Going on pilgrimage after pilgrimage
Does not wash away doubt,
Nor cure the ills of birth and death
That beset the entire world;
Only God's seat is immune
From this worldly ailment;
So, the truly wise meditate on the Name.   4

The world is ensnared in the meshes
Of lust and attachment.
It suffers the anguish
That birth and death do bring;
Hasten to the true guru's sanctuary
And be saved;
In thy heart repeat the Name of the Lord.   5

The guru's teaching brings
Stability to thy mind,
Meditate in the tranquillity of *sahaj*.
Pure is the mind which has Truth
And the priceless ruby that is knowledge.   6

Let the fear and love of the Lord
Be thy worship.
Fix thy mind on the feet of the Lord
When thou meditatest,
And thou wilt cross the fearful waters of life.

Lord! In my heart be Thy Name,
It is the purest of the pure;
My body I place under Thy protection.   7

The Name of the Lord
Is like a mighty wave
That swamps greed and avarice
In the mind;
Pure One,
Chasten and purify my wilful mind!
Nanak craves Thy protection.   8:1:5

Gujari, pp.505–506

Dear Is the Lord's Name

Just as opium is dear to the opium addict and water is dear to the fish, so is the Lord's Name dear to the lover of the Lord. It is his very life breath.

Guru Nanak compares the Lord to a tree that bears the fruit of nectar. Whosoever drinks it becomes immortal. He is completely fulfilled.

What a pity that the Lord is present everywhere and yet remains unseen! It is the wall of ego that separates man from the Lord. How can the thirsty slake their thirst, when a wall separates them from the lake?

Guru Nanak says that he is the tradesman of his Lord, who is at once his Lord and his goods. He adds that it is only His grace and help that can take him out of delusion.

Amlee amal na ambaari

To the addict
There is nothing like an intoxicant.
To the fish
There is nothing like water.
Those imbued with the Name of their Lord
Find every prospect pleasing.   *1*

May every moment of my life
Be a sacrifice to Thy Name, O Lord!   *1:P*

The Lord is like a tree that bears fruit;
Thy Name is immortal nectar.
Those who drink it are truly satiated.
May my life be sacrificed to them!   *2*

Thou livest amongst all creatures,
Yet I see Thee not;
How can the thirsty their thirst slake,
If a wall separates them from the lake?   3

Nanak is Thy tradesman;
Thou art my Lord and my treasure.
My mind would rid itself of delusion
If to Thee I addressed my prayers
And to Thee my petition.   4:1

Vadhans, p.557

Merging in the Lord's Name

Mind resides in the body, which has six centres or *chakras*. In it resounds the divine melody. Guru Nanak says that his mind is attuned to this divine music. He is now in a state of bliss, which is beyond description. This blessing he received from his master, and he abides in the Lord's Name.

In order to merge in God, it is first of all necessary to still one's mind and conquer one's cravings for worldly things. He must also eradicate his ego from within himself. Only then will he be free from the fear of death.

It is through practice of the Word that one attains to the Lord. By such practice all stains of vice are washed away and the wisdom of his master is awakened in the disciple.

Such a realized being becomes detached from all worldly desires, although he still lives in the 'cave' of his body, because he has slain the five demons of the passions. He is no longer lured by another's possessions. He now revels in the state of *sahaj*.

Khaee maee dehee man bairaagi

The body of six *chakras*
Is the seat of the detached mind,
Within which rings
The melody of the Word.
The unstruck melody
Has enchanted my mind,
And through the guru's instructions
It revels in the true Name.   *1*

O man, one attains bliss
Through devotion to God;

By the guru's grace,
The Lord seems sweet
And one merges in His Name.   1:P

Stilling the craving for *maya* and attachment,
One merges in the Word;
Meeting with the true guru,
One unites with the supreme Lord.
I am blessed with the invaluable jewel of *Nam*;
Imbued with it, my mind is stilled.   2

I am afflicted not
By the malady of ego and attachment;
Being the devotee of God,
I am rid of the fear of death.
The tyranny of death no longer affects me,
And the immaculate Name adorns my heart.   3

By practice of the Word,
I now belong to the absolute Lord;
Erased is vice from within my mind,
And guru's wisdom has taken its place.
I am awake to God day and night,
And am eternally attuned to Him.
I have now attained liberation
While still alive.   4

I remain detached in the cave of the body,
And through the Word
Have slain the five demons within.
I am lured not by what belongs to another,
And abide deep within in the state of *sahaj*.   5

The *gurmukh* is forever awake to God,
Detached from the world;
And being ever detached,
Is woven into the Lord's quintessence.
The world is asleep and dies to be reborn,
For without the guru's Word
It is not awakened.   6

The unstruck melody of the Word
Rings within night and day;
It is by the guru's grace that one hears it.
The Lord is revealed when one hears the Word;
Detached from all, He is seen pervading all.   7

One then enters into the Sunn trance,
And attains to the state of *sahaj*;
Abandoning ego and greed,
One knows the One alone.
The disciple,
Having tamed his mind, O Nanak,
Merges in God,
Obliterating all sense of 'other'.   8:3

Ramkali, pp.903–904

True Is the Lord's Treasure

This hymn is mainly in praise of the Lord and the master. Guru Nanak implores us to treasure the Lord and to serve the master. For saints are dear to the Lord, and it is the master who unites us with the Lord, who is eternal, infinite and priceless.

The human body has been compared to a beautiful township in which reverberate the five divine melodies. The Lord Himself resides in it. This township has nine gates. The Lord has bestowed every human body with them. Yet, it is through the tenth gate that the Lord can be found. And it is only through His grace that we can get this realization.

The purpose of human life is to search for our true home in this township. Our true home can be attained through contact with the Word.

The evil passions in us, such as ego, lust and anger, are the main obstacles on the way to our destination. These obstacles can be overcome by following the guru's instructions. It is through his grace that the mind becomes steady and ceases to be affected by desire. Again, it is through his grace that the five divine melodies are heard and the Lord Himself is realized.

The Lord is present in everyone and in everything. He is the merchant as well as the peddler. He Himself judges all, laying down His own criteria.

Through His grace, the Lord rids us of ego and the sense of duality. Through His grace we are able to remain detached from the world even while in the human form.

At the end, Guru Nanak says that he alone is wise who has rid himself of ego, attained bliss through the Word and achieved self-realization.

Har dhan sanchoh re jan bhaai

O brothers,
You will gather the riches of the Lord,
If you serve the true guru
And remain in his refuge.
The Lord's riches are not stolen,
For the melody of the Word
Keeps one ever awake.   *1*

O God, the only Supreme Being,
The detached King!
Thou Thyself accomplishest
All deeds of Thy saints.
Eternal art Thou,
And motionless and infinite and priceless;
Ever-abiding is Thy beauteous abode.   *2*

Blessed is that township of the body
Wherein the five melodies* reign supreme,
And where resides
The one supreme, detached Being,
Sitting in the trance of Sunn.   *3*

The township of the body has nine gates,
The Creator-Lord has endowed all with these.
But within the tenth abides
The detached, unfathomable One,
Realized only
If He makes us realize.   *4*

---

*The five melodies pertain to the five spiritual regions within, or the spiritual sounds within.

Indescribable is the supreme Lord;
True is His court
And true is His standard,
And His writ runs over all.
Says Nanak: Search thy true home
And find the Name
Of the all-pervading Lord.   5

He, the Lord, is all-wise,
Detached from all.
He is merged in the guru's wisdom
And does justice to all;
He strikes one's lust and wrath in the neck,
And purges one of ego and greed.   6

In the true abode
Resides the formless Lord,
And he who meditates on the Word
And knows himself, realizes Him;
Deep within the true home
Abides He ever,
And emancipates one
From transmigration.   7

And then one's mind wavers not,
Nor does the wind of desire
Send him adrift;
Within himself the yogi rings
The unstruck melody of the Word,
Yea, the symphony of the five sounds
Rings sweetly within,
And the detached Lord Himself
Makes the divine music.   8

With fear and love for the Lord,
One merges in *sahaj*.
He is purged of ego
And revels in the unstruck melody.
And through the collyrium of knowledge
He knows the detached Being
And sings praises of Him.   9

The eternal Lord rids us
Of our woes and fears;
Rid of all maladies,
Yama's noose is no more for us.
Says Nanak:
The Lord is the dispeller of fear,
And one who meets the guru
Attains unto Him.   10

He who knows the detached Lord
Devours Kal;
Yea, to whom the grace
Of the Lord is revealed,
Realizes the Word.
He knows his self
And he knows the world as His play.   11

The Lord Himself is the merchant
And the peddler too,
And He it is who Himself judges all;
Testing each on His touchstone,
He evaluates each Himself.   12

Compassionate and merciful is our Lord;
He, our creator, pervades all hearts.
And yet our Lord remains detached;
It is the powerful guru
Who makes us meet
With the all-powerful Lord.   13

The all-wise and all-seeing Lord
Purges us of our ego
And rids us of the sense of duality,
And makes us see the One alone;
And despite the human garb,
We remain detached from the world of hopes
And sing of the one absolute Lord
Without ancestors.   14

Ridding oneself of ego,
He who attains bliss through the Word
And knows himself,
Is indeed the man of wisdom.
Says Nanak: He reaps the eternal fruit
Of the Lord's glorious praise,
Who associates with saints.   15:2:19

Maru, pp.1039–1040

The Word

If one keeps silent, men take him to be stupid. Much talk, on the other hand, is a waste of time and energy, for he is bereft of meditation on the Lord. Without the practice of the Lord's Name there is no piety.

Guru Nanak says that he loves those who slander him, because they take his sins without charging any wages. He is here referring to the Indian belief that the slanderer takes on himself the karmas of the person he slanders.

Salvation is attained through the Word of the master, which comes through the grace of God.

Excellence is acquired through practice and not merely by repeating the word 'excellent'. The man of God practices on the holy Name, but the worldly man thoughtlessly consumes poison. The Name is an elixir for the blind and the deaf, the moron and the outcast, the thief and the murderer. It is gold for all of them, whereas worldly wealth is dust and poison.

Guru Nanak says that some see goodness in others and some see only faults. But the best is he who is exclusively engaged in practice of the Word.

Masee karo moorakh jag kaheea

If I keep silent,
Men think me stupid;
If I talk much,
How can I meditate on Thee?
Lord, who art the judge
Of all my omissions and commissions,
Without Thy holy Name
There is no true piety.

1

Worldly men are so enmeshed in falsehood
That I love those who condemn me.   *1:P*

The pious
Are often condemned by the world,
The Word of the guru alone
Shows one the path.
He knows within that *Nam*
Is the ground of all existence.
That one alone knows it,
Who has the grace of the Lord on him.   *2*

I am soiled,
The true One is spotlessly clean;
And alas,
By repeating the word 'excellent'
One does not attain
To excellence oneself.
Thoughtlessly the self-centred man
Consumes poison,
But the man of God
Is immersed in His Name.   *3*

For the blind, the deaf,
The slow-witted;
For the outcast, the thief,
The murderer, the wretched,
The love of the Lord's Name
Is glory and wealth:
The holy Name for them
Is the only gold;
All of the world's wealth
Is venom and dust.   *4*

Some see goodness in others,
Some only faults;
Others meditate entirely on the Word.
All these are God's gifts
And glory to Him.
With Thy grace,
Honour and esteem are achieved.
Nanak speaks
But his words are inspired
By Thee.   5

Prabhati, pp.1330–1331

Rituals

Wander Not from Place to Place

Wandering from place to place does not extinguish the inner fire of passions; nor does wearing clean clothes wash away the dirt of the mind. Alas, men lead a life of falsehood and hypocrisy! They put on a mask to conceal their interior.

Nothing will make one a true devotee except the teaching of a true guru. If the guru's Word dwells in the heart, one's ego and cravings disappear. The mind is a priceless gem only if the Lord's Name dwells in it. The rebellious mind of the disciple is tamed by the guru. Eventually the soul gets released from the grip of the mind and goes back to its source, like a wave merging in the ocean.

Guru Nanak emphasizes that those who do not find a living master and do not meditate on the Lord flounder in the stormy waters of life and keep on moving in the cycle of birth and death. He reminds us that human life is a priceless jewel and should not be wasted away like worthless shells. The secret of escape from this world is acquired from the master. Those who have obtained it become perfect beings, full of wisdom. Their faces radiate bliss, for they hear the sweet melody of the Word.

Bharmai bhaah na vijhvai

By wandering, fire is not extinguished,
Even if thou wanderest from land to land.
The dirt within thee is not cleansed.
Fie on such a life! Fie on such a mask!
There can be no worship of the Lord,
Save through the teaching of the true master.   *1*
O my mind,
Through the master, extinguish thy fire.
Let the master's Word find abode in thee,
Then thy ego and thy cravings
Will be destroyed.   *1:P*

The mind is a priceless jewel,
Through the Lord's Name it finds honour.
In the company of the True, find the Beloved,
Become absorbed in God
Through the guru's grace.
Thy ego will go, thy bliss will come,
The wave will merge back into the waters.   *2*

Who have not meditated on the Name,
They will suffer the cycle of birth and death.
Who have not found a true master,
They will flounder
In the turbulent waters of life.
Human life is a priceless, peerless jewel;
Do not throw it away for a worthless shell.   *3*

Who have acquired the secret
From their master
Are perfect beings
Saturated with wisdom.
The master takes them across
The stormy ocean,
And they are received with honour
In His court.
O Nanak, their faces are radiant
Within whom arises
The sweet melody of the Word.   4:22

Sri, p.22

The True Muslim

In this short poem, Guru Nanak enumerates the qualities of a true Muslim. A true Muslim need not go to a mosque and pray on a specific prayer mat. Nor is it necessary for him to recite verses from the Quran and undertake fasts in the month of Ramzan. For a true Muslim, sympathy and kindness are his mosque. Faith is his prayer mat. Honest living is his Quran. And to live a pure and pious life is keeping his fasts.

Continuing further, Guru Nanak says that right conduct is his Ka'aba, and Truth is his Prophet. Good actions are his prayer and submission to the Lord's will is his rosary. If one imbibes these qualities, he is a true Muslim and the Lord is his protector.

Mihar maseet sidak musalla

> Let compassion be thy mosque,
> Let faith be thy prayer mat,
> Let honest living be thy Quran,
> Let modesty be the rules of observance,
> Let piety be the fasts thou keepest;
> In such wise, strive to become a Muslim.
> Right conduct the Ka'aba,
> Truth the Prophet,
> Good deeds thy prayer,
> Submission to the Lord's will thy rosary;
> Nanak, if this thou do,
> The Lord will be thy protector.

Panj nivaaaja vakht panj

Five prayers, five times a day,
With five different names:
Make the first prayer truth;
The second, to lawfully earn your daily bread;
The third, charity in the Name of God;
The fourth, purity of mind;
The fifth, adoration of God.
Practice these five virtues,
And let good deeds be
Your article of faith, your *kalma*;
Then you can truly call yourself a Muslim.
By practicing hypocrisy, O Nanak,
A man is false through and through.

Majh-ki-Var, pp.140–141

The Door to Salvation

The material elements together with the mind combine to form the human body. God has given it nine doors* but the tenth door† He has kept hidden, which leads one to His mansion. Guru Nanak implores the learned to realize this, for in this knowledge lies the essence of wisdom. One can be an eminent speaker and a good listener, but the one who has realized himself is the true knower.

Guru Nanak raises the question: What dies at the time of death, besides the body which is but dust, and the breath which is but air? He himself answers: What dies is the ego and the demon of ignorance. The soul within does not die.

He then admonishes man not to go to holy places to search for the jewel that he seeks, but to look for it within his own body. The pedantic scholar indulges in much hair-splitting and debate because he does not know that the real treasure lies within.

Guru Nanak concludes with the statement that he realized the Lord through his master, thus triumphing over birth and death.

---

* Two eyes, two ears, two nostrils, one mouth and the two lower orifices of elimination.
† The third eye.

Paunai paanee agnee kaa mel

Air, water and fire combine,
On these plays the restless mind,
And thus is our body made.
Nine doorways it has,
But the tenth is the one
That leads to the Lord.

O learned one, know thou this,
For in this lies the essence of wisdom.   *1*

Speak, discourse and listen, everyone can;
But who realizes himself
Is the true knower.   *1:P*

The body is but dust,
The breath is but air;
What then, O learned one,
Dies when death doth come?
The death is of the ego in man;
But the seer* within doth not die.   *2*

That for which thou goest to holy places,
That jewel thou wilt find within thy body.
The learned pundit reads much,
Debates much,
For he knows not of the treasure within.   *3*

---

* The soul.

I die not, only the demon* within me dies;
The soul that sustains me
Is beyond death.
Sayeth Nanak:
The master hath shown me the Lord;
There is now no birth or death for me.   4:4

Gauri Guaveri, p.152

---

* Of ignorance.

Leave All Prayers and Penances

All prayers, penances and other external observances are like wandering in the wilderness without finding a path. Without understanding, the destination cannot be known and without the practice of *Nam* there cannot be understanding.

The Lord alone is permanent. All else is transitory. It is through service of the master that release from the bondage of impermanence can be attained.

The world is caught in the web of hope and attachment. Only the teaching of the master gives release from it. With the gift of *Nam* the master bestows, the mind of the disciple gets illumined and it opens out like the bud of the lotus flower. The guru's disciples no longer have any fear of death.

Men are victims of their evil passions and are dominated by their worldly attachments. They forget that the human birth is a very rare gift, the only one in eighty-four lakhs of life forms for attaining release from birth and death. They also forget that service of a true master is the noblest of acts. Through service of their master they become liberated souls, and are no longer soiled by the dirt of ego. They are able to burn the love of worldly things and find the unsullied *Nam* firmly established in their heart. Their mind ceases to wander and becomes motionless. It is rarely that one comes across such persons.

In the next stanza Guru Nanak stresses the importance of the living master in attaining God-realization. Without the master, one is lost in the cycle of birth and death. Without him there is no realization of the Word and therefore no attainment of bliss. Without his help, one cannot hear the unstruck music, the divine melody.

Such a God-realized person gains the three worlds, although he loses himself. He becomes one with the Divine. He attains this state through single-minded attention on practice of the Word.

Sabh jap sabh tap sabh chaturaaee

All repetition of holy words,
All austerities, all cleverness,
All other devices
Lead one to the wilderness
Without showing the path.
Without understanding
One cannot reach one's destination.
And without the Name
There is no understanding;
One's forehead is smeared
With the ashes of shame.   *1*

Our Lord is true,
Immortal is He;
The rest of the world is born to die;
By service of the guru
We gain release.   *1:P*

The world is bound in cords
Of attachment and much hope;
Only the teaching of the guru
Gives a sense of detachment.
The Name illumines the mind within,
It opens like the bud of the lotus flower.
The guru's disciples fear not
The clutches of death.   *2*

Since men lust after women,
The world is dominated by womankind.
Men love their sons and wife
But forget the Name.

They waste the human birth
And lose the gamble of life.
They forget that service of the true guru
Is the noblest of acts.   3

Men who serve the guru
May act with seeming pride
And sense of self respect,
But inwardly they are liberated souls
And are not soiled
By the muck of ego.
They burn the love of worldly things
By the guru's teaching,
And find the Name unsullied
Ensconced in their hearts.   4

Their mind ceases to wander
And is stabilized;
One meets such as they
By the grace of God.
Without the guru one is lost
In the cycle of birth and death,
And by the grace of God
We meet with the guru.   5

Fain would I describe
The handsome One
But words fail me.
How can I speak of One
Who is beyond the power of speech?

How can I evaluate One
Who is beyond all evaluation?
In Thy will all sorrows
Are turned into joy,
But the true Name
Annihilates every sorrow.   6

He who realizes the Word
Achieves bliss;
For him music is played
Without hands,
For him there are beats of time
Without feet,*
He knows the Word;
All joy is his;
By His grace
The Protector protects him.   7

He loses his self
But gains the three worlds;
He realizes the Word
And merges in the True.
He meditates on the Word
With exclusive attention.
Sayeth Nanak: thank Him
Who sets straight our affairs.   8:2

Asa, p.412

---

* *Anahad Shabd* or unstruck music.

On Rituals

Guru Nanak denounces rituals not only in the strongest possible terms, but also in great detail. And he is critical as much of Hindu ritualism as of Muslim or any other orthodox religion. All religions have their own sets of external observances and all of them have been equally rejected in the writings of Guru Nanak. For instance, bathing in holy waters, offering flowers to idols, burning incense before them and wearing the sacred thread by Hindus are as strongly censured as the rituals of Muslims.

In equally unambiguous terms Guru Nanak disapproves of all ascetic practices, such as walking barefooted on thorny ground, remaining unclad in severe cold and renouncing one's home to bear the hardships of jungle life. They do not bring one any nearer to spiritual realization.

Nor is the Guru happy with mere debate and argument often resorted to by learned pundits and scholars. Even their reading of scriptures, without putting into practice what they read, is prominently brought out in Guru Nanak's compositions as sheer hypocrisy and cant. In fact, there is a wide chasm between their speech and their actions.

The following hymns of Guru Nanak serve as representative samples of the points mentioned above.

Par par gadi ladeeyai

If we were to carry cartloads of books,
And the carts contained nothing but their load;
If we were to fill boats with these books,
And stuffed all pits and crevices with them;
If we were to recite scriptures year after year,
If we were to recite them month after month;

Nay, if we were to recite them all our life
And spend every breath in this pursuit,
Only one thing will count in the end, O Nanak,
All else is futile, sheer waste and strain.

Asa-di-Var, p.467

Musalmaana sifat sareeyat

The Muslims praise their religious rites
And remain content with reading
And dwelling on them,
But the real lover of the Lord
Is one who has experience of His vision.[*]
The Hindus praise the Lord
Who is invisible and infinite;
Nevertheless they bathe in holy waters,
Offer flowers to idols
And burn incense before them.
The yogis dwell on the void
And call the Creator unknowable,
And yet they give the form of a body[†]
To the Absolute.

Asa-di-Var, p.465

Lakh nekeeya changiyaaia

Countless austerities at holy places
And yogic practices in the wilderness,
Countless brave deeds
And laying down one's life on battlefields,

---

[*] Realizing the Lord within.
[†] Idols or images.

Countless repetitions of scriptures
And even their comprehension,
Are all in vain to realize Him.

Asa-di-Var, p.467

Likh likh pariya teta kariya

I wrote and wrote
And read what I wrote;
The more I did so,
The more I was burned.
I roamed round many a pilgrim place;
The more I roamed
The more I prated.
Many a garb of piety did I wear,
And much torture I inflicted
On my body.
What I suffer
Is the result of my own doings:
I ate no food
And lost the taste of my tongue.
In love of other than God,
I suffered much anguish;
I wore no clothes
And shivered day and night,
I wasted myself away
By keeping a vow of silence.
How could I awake from slumber
Without the master?
Barefooted I walked,
I reaped what I sowed;
I ate dirt and rubbish
And threw ashes on my head.

The purblind fool that I was,
I lost all honour,
For without the Lord's Name,
All was futile.

Asa-di-Var, p.467

Moorakh pandit hikmat hujat

The foolish pundit revels in argument
And loves victory in debate.
The virtuous one practices virtue,
But loses all merit
By asking for reward.
One who calls himself continent
Knows not the way
And abandons his home.
All are complete within themselves
And lack nothing;
But he alone, O Nanak,
Is weighed with honour*
Whom God Himself accepts.

Asa-di-Var, p.469

Par pustak sandhya baand

They read scriptures, offer prayers
And then they fight;
They worship stones
And heron-like assume a trance;

---

*In India a great person is sometimes honoured by weighing him on a scale balanced with gold or silver; here the devotee is weighed against the weight of honour, that is, he is received with honour in the court of the Lord.

They utter falsehood
And their bodies are adorned with piety;*
They recite the three lines of *gayatri*
Three times a day;
They put a rosary round their neck
And a saffron mark on their forehead;
They fold a *dhoti* round their loins
And put a cloth to cover their heads.
If they had known the divine law,
They would have known
All these beliefs and deeds
To be futile.
Meditate on the everlasting Lord,
O Nanak;
But without the true master
How to find the way?

Asa-di-Var, p.470

Lakh choreeya lakh jaareeya

Myriads of thefts,
Myriads of illicit loves,
Myriads of deceits and abuses,
And myriads of secret frauds,
Day and night he perpetrates;

Still the Brahmin twists and spins out
Thread from cotton.†

---

*Indian sadhus smear their body with ashes and wear earrings in their ears, *tulsi* beads around their neck, etc.
† Sacred thread.

He kills and cooks a goat
And eating it says to all:
"O wear thou the sacred thread."
When the thread is worn out,
It is thrown away
And replaced by another,
But it would not have sundered, O Nanak,
If it had power.

Asa-di-Var, p.471

Maanaskhaane karaih nivaaj

The man-eaters* say their *namaz*,
And those who wield the knife
Wear the sacred thread.
In their homes the Brahmins blow the conch,†
But they too relish the taste of meat.
False is their property,
False their profession,
False is their speech,
False their repast;
Far removed are they from shame and truth.
They are all filled with falsehood, O Nanak.
On their foreheads is the saffron mark,
Round their loins are the folds of a *dhoti*,
But in their hands is a knife
And they are butchers of the world.

Asa-di-Var, pp.471–472

---

* 'Man-eaters', an expression meaning those who are extremely cruel to
other people.
† For prayers.

Je mohaaka ghar muhai ghar mahi

If a thief robs a house
And offers the loot in charity
To his ancestors,
The spoil is recognized in the next world
And the ancestors are charged with theft.
The hands of the broker* are chopped,
Thus is justice done.
That alone is received hereafter, O Nanak,
Which is earned with one's own labour.

Asa-di-Var, p.472

Andarahu jhoothe paij baahar

False within, famous without,
If such be thy way of life,
Thy filth will not go,
Even if thou bathest
In all the holy waters.

Asa-di-Var, p.473

---

*It is a Hindu tradition to give alms and free meals to propitiate the gods and ameliorate the condition of one's dead relatives in their after-life. The living are thus 'brokers' for their dead relatives. But if their offerings are made with dishonestly earned money, the dead relatives and the living both have to suffer for it.

Ambrosia Is Within

The elixir that man comes to seek in this world is nowhere outside, but within his own 'home'. It is within his body and the key to open the lock containing the treasure is with the living master.

All external observances and rituals are a sham. Guru Nanak entreats the seeker to give up these 'masks and disguises'.

It is incumbent upon man to distinguish between good and evil, to give up the path of evil and to follow the path of virtue. In the absence of such distinction, the further one goes the deeper one sinks in the mire.

Washing the body at pilgrim places is of no use when the mind is full of greed and falsehood and the mouth is full of calumny. What can cleanse him of sin is practice of the Word under the guidance of the master.

Jis jal nidhi kaaran

The treasure of the Name
You came into the world to seek,
That sacred font of nectar
You'll find through your master;
Take off your mask and other disguises,
Give up trickery and all other pursuits.
Doubt and duality bear no fruit.   1

O my mind, be firm, go not astray.
If elsewhere you look,
Yours will be frustration and grief,
For the ambrosia you seek
Is within the home.   1:P

Abandon the path of evil,
Take the path of virtue;
You'll regret the evil acts you do.
If you know not good from evil,
Again and again in the mire will you sink.*   2

Of what avail
Is external washing of the body,
When the grime of greed and falsehood
Is within?
If under the guru's guidance
You meditate on the pure Name,
Your inner self will be cleansed of sin.   3

Discard greed and calumny,
With falsehood make no compromise.
With the guru's teaching
Pluck the fruit of Truth.
As be Thy will, O Lord,
So keep me, I pray.
Praises of Thy Word I'll sing,
Nanak is Thy bond slave.   4:9

Sorath, p.598

---

* In the wheel of transmigration.

The Anchorite

In this powerful hymn Guru Nanak strongly denounces the mode of life of a *jogi* in which there is no conformity between his proclaimed ideals and his actions. Guru Nanak brings to the surface the hypocrisy involved in the anchorite's renunciation of the world. In his heart lie love for mammon and woman, although he has withdrawn from the city to the jungle. He is thus neither a true anchorite nor a worldly man. He gives sermons to others, but has not been able to extinguish the fire of carnal desire raging within him. He puts on the garb of piety and wears rings of crystal in his ears, but has venom within which poisons and deceives mankind. The ritualistic application of ashes on his body is all a sham and it will not save him from the cycle of birth and death. Above all, he begs from door to door shamelessly and becomes a parasite on society. There is only one way that can give him deliverance from suffering and transmigration: he must find a perfect master and scrupulously abide by his instructions. His mind will then be purified and become fit for containing the love of God. By persevering in the practice of *Shabd* under the guidance of his guru, he will eventually realize God.

> *Jag parbodhai marhi badhaavai*
>
> O *jogi*, thou preachest to the world
> As also fattenest thy body.
> If, abandoning thy posture of meditation,
> Thou beg from door to door,
> How shalt thou obtain the true One?
> Thou lovest mammon and woman,
> And art neither an anchorite
> Nor a worldly man.   *1*

O *jogi*, still your mind
So that pain and duality depart.
Thou art not ashamed to beg
From door to door.   1:P

Thou singest songs,
But knowest not thyself.
How shall the great fire
Which burneth thee be extinguished?
If thou dwellest in the guru's Word
With devotion,
Thou shalt easily receive
The alms of *sahaj*.   2

Like a hypocrite
Thou appliest ashes to thy body,
Thou shalt suffer the blows of death
For thy worldly attachments.
The vessel of thy heart is broken
And cannot hold the alms of love.
Thou art bound by bonds
And shall suffer transmigration.   3

Thou dost not restrain thy seed
And yet thou callest thyself continent.
Tempted by the three attributes,
Thou beggest for mammon.
God's light shineth not in one
Who is devoid of compassion;
Such a one is involved in entanglements
And keeps on sinking.   4

Thou wearest many garbs;
Thou changest many colours.
Like a juggler thou performest tricks
To deceive men.
The fierce fire of anxiety
Burneth thy heart;
How shalt thou be saved
Without good works?   5

Thou makest rings of crystal for thine ears,
But without divine knowledge
There is no emancipation.
Thou art beguiled by the pleasures
Of the tongue and sex;
Thou hast become a beast,
And the mark of it shall not be erased.   6

The *jogis* too are involved
In the three attributes of Maya,
Even as the householders are;
Those alone will be delivered from anguish,
Who practice the Word.
For he who practices the Word is a true yogi. 7

Thou art the possessor
Of nine treasures, O Lord;
Thou art the all-powerful One.
Thou createst and Thou destroyest
As Thou wilt;
Thou art chaste, true,
Self-controlled and pure;
Thou art, indeed, the true yogi,
Friend of the three worlds.   8:2

Ramkali, p.903

Futility of Ascetic Practices

Ascetic practices connected with *hatha yoga* have been criti-
cized by Guru Nanak. What is required in the way of spiritual
realization is taming the mind, not torturing the body. And
mind can be disciplined only in the company of saints. *Pranayam*, which implies control of breath, can only purify the
body, but cannot rid the mind of the five passions of lust, anger,
avarice, attachment and egotism, nor can it remove the cover-
ings of the three attributes. Likewise, pilgrimages to holy places
are useless for purifying the mind, for water at best can only
clean the body. What can bring God-realization and release
from the bondage of birth and death is only practice of the
Name of the Lord. And the method to practice it rightly comes
only from a living perfect master, for he alone has knowledge
of this path, having himself trodden it.

Hath nigrah kar kaaiya chheejai

To subdue desire through *hatha yoga*
Wears down the body;
But through fasting and penances
The mind is subdued not.
There is nothing that equals
Practice of the Lord's Name.   *1*

Serve the guru, O mind,
And seek the company of saints,
Then the tyranny of Death
Can overawe thee not;
Nor Maya sting thee,
If thou drinkest the divine nectar.   *1:P*

The world is involved in debate
And is charmed by false music;
Abiding with the *maya* of three attributes,
It comes and goes.
Yea, without the Lord's Name
One suffers pain.   2

The yogi sucks in his breath
And relishes his success,
And through internal washing
And six other practices,*
He cleans his insides;
But without the Lord's Name,
Vain is the breath he breathes.   3

If within burns the fire
Of the five passions,
How can one be content?
If within is the thief,
How can one attain to God?
Only the God-man conquers
The fortress of the body.   4

If one's within be soiled,
Why should one wander at pilgrim places?
If the mind is not pure,
What good is bathing the body?

---

* The yogi sits erect, and with drooping shoulders moves the muscles of his stomach from left to right and from right to left in order to clear his intestines. This is called the *neoli karam*. The six other practices are to cleanse the body within with (a) water, or (b) cloth, or (c) thread; by (d) fixing one's gaze on something, (e) inhaling, and (f) exhaling swiftly like the bellows of an ironsmith.

If such be one's actions,
Then who is one to blame but oneself?   5

If one eats not food,
One tortures the body.
Without knowledge from the guru,
One is never content;
The worldling is born only to die
And be born again.   6

Ask the true guru for knowledge
And seek the company of saints.
If the mind is imbued with God,
One comes not nor goes.
There is no deed better
Than practice of the Lord's Name.   7

Quieten the clamouring
Of the mice of thy desires
And repeat the Lord's Name,
Thy primal service to Him.
Nanak, when God is merciful,
He blesses us with His Name.   8:5

Ramkali, p.905

The Fake Pietist

The anchorite leads a futile and unhappy life, begging at others' doors. He shrinks from his duties as a householder and becomes a prey to his cravings and evil desires.

He sometimes assumes the form of a *sannyasi* by wearing saffron robes and putting on the distinctive garb of a mendicant. He begs from door to door and does not earn his own living. He is ridden with doubts, for he does not know the mystery of the Word.

Going to holy places and smearing his body with ash do not save him from falling into delusion and being caught in the web of Maya. Although he recites scriptures, he lives in untruth. He does not know that God is realized within and that He also pervades everywhere outside.

By cropping his hair close, leaving a knotted tuft on his crown, he gains nothing spiritually. Nor does it benefit him to keep silence, except that such acts inflate his ego. His mind wanders in all directions and does not become still to enable him to drink the Lord's nectar.

Although he has abandoned his own wife, he is attracted by other women, enthralled by lust.

He gives sermons to others, but himself does not know the Word, being entangled in worldly affairs. From the outside he may appear to be calm, but he is full of venom within.

In contrast, a true *sannyasi* is attuned to the Word and lives in bliss. Through the grace of the master, he has conquered his evil thoughts and carnal desires. By serving the master, devotion for God has been awakened in him. He has been able to annihilate his ego and attain self-realization. Such a one begs neither food nor clothes. He does not speak in vain and is full of compassion for others. He is emancipated and remains in bliss by hearing the divine melody within.

Manmukh lahar ghar

The anchorite abandons his home
In a fit of despair
And he begs at the doors of others.
Yea, he shrinks from his duty
Towards his household,
Being instructed not by the true guru;
And lo, he is caught
In the whirlpool of an evil mind.
He wanders from land to land
And reads the sacred texts,
But his craving goes on increasing.
Yea, he practices not the Word
Within his fast-dissolving body,
And fills his belly like a beast.   *1*

O friend, a true *sannyasin*
Lives his life this way:
He is attuned to the one God,
Through the guru's Word in his very home,
And is satiated with His Name alone.   *1:P*

If he dyes his robes in ochre
And dons the distinctive coat of a mendicant,
And, tearing his usual wear,
He makes a cloak,
And holds out his bag to gather coins,
And begs from door to door
But instructs others in wisdom,
Lo, the blind of mind
Loses all his honour this way.

He is confused by doubt,
And practices not the Word,
And gambles his life away thus.   2

Within him the fire of desire
Is quenched not without the guru's grace,
And outside too he raises a fire
To warm his limbs.
Oh, how can he have devotion for God
Without serving the guru,
And how can he know himself?
And he slanders others
And falls into hell;
For within him
Is the darkness of ignorance.
And his pilgrimages to the holy places
Throw him into delusion;
Then how can he wash his sins off?   3

He walks on the path of *maya*
And besmears his body with ashes
And wallows ever in dust;
And he knows not the One
Within and without;
And if someone utters the truth to him,
He is angered.
Being guru-less,
He utters the sacred texts
But speaks untruth;
And as he meditates
Not on the Lord's Name,
He is blessed not with glory nor peace.   4

He close-crops his hair
But keeps a knotted tuft,
And keeps silence, proud of himself;
But his mind wanders in ten directions,
Without any love for self-knowledge.
He abandons the Lord's nectar
And tastes poison,
Being intoxicated with the wine of *maya*.
His destiny is not erased;
And as he knows not the Lord's will,
He is counted among beasts.   5

In his hands is the begging bowl
And he wears a patched coat
Like a mendicant,
But within him is immense craving.
And though he abandons his own wife,
He is attracted by another's;
Lured by sex desire.
He instructs others
But knows not the Word,
Being entangled in mundane affairs.
From without he is calm,
But within he has poison,
And so he is brought to ruin by Yama.   6

He alone is a *sannyasin*
Who serves the true guru,
Eliminating his ego,
And demands neither food nor raiment,
And whatever he receives unasked
He accepts;

And barks not in vain,
And treasures compassion,
And silences his wrath
Through the Lord's Name.
Oh blessed is such a householder,
Yea, a *sannyasin*, a yogi,
Who dwells at the Lord's feet.   7

The *sannyasin* remains detached
From hope and despair,
Being at one with the One alone,
And is comforted in drinking
The Lord's essence,
And lives in his true home
Wrapped in a holy trance;
And his outgoings cease
And his mind wavers not,
And he knows his God
By the guru's grace,
And searches his body, his home,
And finds the Name revealed within.   8

Brahma and Vishnu and Shiva are sublime
Only if they meditate on the Lord
And are imbued with His Name.
For it is Thy light, O Lord,
That animates the four sources of creation
And the speech of man,
And pervades the sky and the underworld.

Yea, all gladness and emancipation
Is in hearing the divine melody within
And cherishing it in the heart.
Says Nanak: Without the Lord's Name,
One is released not;
So swim thou across
The true way of the Name.   9:7

Maru, pp.1012–1013

Mind

Fish in the Net

Just as a fish, which is seemingly wise and clever, is caught unawares in the net by the fisherman, so also are we entrapped by the ruthless Messenger of Death. Both fish and men are caught in the noose of Death by their own follies.

The entire world is within the bounds of death. None can escape it. The only way to combat and triumph over it is by seeking the guidance of a master. He imparts the technique of forming contact with the Word that gives liberation from death. Guru Nanak says he is a sacrifice unto such a master.

Using other analogies, Guru Nanak compares man to a small bird caught in the talons of a hawk, or a beast caught in the hunter's snare. He is enthralled by the bait of Death. Only such can be saved who have the protection of their master. The master gives the boon of the Name, which saves man from being doomed to further births and deaths. No friends or companions can render such help.

God is True; His realm is True and the minds of those who have realized Him are absorbed in Truth. Those who have gained this knowledge from their master, their minds and mouths are pure; that is, their thoughts, words and deeds are now beyond karmic bonds. They become immortal, for death itself will cease to exist for them.

Without the master as guide we stumble in the dark, and without the Word we cannot see. Through the master's grace, we get enlightened and take abode in Truth. Our light blends with the eternal light.

Guru Nanak ends the hymn by saying that all happens according to the Lord's will. By His command the whole creation comes into existence. By His command death occurs. And it is by His will that we unite with Him. In short, whatever pleases the Lord comes to pass, for nothing is under the control of man.

Machhlee jaal na jaania

The fish in the deep and salty sea,
Wise and pretty as she was,
How was it that she was taken unawares
And knew not of the net?
She was entrapped in her own folly,
And escaped not the noose of Death.   *1*

Brothers, so are you caught
By the Angel of Death.
As on the fish so on us men;
When we least expect it,
The net will fall.   *1:P*

The entire world is within death's compass.
Without the guru
There is no means to conquer it.
Who are imbued with Truth are saved;
They dispel doubt and duality.
I am a sacrifice unto those
Who have reached the gate of the true One.   *2*

As a small bird
In the talons of a hawk,
Or on the ground
Caught in the huntsman's snare,
So is man enthralled by the bait of Death.
Only those the guru protects are saved.
If you have not the Name,
You will be picked out and cast aside;
You will have no friends or companions
To help you.   3

True is He called,
True is His realm.
Those who have accepted Him as True,
Their minds dwell in Truth.
Those who have gained this knowledge
From the guru,
Their minds and mouths are pure.   4

Pray to the true guru:
"Take me to the Lord and unite me with Him."
Union with the Beloved will give you peace,
The Demon of Death will poison himself and die.
"Let me abide in the Name
And let the Name abide in me."   5

Without the guru we stumble in the dark,
Without the Word we see not.
Through the guru's grace we are enlightened
And take abode in Truth;
There Death has no dominion.
Our light blends with the light eternal.   6

Thou art our friend,
Thou art the wise One,
Thou art Thyself the uniter.
Through the guru's Word we praise Thee,
But there is no end to Thy praise.
Where the immortal Word of the guru abides.
There Death shall have no access.   7

By His decree
Comes all creation into being,
By His command
All labour and earn.
By His ordinance
Occurs death.
By His will
We merge with Truth.
O Nanak,
Whatever pleases the Lord
Comes to pass,
For nothing is in the hands
Of mortal men.   8:4

Sri, p.55

The Ten Stages of Life

The hymn begins and ends with praise of the master. The master is the giver. He is the haven of peace. He is the lamp whose light illumines the three worlds. When he bestows the gift of the Word on someone, his mind is tamed and he finds eternal bliss.

Guru Nanak describes the ten stages of life, all of which are steeped in ignorance, cravings, desires and the passions. When at last the individual dies and is cremated, his friends lament for a while and then forget him. Some obsequious ceremonies, such as feeding the Brahmins, are performed and then all is forgotten. The soul of the dead man has gone, no one knows where. Thus begins and ends the purposeless life of the man of this world.

Guru Nanak ends by saying that the world remains sunk in ignorance without the enlightenment that comes from the master.

Gur daata gur hivai

The guru is the giver,
The guru is the haven of peace;
The guru is the lamp
That lights the three worlds.
O Nanak,
When he vouchsafes you
The eternal gift of the Word,
Then alone is the mind tamed
And bliss found.   *1*

The ten stages of life
Are steeped in ignorance.
First, the child's craving
For the mother's breast;
Second, his awareness
Of his father and mother;
Third, he knows his sister,
Brother and brother's wife;
Fourth, he takes to games and sports;
Fifth, he is inclined to food and drink;
Sixth, he wallows in lust,
Unrestrained by caste;
Seventh, he hoards wealth
And builds a house;
Eighth, anger afflicts his body;
Ninth, his hair turns grey,
His breath becomes wheezy;
And tenth, he dies
And is burned to ashes.
His friends lament for a while
And leave.
The swan has flown,
Not knowing whither.
He came and he went;
His name is dead.
Then were fed the crows,
Out of leaf-plates the Brahmins.*
O Nanak,
So do the worldly grope in the dark;
Without the guru
The world remains sunk in ignorance.   2

Var Majh, pp.137–138

---

* See Glossary: *Pittripuja.*

One against Five

The five passions have been depicted in this hymn as five dacoits. The soul has to fight by herself against all five. She is repeatedly overpowered and looted by them. She feels forlorn and helpless. Guru Nanak implores the soul to repeat the Name of the Lord, for it is only by repetition of His Name that the onslaught of the five can be successfully met. Practice of the Name will also help in warding off the attack of the Couriers of Death; without it the soul will be ruthlessly tortured by them. Guru Nanak ends with the advice that one should avoid committing sins for the sake of one's wife and friends.

Avar panch ham ek janaa

They are five, I am one.
How can I guard my house, O my mind?
They beat me and loot me
Again and again.
Before whom shall I lodge my complaint?   *1*

Repeat thou the Name of the Lord,
My mind,
For facing thee is a cruel gang
Of the Couriers of Death.   *1:P*

He raised the temple with many doors;*
Within it sits the soul as its dweller.
Taking the body to be immortal,
She disports herself with many a game
While the five are constantly plundering her.   *2*

---

* He created the body with nine outlets.

Death demolishes and robs the temple,
And takes the occupant captive.
Death beats her with a mace
And puts a chain round her neck.
The five take to their heels and flee.   3

One's wife seeks silver and gold,
One's friends need food to eat;
O Nanak, who sins for such causes
Will be bound and dragged
To the city of Death.   4:2:14

Gauri Cheti, p.155

Wasted Chance

Human birth is the only opportunity to meet the Lord. It provides the only outlet from the prisonhouse of eighty-four. Bringing out the significance and importance of this birth, Guru Nanak regrets that it is wasted in worthless activities such as sleeping, eating and amassing perishable goods. All effort should have been directed towards attaining God and His Name, the only lasting verities.

At the end, Guru Nanak states that human effort by itself is not sufficient, for without the grace of the Lord, He cannot be realized.

Rain gavaai soi kai divas gavaaya khaae

You have lost your nights, sleeping;
You have lost your days, eating.
Human life was a precious jewel;
You exchanged it for a cowrie.   *1*

You didn't realize the Name of the Lord,
Now you regret it, you foolish one.   *1:P*

You buried your precious wealth
In the earth,*
But the perishable cannot be loved;†
Those who leave with desires
For perishable things
Return, losing the Lord,
Who lasts forever.   *2*

---

* In olden times, people would bury their wealth to keep it safe.
† *Or:* "But desire not the imperishable Lord."

If by one's own efforts one could attain,
Then everyone would be blessed
With good fortune;
All depends on our past deeds,
Even though our wishes may be different.   3

Nanak, the One who has created
Alone takes care of His creation.
No one knows
On whom He will bestow greatness
Through His will.   4:1:18

Gauri Bairagan, pp.156–157

The Plight of the Worldly

The lovers of God have all their interest fixed on Him. They are indifferent to the world of the five elements. They have no bitterness and strife in their minds. Through love they have merged in the Lord and are at peace with themselves and the world.

The crucible of the heart of worldly people is inverted. They cannot receive divine grace. The conflagration of their wicked deeds ever consumes them. They are slaves of their cravings even as the bumblebee, the moth, the elephant, the fish and the deer are servile to their urges. Men's hearts are filled with lust and they run after women. They lose their poise and their sense of honour. They get frustrated and angry and then come to grief. Some are lured by others' wealth and burn in envy.

Only those who dwell in the Word are saved from such calamities.

A widow may sell her person for the sake of money or carnal gratification, but she will never be satisfied in the absence of her husband. So also, no real satisfaction can come to a seeker by reading scriptures and observing rituals unless he experiences spiritual union with the Lord.

Seva ek na jaanas avre

He who serves the One
Knows no other.
He rejects this world of five elements.
He gives up bitterness and strife.
Through love he merges in Truth.

1

Such is the devotee of the Lord;
He sings His praises;
He washes away the dirt on his mind
And gets united with Him.   *1:P*

The heart's lotus of the whole world
Is inverted;
The fire of evil deeds
Thoroughly burns mankind;
Only he who dwells in the guru's Word
Will be saved.   2

The bumblebee and the moth,
The elephant and the fish,
As also the deer, meet their doom
Because of their own doings.
Their cravings make them blind to reality.   3

Lust fills men's hearts;
They become lovers of women.
Then frustration and anger
Prove their undoing:
They lose their poise
And their sense of honour,
For they forsake the Name.   4

The wealth of others
Lures the minds of the worldly;
They put halters round their necks
And are enmeshed in anguish.
Only the godly
Who sing praises of the Lord
Escape.   5

A widow offers her body to another;
Under the sway of lust or money
She acts thus,
But without her spouse
She is not satisfied.   6

Study all the scriptures,
All litanies recite;
Read all the religious epics
And have them explained;
Unless you are dyed
In the essence of Truth,
Your mind will wander in delusion.   7

As the rainbird thirsts for drops of rain,
As the fish gambols in water in delight,
Nanak is athirst for the Name of the Lord.
He drinks and his heart is filled with joy.   8:11

Gauri, pp.225–226

Kal

Kal, the Negative Power, the King of Death, spares no one who is born in this world. Not even kings and chiefs, or qazis, sheikhs and faqirs can live forever. None can escape the clutches of Kal.

Kal lures us by putting temptations before our eyes, ears and tongue. The senses fascinate the mind, making it their slave.

Kal runs this world on the triple principle of creating, sustaining and destroying, manifested through the three gods, Brahma the creator, Vishnu the sustainer and Shiva the destroyer. Maya as the mother has borne these three deities. But all work under the Lord's will, without any say of their own. Guru Nanak enjoins the worship of the Highest only, and not of gods and goddesses of a lower order. Though the Lord watches over these agents, yet paradoxically they cannot know Him. He is subjective and formless, while they are part of the objective creation.

Prathme brahma kaalai ghar aaya

Firstly Brahma was begotten by Kal.
Brahma entered the lotus,
Searched the underworlds,
But found not the Lord;
He obtained not the Lord's sanction
And was led astray in delusion.   *1*

All that is born is destroyed by Kal;
But I have been saved,
As I practiced on the guru's Word.   *1:P*

Maya has deluded all gods and goddesses;
Kal spares none who serves not the guru.
The Lord alone is imperishable,
Invisible and inscrutable.   2

Kings, chiefs and emperors
Will not remain;
Forsaking the Name,
They will be tortured
By the Couriers of Death.
My mainstay is the Name;
As the Lord wills,
So do I live.   3

Neither kings nor chiefs
Stay forever;
Even the opulent die
After amassing much wealth.
Give me, O Lord,
The wealth of Thy ambrosial Name.   4

Subjects and lords, leaders and chiefs –
None are permanent in this world;
The inevitable Kal strikes the false ones
On the head.   5

The One alone,
The Truest of the true,
Is ever stable.
He who has fashioned and created,
He will destroy all.

When He is known through the guru,
Then alone honour is obtained.   6

The qazis, the sheikhs
And faqirs in religious garb,
Think themselves to be great,
But they too suffer
The pangs of ego.
But Kal does not spare those
Who do not have the support
Of the guru.   7

Kal traps us
Through our eyes and tongue;
Kal is over our ears
When we hear poisonous talk.
Without the Word,
We are being robbed
Day and night.   8

Kal cannot slay,
If the true One
Dwells in our heart,
And we sing His praises.
O Nanak,
Through the guru
We merge in the Word.   9:14

Gauri, p.227

The Rogue Elephant

Mind has been compared in this hymn to a rogue elephant, drunk with power and yet in dire fear of death. He can reach his sanctuary only if he finds a living master.

Without the teachings of the master the mind will not be stilled. The master asks the seeker to give up all ritual and to practice the Word.

How can the wayward mind be made motionless? Guru Nanak answers that the Lord in His mercy makes the seeker meet a true master. The master can draw the thorn of death out of his flesh. He can make Truth triumph.

The mind commits evil as well as virtuous deeds, because it is made up of five elements and is subject to the law of karma. The mind of the fool worships power and wealth. But under the master's advice, it practices the Name and is thus emancipated from suffering and the cycle of eighty-four. Under the master's instructions, the mind can comprehend the three worlds and it can realize God.

When the mind, under instructions from the master, becomes detached and is freed from the contagion of desire, it tastes the divine ambrosia. Such a one is welcomed with honour at the tenth door or the third eye. Thanks to the gift of Nam bestowed by the master, mind becomes fearless and conquers the five enemies of lust, anger, greed, attachment and pride. It now relishes the 'unstruck' music and relinquishes all other music.

It is at the door of the Lord's mansion (the third eye) that man begins to understand his spiritual self, gets immersed in devotion and love for the Lord and listens to the divine melody.

Guru Nanak concludes the hymn with a prayer to the Lord to give him an abode at the feet of the master so that he can find Him.

Man maigal saakat devaana

The mind is like a rogue elephant,
Wild and intoxicated with its own power.
It wanders about in the jungle
Of delusion and attachment.
It runs hither and thither
In terror of death.
If it finds the guru to guide it,
It will find its home.   *1*

Without the guru's Word,
The mind will not be stilled;
Repeat the Name of the Lord –
It is utterly pure –
And abandon the bitter ways of thy ego.   *1:P*

How can this wayward mind be stilled?
Unless it is tamed,
It will suffer at the hands of death.
God is our saviour,
In His mercy He makes us meet
A true guru.
He can draw the thorn of death
Out of our flesh;
He can make Truth triumphant.   *2*

The mind commits evil deeds
And the mind performs virtuous acts.
The mind is born out of five elements
And is subject to the law of karma.
The foolish mind worships power
And is full of greed;

By the guru's advice
It meditates on the Name
And attains eternal felicity.   3

Under the guru's instruction
The mind finds its true destination.
Under the guru's instruction
The mind comprehends the three worlds.
The mind can be a celibate yogi
Or a householder,
The mind can be a performer of penances;
Under the guru's instruction
It can also realize God.   4

The mind can become detached
And renounce the ego.
Every mind suffers
From desire and duality;
Under instruction of the guru
It tastes the nectar of the Lord.
At the door* of the body-palace
Is the soul welcomed with honour.   5

This mind of ours can be a monarch
And the hero in the field of battle,
The guru gives it the gift of the Name
And makes it fearless.
It can conquer the five enemies –
Lust, anger, greed, attachment and pride –
And reduce them to servitude;

---

*The third eye behind the two eyes.

And devouring the ego,
Bundle them into one!   6

The guru-intoxicated
Relinquishes all other music*
And allurements.
He loses his taste for all other fare;
In his mind is awakened love of God.
He hears the unstruck music
And revels in the Word.
He realizes his self
And becomes formless.   7

At the door of the Lord's mansion
Is our mind purified,
And it is immersed in devotion,
Love and the divine melody.
Day and night it sings praises of God –
Such grace the guru brings.
Within every body abides God
Who is without end
And without beginning.   8

This mind is drunk
With the elixir of God.
From the guru it found the cure
For all maladies.
To attain His love,
Seek abode at the guru's feet.
Nanak is the slave of the slaves
Of the devotees of God.   9:8

Asa, pp.415–416

---

*Other than the unstruck music.

Bondage

Only through service to the master can the Lord be known. The master imparts the secret of the Word. One who practices the method taught by the master gets rid of sorrow and suffering.

All relatives, attachment for whom ties us down to this world, are a bondage. Thus the father, the mother, the sons and daughters and wife are all bondages.

Even our deeds, performed in ego, serve as bondage, for they bring us back to this world according to the law of karma.

All possessions, such as the land of the farmer, the revenue of the king, the riches of the wealthy, are bonds.

Even our learning and scholarship, the study of scriptures and discursive knowledge act as bonds, for they inflate our ego. Thus does Maya cast her net wide and catch us all. Nothing gives us release and is acceptable to the Lord except His devotion.

Guru Nanak ends the hymn by praying to the Lord to grant him the shelter of the true guru and his refuge.

Guru seve so thaakur jaanai

He who serves the guru,
Knows the Lord;
His sorrows depart,
And through the Word
He realizes the Truth.   *1*

O my confidant,
Dwell thou on thy Lord,
And serve thy true guru,
And see thy Lord with thine eyes.   *1:P*

Father, mother and the world
Hold thee in bondage;
And so do thy sons, daughters
And thy wife.   2

All deeds, all righteousness
Performed in ego
Are like fetters;
Since they lead to duality,
Thy sons and wife too
Are thy bondage.   3

The farmer attached to his farm
Is in bondage.
And so is the king
Who demands revenue;
Such is the price they pay
For their ego.   4

All dealings,
Made without thought
Are nothing but bonds;
They satiate not our desire,
And the net of Maya and attachment
Is cast wide.   5

The riches men of substance gather
Leave them;
And so these too are a bondage.
Nothing is acceptable to the Lord
Except His devotion.   6

Thy study of the Vedas
And discursive knowledge,
Which inflate one's ego,
Forge new bonds,
And one is brought to ruin
Through attachment and sin.   7

Says Nanak:
I seek the refuge of the Lord's Name.
For when the true guru saves,
One is not held in bondage.   8:10

Asa, p.416

Deluded Mind

Various analogies and epithets have been used in this hymn to describe the mind. To begin with, it has been compared to a black deer, which craves to break into forbidden fields. The pleasure of eating the prohibited herbage is only short-lived. It is followed by suffering, which is long. Mind hankers after sense pleasures, which last for a short time but which bring sorrow and pain in their wake.

There is no lasting peace for mind and soul except in the Lord, except in meditation on His Name. By treading any other path, one meets death and destruction.

Again, mind has been compared to a honeybee, which hovers around worldly flowers and comes to grief. Guru Nanak says that he has heard in explicit terms from his Master that all roads other than the practice of the Word lead to ruin. Without the Word, man remains stupid, cannot find the way and keeps groping in the dark.

Guru Nanak reminds the soul that she is not a native of this world. He admonishes her not to get caught in the net like the fish, which in consequence has to suffer the agony of death. Only by absorption in the Lord's Name can the soul escape the net of death and be released from delusion and baseless fears.

As rivers are separate at the source but meet in the ocean, so do souls meet in the Infinite.

It is a rare one who realizes the illusory nature of the world's allurements. The one who learns this lesson, does so from his master. Those who keep away from the Name of the Lord wander aimlessly and remain bewildered in this world. Remorse and anguish are in store for them.

Guru Nanak ends the poem with the utterance: Through practice of the Word given by the master, the long separation of the soul and God ends in union.

Toon sun harna kaalia

O black buck, listen to me!
Why dost thou crave to break into
The fenced-off fields?
The delight of cropping forbidden fruit
Lasteth but a few days;
Thereafter there is sorrow in store.
Sorrow is the wages of sin
On which thou art intent.
Those who forsake God's Name
Suffer in the flames of evil;
The delight of the senses lasts no longer
Than a surface ripple on water,
Than the lightning's sudden flash.
Black deer, O my mind,
Thou forgettest the Lord;
There is no peace
Except in the Lord;
Forsake Him not!
O black deer,
O heart of a fool,
Hold on to the Lord:
Nanak warneth thee,
By the other road
There lieth but death,
But destruction.   *1*

O my mind, thou honeybee,
Buzzing around the blossoms
To rifle their sweets,
Hear me, thy sorrow is great:

I asked the guru in so many words,
"What is the true path?"
And the guru in so many words answered me:
O honeybee,
Thou art lost in worldly flowers;
When the sun rises after death,
Thou wilt suffer
As a body scalded by oil.

Without the Word of the guru
Thou art stupid and cannot find thy way,
Thou shalt suffer agony
From Yama's blows.
Forget not God, O heart of a fool,
O honeybee:
On the other road lieth death,
On the other road lieth destruction,
Saith Nanak.   2

My soul,
Thou art not a native of this world,
Wherefore then get caught in the net?
Entertain within thyself
The holy Name of God.
The fish, like the human soul,
Is ensnared in the net of death,
It weeps and gasps in agony,
And now she knows
That life ever pleasant
Was a delusion.
Adore and cherish the Lord
And cast out baseless fears.

Pay heed, O my mind,
To this admonition of Nanak:
My soul,
That art not native to this place,
In thine inner depths
Cherish the true Lord.   3

As streaming rivers
That start from the same source
Are separated but meet in the ocean,
So do souls meet in the Infinite.
One in a million knows
That age upon age
The world's illusions enchant
And poison the soul.
Those that contemplate the guru
Attain the state of *sahaj*
And realize God.

Those who are devoid of the Lord's Name
Wander, deceived and bewildered;
Without such realization of the Lord's Name,
Without the love of His eternal Being,
Man can have no destiny
Except remorse and anguish.
Nanak utters a truth:
Through the Word of the guru
The long estrangement
Of the soul and God
Ends in meeting.   4:1:5

Asa, pp.438–439

The Book of Our Deeds

A graphic analogy has been used in this poem to bring out the significance of the law of karma. Our deeds are compared to the leaves of the book of our life. The writing in it is of two kinds corresponding to our good and bad deeds. As the deeds are repeated, they become our habits.

Guru Nanak implores our rebellious mind to meditate on the Name of the Lord and revive those virtues that withered away by forsaking His Name.

In another analogy, night and day are compared to the nets that entrap us. Our body is the furnace, which is being heated by the fires of our five passions; our sins serve as the fuel and our mind gets burned. But mind, the rusted iron, can be turned into gold if it is transmuted with the touch of the philosopher's stone, the master. For the master bestows on one the nectar of *Nam* which ends once and for all the cycle of birth and death.

Karnee kaagad man maswaani

Our deeds are the leaves,
Mind the inkpot,
And the writing is of two kinds:
Good and bad.
As mind drives us on the writ of habit,
So are we driven;
But God has infinite virtues
Through which one overcomes the habit
Of one's mind.   *1*

O crazy mind,
Why dost thou not meditate?
Forsaking thy Lord,
Thy virtues wither away.   *1:P*

The night and the day
Are the nets cast for us,
And all moments too
Are but a snare:
As one pecks at the bait,
One is trapped;
Then how is one to be saved?   *2*

The body is the furnace,
In which is cast
The iron of the mind,
And it is heated
By the five fires;
The coals are the sins
Stacked with the tongs of care:
And lo, the mind is burned!   *3*

Rusted iron, too, is transmuted into gold
If it meets with the philosopher's stone,
The guru,
For he blesses one
With the nectar of *Nam*
And therewith ceases the cycle
Of birth and death, O Nanak.   *4:3*

                    Maru, p.990

The Manmukh

The Lord is the destroyer of demons. He abides within all and yet is invisible. He becomes visible and is realized if one lives in accordance with his master's instructions. The *gurmukh* is thus able to cross the ocean of phenomena.

The *manmukh*, in contrast, constantly suffers the cycle of birth and death. Since his destiny cannot be erased, he is gravely dishonoured by the Courier of Death.

A bride who makes merry with a stranger, forsaking her Lord, can never be accepted by Him.

Imprisoned in the body, a *manmukh* suffers from countless sorrows in this life and burns in the fire of hell after death. For the King of Death shows no mercy on sinners.

The *manmukh* is afflicted by desire. Having lost all sense of honour, he degrades himself to the level of beasts. He gets immersed in vice and sin.

The world is entangled in earthly attachments, love of wife, children and family. All this is illusory and this illusion can only be broken through the master's grace.

While the *manmukh* goes astray and burns in the fires of hell, the *gurmukh* becomes immortal by drinking the nectar of *Nam*, bestowed on him by his master.

The master's teachings give the disciple an inner strength and resilience, which enable him to bear the misfortunes of destiny with fortitude. The thorns of the world do not prick him. The *manmukh* does not realize that death is inevitable, just as a stone cannot absorb water.

The sense of duality, born of Maya, is the cause of our undoing. We can never be rid of this illusion, except through love, which comes from the master.

One who worships Maya has been compared to a bitch or a swine, lured by vice and ridden with fear. It is the master who can still his mind by bestowing on him the gift of *Nam*.

Asur saghaaran raam hamaara

Lo, our God
Is the destroyer of demons,
And He, our beloved Lord,
Abides within all.
He is ever with us, yet not seen:
But if one dwells upon
The writ of the guru,
One comes to know Him.   1

O God,
They who are turned towards Thee
Are ever in Thy refuge,
And Thou in Thy mercy
Ferriest them across.
For the sea of fire is deep,
And it is through the true guru
That one crosses it safely
To the yonder shore.   2

The egotists are blind
For they know not,
And they come and go
And are born only to die.
The writ of the past
Is erased not,
And one is piteously dishonoured
At Yama's door.   3

Some there are
Who but come and go
And find not refuge
In their home;

Bound to their past,
They commit sin upon sin:
Yea, the blind ones,
They know naught,
Being trapped by ego and greed.   4

Oh, how can a bride embellish herself
Without her spouse,
If she forsakes her lord
And enjoys the bed of another?
And as one knows not
Who is the father of a harlot's son,
So vain are the deeds
Of the one without God.   5

In the cage of the body
There are countless sorrows,
And in the darkness of ignorance
One burns in the fire of hell.
And to Dharamraj one has to pay
The balance for one's deeds,
Having forsaken the Lord's Name.   6

Within him blazes
The scorching sun of desire.
Yea, the egocentric is without honour,
An animal, out of step with life;
And lured by worldly hope and desire,
He practices falsehood
And is afflicted with the disease of vice.   7

He carries on his head the load of saltpeter;*
How can he cross the sea of phenomena?
It is the true guru who is the eternal boat,
And with the Lord's Name
One is rowed across.   8

The world is bound
To the loves of sons and wife,
But all this is the expanse of illusion,
Born of attachment.
Yea, the bonds of Yama
Only the true guru breaks,
If one reflects on the quintessence.   9

Beguiled by falsehood,
One goes this way and that;
And lo, the egocentric is burned up,
Being cast into the blaze.
But if one practices the nectar-Name
Ministered by the all-wise guru,
One attains to pure bliss.   10

The true guru, in his mercy,
Ministers to us the Truth;
He dispels all one's woes
And puts one on the path.

---

*Literally, 'with loaded forehead he carries the weight of saltpeter on his head'; that is, one's destiny or *pralabdh* karma is written on his forehead and he is weighed down by the load of past karmas, the 'saltpeter' that prevents him from attaining liberation. *Kallar*, saltpeter, found in barren soil, prevents the growth of crops.

Yea, no thorn pricks the foot
Of one whom the true guru
Protects and redeems.   11

When the body wears out
It returns to dust,
But this enters not
The mind of the egocentric,
Even as water seeps not into a stone.
And he wails incessantly,
And is now in heaven,
Now in hell.   12

The snake of Maya stings everyone:
Yea, this sense of duality, born of Maya,
Has destroyed many homes.
But without the true guru,
Love does not well up in one;
And it is devotion to God
That brings one the coolness of comfort.   13

The worldling runs after illusion,
But how can he find peace,
Forsaking the Name?
And so he is consumed
By the fire of the three attributes
And is not ferried across.   14

The man of falsehood
Is like a bitch,
Like a swine,
And riddled with fear
He barks himself to death.

And he practices falsehood
Through body and mind;
And being lured by vice,
Loses the Lord's court.   15

If one meets the true guru,
One's mind is stilled.
He who seeks the guru's refuge
Is blessed with the Lord's Name.
Yea, he is blessed
With the priceless gift of Nam;
He is dear to the Lord
And is praised in His court.   16

It is in the Saint's refuge
That one is blessed with the Lord's Name:
Yea, it is through the guru's Word
That one knows the state
And extent of God.
Says Nanak:
O mind, contemplate on the Lord:
For He it is who unites thee
With Himself.   17:3:9

Maru, pp.1028–1030

Counsel to the Mind

Mind is advised in this poem not to wander in the world outside. It should get attached to the Lord's Name within. It must remember that death is inevitable. Pain and suffering are in store for it if it neglects to meditate on the Name of the Lord. And it is through the guru's grace that it can learn to dwell on His Name. The guru imparts the method to attain this goal. After that, what is needed is regular practice of the Word, which the master has imparted. Guru Nanak also denounces penances and austerities in this hymn, for the goal lies within and all search outside is futile. After shelter has been taken with the true guru, no harm can come from the Courier of Death. For the true guru is all-wise and in him the Word has taken abode. In contrast to the guru's disciple, the worldly man remains enthralled in worldly attachments, the victim of his own ego. He ever lives in fear of death and ceaselessly suffers the cycle of transmigration.

> *Ghar raho re man mugad ayaane*
>
> O my ignorant and foolish mind,
> Stay in thy home
> And meditate on the Lord's Name,
> Immersed in contemplation within.
> Abandon thy greed,
> And be absorbed in the infinite Lord
> That thou be emancipated.   *1*
>
> By forsaking the Lord,
> The Angel of Death
> Keeps his eye on thee,
> And thou art denied all peace here,

And sorrow confronts thee
In the hereafter.
Dwell thou on His Name,
Through the guru's grace:
For this is the quintessence
Of all wisdom.   2

Practice thou
The sweet Name of the Lord,
And find the quintessence of God within,
Through the guru.
Day and night be imbued
With thy Lord's love,
For this contains all chantings,
Penances and austerities.   3

Utter thou the Lord's Name,
Through the guru's Word,
Search thou for this essence
In the company of saints.
Through the guru's wisdom,
Arrive at thine own home,
And thereafter be not cast
Into the womb.   4

Bathe thou at the pilgrim-place of Truth
And utter the Lord's praise;
Dwell on the quintessence,
And be attuned to the Lord;
Then the Angel of Death
Can eye thee not when thy days end;
So utter thou the Name
Of the beloved Lord.   5

The true guru is beneficent and all-wise:
In him the Truth and the Word
Have taken abode.
Whosoever the guru unites
With himself and the Lord,
He is rid of the overpowering
Fear of death.   6

The five elements conjoin together
To build our body,
And within it we realize
The jewel of God.
For the soul is God,
And God is the soul,*
And He is beheld
By dwelling on the Word.   7

O brothers, remain true and contented,
And acquire compassion
In the refuge of the true guru.
Within thy soul, know thy Lord;
This benefit thou gainest
From the company of thy guru.   8

The worldly man leans
On falsehood and deceit;
Day and night
He slanders countless people.

---

* The soul and God are in essence one.

But without meditation
He comes and goes,
And is cast repeatedly
Into the hell of the womb.   9

The worldly man lives ever
In the fear of death;
The rod of Death ever hangs
Over his head,
And the balance of his misdeeds
He has to account for
Before the Lord of Law,
For he carries an immense load
Of evil upon his head.   10

Without the guru,
The worldling is saved not,
Lured by ego, he is tossed about
On the sea of phenomena;
Without the guru, he is not ferried across:
Yea, only through meditation
Doth one cross safe to the other shore.   11

No one can cancel out the gift of *Nam*
Bestowed by the guru;
He alone is ferried across
On whom the guru bestows this gift.
The pain of birth and death
Comes not near him,
For he transcends the limits of mind.   12

He who has gone astray from the guru,
Comes and goes;
He is born and he dies,
And he goes on committing sins endlessly.
The ignorant worldling
Cherishes not his Lord,
But cries out to Him
When overcome by suffering.   13

The pain and pleasure we experience
Are the result of our past deeds,
And He, the giver,
Who has bestowed them on us,
Alone knows.
O man, whom then can you blame?
You reap whatever you yourself have sown.   14

You have been indulging
In ego and attachments;
You have been driven
By hope and desire;
And you have been calling things
'Mine, mine';
So you have been carrying poison of sins
And the ash of vices with you.   15

Meditate on the Lord, O brothers,
And let the unutterable utterance*
Take abode in the inner recesses
Of your mind.

---

* *Akath Katha*, that is *Anahad Shabd*, the 'unstruck music'.

Hold the reins of your refractory mind
So that it stays at home
And the Lord ends your pain.   *16*

I seek the refuge of the perfect guru;
By his grace I shall be attuned to the Lord.
Says Nanak: Through the Lord's Name
My mind has become sublime,
And in His mercy
He has ferried me across.   *17:4:10*

Maru, pp.1030–1031

Shed the Five Passions

In order to attain inner spiritual experience and realize God it is necessary, first of all, to give up the passions of lust, anger, avarice, attachment and ego. Without fulfilling this preliminary condition, it is not possible to drink the nectar within.

The initial mystic experience comes in the form of flashes of lightning. This is followed by the vision of the resplendent flame and the sun and the moon in the inner regions.

The living master is an indispensable intermediary between man and God. Without the grace and the guidance of the master, it would be impossible to realize Him. It is the master who enables the disciple to see the invisible and be blessed with the ambrosia, which bestows immortality.

The highest mystic experience is attained through the practice of the Word. It is unitive and transcendental in character, as it is beyond the range of the senses and the intellect.

At the end of the hymn, Guru Nanak says that one who has realized God within also sees Him without, immanent in everyone.

Kaam krodh par har par ninda

Shed thou thy lust and wrath
And the slander of others.
Abandon thy avarice and be carefree;
Yea, break the chains of illusion
And be detached:
For this way
One drinks God's nectar within.   *1*

As at night one sees the light
Of the lightning flash,
So see thou the light of God,
Night and day, deep within thee;
Of unparalleled beauty is He,
The embodiment of bliss.
The perfect guru hath shown Him to me.   2

If one meets the true guru,
God himself will ferry him across.
In the inner skies one beholds
The resplendent flame,
And the sun and the moon.*
Seeing the Unseeable,
One is attuned to Him
And sees Him pervade
The three worlds through.   3

He is blessed with nectar,
His craving and fear are dispelled,
And he enters into the state
Of unitive experience,
Shedding his self;
Practicing the immaculate Word,
He becomes the highest of the high.   4

Infinite is the Lord's Name,
Beyond the senses and the intellect.

---

* In the spiritual journey within, one comes across the light of the lamp in
the first region, the reddish light of the morning sun in the second region,
and the light of the full moon in the third region.

Sweet, O sweet, is its essence,
Ever dear to me!
O God, bless me with Thy praise,
Age after age;
However much one may contemplate,
Thy greatness cannot be fathomed.   5

Within one can be found and attained
The jewel of the Lord's Name:
Contemplating God,
The mind is comforted
By the mind itself;*
One attains to God,
The destroyer of fear,
And one comes not into the womb again.   6

O God, I seek the zeal for Thy devotion
Through the guru's Word:
Yea, I seek to sing Thy praise,
To attain to the bounty
Of Thy Name,
And, if Thou so willest,
Thou wilt lead me on to the guru;
In this way,
Thou liberatest the whole world.   7

He who has meditated
And attained his guru's wisdom,
The Couriers of Death
Serve at his feet;

---

* The universal mind gives solace to the particular mind.

Yea, through the company of the holy,
His state and ways become sublime,
And he swims across
The ocean of phenomena.   8

This sea of the world one crosses
Through the guru's Word,
And then one's duality
Is burned within one,
And one aims the five arrows*
At the Messenger of Death,
Stretching the bow in the sky within.   9

How can the *manmukh* have access
To the path of *Surat Shabd*?†
And without the *Surat Shabd* path,
One but comes and goes.‡
Says Nanak:
It is through the guru
That one gets the refuge of deliverance;
Yea, it is by perfect good fortune
That one gets united with the Lord.   10

The true guru is fearless,
The refuge of all;
And it is through
Loving adoration of him
That one attains unto God.

---

* The five virtues: continence, forbearance, contentment, detachment and
humility; some scholars also interpret 'the five' to mean the *panch shabd*
or five *Shabds*.
† The method of connecting the soul with the Word.
‡ In the cycle of birth and death.

Within one rings
The blissful unstruck melody,
And it is through the guru's guidance
That one beholds the supreme Lord.   *11*

The Lord alone is fearless
And He has to render no account;
Himself remaining uncaused,
He is seen through His wondrous creation;
Detached is He, free of all bonds,
Not cast into the womb,
And attained only through
The guru's wisdom.   *12*

The true guru knows the secrets
Of the inner realms,
And it is through the guru's Word
That one realizes the fearless One.
Looking within thyself, find thy Lord
And stray thou not elsewhere.   *13*

He alone is free of fear
Who has taken abode within himself,
And is imbued, night and day,
With the immaculate Name of the Lord;
Yea, the Lord's praise one finds
In the company of saints
Through whose grace one attains
To the state of *sahaj*.   *14*

He who sees God
Both within and without
And remains detached,
Bringing back to its home
The outgoing mind,
He drinks the true nectar-essence
Of Him who is above all,
Has been since the beginning of time,
And pervades the three worlds.   *15:4:21*

Maru, pp.1041–1042

Love

Talk of Love

The soul is depicted as the bride and God as the bridegroom in this hymn. One devoted soul invites another one to join her in talking about their Spouse and to praise Him. They say that their Lord is a mine of goodness, while they are the repositories of evil. He is the creator, all-powerful, perfect in all respects. Why then think of any other? Although He is One, He has a multiplicity of shapes and colours, castes and races. And manifold are His creatures who are engaged in His praise day and night.

What virtue earns the Lord's favour? It is calmness of manner and sweetness of tongue that help to win His favour. It is by meeting and by being instructed by a master that one gains true knowledge and eventually merges into the truthful One.

Aavahu bhaine gal milah

Come, dear sister,
Clasp me in your embrace!
Come beloved friend,
Let us speak of love!
Let us sit together
And talk of our Husband,
The perfect, powerful Lord.

O my true Lord,
Thou art the repository of goodness,
We the repositories of evil.   *1*

O my Creator, all is within Thy power.
In Thy Word we abide.
When Thou art with us,
Why need we think of anyone beside?   *1:P*

Go ask the happy spouse
What virtues earned her
The favour of the Lord.
She will tell you,
"I was adorned with calmness
And contentment
And sweetness of tongue."
If you hearken to the guru's Word
You will meet your Husband,
The beauteous Lord.   *2*

Manifold is Thy nature,
Great is Thy bounty;
Manifold Thy creatures
Who praise Thee day and night.
Manifold Thy shapes and colours,
Manifold Thy races and castes.   *3*

On meeting the true guru
One gains knowledge of the Truth,
Then one merges into the truthful One.
From the guru's teaching we learn
The fear of the Lord.

From realization of the Truth
We gain honour.
O Nanak! The true King of kings
Himself unites us with Him.   4:10

Sri, pp.17–18

Forget Not the Lord

For the devotee to forget the Lord even for a moment is to invite serious sickness. If He does not abide in the mind, how will one find admittance in His court?

To realize God, the guidance of the master is essential. It is through the master that the fire of evil passions is extinguished and peace enters the mind.

It is a rare person who never for a moment forgets His Name. With the master's help one should merge his finite light with the infinite light and blend his individual consciousness with the divine consciousness. Then alone can one become free from violence, egotism, doubts, woes and restlessness of mind. Thanks to the master, one also meets those in whose hearts shines divine light.

Guru Nanak warns us against getting attached to people of this world, who are here only for a short time and will then depart. Love of the worldly will bring only grief in its wake. He ends with the advice that we should make the true guru our friend, for he will take us to the Lord's presence.

Ik til pyaara veesrai

If I forget the Beloved
Even for a moment,
A grave malady afflicts my mind.
How shall I find a place of honour
In His court,
If within, my mind
Dwells not the Lord?

On meeting the guru
Peace is found;
The fire of passions
Is extinguished
And virtue enters.   *1*

O my mind, day and night
Sing praises of God.
Rare in the world are those
Who forget not the Name
Even for a moment.   *1:P*

Merge your light
With the light eternal,
Blend your consciousness
With consciousness divine.
Then be free
From violence and egotism,
From restlessness of mind,
Doubts and woes.
By the grace of the guru,
Meet the ones
In whose heart dwells the Lord.   *2*

If I offer my body
As if it were a bride,
The Lord will take it
As if He were the groom.
Love not the one
Who is here for a while,
Love not that
Which is a passing show.

By the grace of the guru,
Attain union with the Lord;
Like a married woman,
Enjoy the bed of your Husband.   3

Extinguish all the four fires*
Within you,
With the sacred water
Your guru did give.
Within you will then blossom
The lovely lotus flower,
And your heart will be filled
To the brim with nectar.
O Nanak,
Make the true guru your friend,
He will take you to the court
Of the true One.   4:20

Sri, pp.21–22

---

* Violence, attachment, anger and avarice.

What Pleases the Lord

The lovers of God are compared to wives who adorn themselves with jewellery and bright red clothes to please their Lord. But deceitful love, like a counterfeit coin, is soon found out and brings disaster.

How does a woman (the soul) please her husband (the Lord)? Guru Nanak says that the Word is her main ornament. With folded hands, longing eyes and truthfulness in her heart she waits on Him. Dyed in His love, her colour is fast and true. As His slave, she is attached to Him.

The devotee gains this blissful state through love for the guru. The one who is absorbed in him, becomes immortal. Such a 'wife' will never become a widow because her husband is immortal. She has lit the lamp of the Word which never goes out. She wears *Nam* as her necklace, and on her forehead she wears the jewel of love. She could have never known her spouse except through love for the true guru.

To spend our human life without seeking and achieving union with the Lord has been compared to a woman sleeping the dark night through without meeting her husband. Guru Nanak ends the poem by saying, "The true guru teaches how to fear and love God and thus be united with Him."

Sabhe kant maheleeya

We are His brides;
We bedeck ourselves for Him.
We count our ornaments
And don bright red clothes.
But love is not won by deceit;
A counterfeit coin gilded with gold
Is soon found out and spells ruin.

How does a woman win
The attention of her Lord?
Lord, she who is pleasing to Thy sight
Is in nuptial bliss;
Thy mercy is her adornment.   *1*

The guru's Word is her adornment;
Her body and mind are with her Lord.
With folded hands she waits on Him,
And longingly she looks
With truthfulness in her heart.
She is immersed in His love;
She lives in fear of the true One;
And when dyed with His love,
Her colour is fast and true.   *2*

She is now counted as one of His devotees.
As His slave she is attached to His Name.
Her true love is unbroken,
And the true One unites her with Himself.
Her soul is plaited with the Word;
I am ever a sacrifice unto her.   *3*

She who is absorbed in the true guru
Becomes immortal,
Never shall she become a widow.
Her Beloved is forever handsome
And ever fresh;
He is never born to die.
She is always dear to Him;
In His grace and will she lives.   *4*

Truth is the decorated braid of her hair,
Love is her dress and ornaments.
God within her
Is the breath of sandal perfume,
And Daswan Dwar is her temple.
She lights the lamp of the Word,
She wears God's Name as her necklace.   5

She is beautiful amongst women of beauty;
On her forehead she wears the jewel of love.
Her glory is that she cherishes in her mind
True and infinite love.
She knows not the Lord, her spouse,
Except through love of the true guru.   6

You stayed asleep the dark night through;
Why did you waste the night in sleep?
How did you pass the night
Without your Lord?
Your body is afire,
Your mind is aflame;
Where your Lord abides not,
Wasted is your youth.   7

You are sleeping on the nuptial couch,
Yet you know not of His presence.
You sleep while your Beloved is awake;
To whom, then, will you turn for advice?
Sayeth Nanak: the true guru teaches
How to fear and love God,
And thus be united with Him.   8:2

Sri Ashtpadi, p.54

Divine Love

This hymn begins with a graphic description of the state of mind of one who has been pierced with the shaft of the Lord's love. He can think of nothing except his Beloved. His soul has become attached to the divine melody within and he dwells in unceasing bliss. In this state of ecstasy he prays to the Lord to keep him as He wills, for His Name is his only succour.

Guru Nanak then enumerates a number of sacrificial acts that cannot cure the malady of the mind, nor yield the fruit of *Nam*. Burning oneself in fire as a sacrifice; cutting one's body into pieces to be used as firewood and burning them ceaselessly; having one's head cut off with a saw;* dissolving the body in the snows of Himalayas, and other such acts of hardship and torture still do not cure the malady of the mind. The treasure of *Nam* would still remain inaccessible. If one were to give away in charity castles of gold, horses and elephants, vast lands and countless cows, one would still not be rid of the malady of the ego. Much learning and scholarship, much intellectual reflection on scriptures, would still not remove the fetters of the soul. If these fetters are to be removed and the door of salvation is to be opened, the guidance of the living master is essential.

Guru Nanak then stresses the practice of the Word, which is higher than all other practices. He also impresses upon the disciple to consider everyone higher than himself. He should remember that all human beings are like vessels made by one potter. The same light illumines the three worlds. It is by the Lord's grace that Truth is found, and what He gives none can take away.

---

* In earlier times the *pandas* of Benaras used to behead devotees under a saw, giving them the assurance that they would go to heaven for their act of sacrifice.

When one has the good fortune to meet a true master, peace takes abode in him. And if he merges himself in the master, he comes to realize the unutterable Truth. He would, then, be admitted to the Lord's court with great honour. Within him would ring the music of the lute, the music of the third spiritual region. There is a rare one who has this knowledge, for it comes only through a living master.

Guru Nanak, at the end, implores the disciple never to forget *Nam*, for deliverance from suffering comes through practice of it.

Raam naam man bedhiya

My mind is pierced with the Lord's Name.
What else is there now for me to dwell upon?
When the soul is attached to the Word,
In bliss doth it abide.
Imbued with the Lord's love,
In sheer joy doth it dwell.
Keep me, O Lord, as Thou wilt,
Thy Name is my only succour.   *1*

O my mind,
Invincible is the Lord's will.
Attach thyself to Him
Who adorned thee
With a body and a mind.   *1:P*

If thou wert to consign thy body
To the sacrificial fire,
If thou wert to cut it into bits
To turn it into firewood,

If thou wert to burn this fire
Ceaselessly every day,
It would not equal the Name of the Lord,
Despite millions of such acts.   2

If thy body were to be cut in two,
If thy head were to be put under the saw,
Or thy torso to be dissolved in the Himalayas,
Still the malady of thy mind will not be cured.
No remedy equals the Name of the Lord:
I have realized it as a tested truth.   3

If thou wert to give in charity castles of gold,
Horses fine and mighty elephants;
If thou wert to gift lands
And cows numberless,
Still the malady of ego
Would not leave thee.
The Lord's Name hath pierced my mind,
A true gift, indeed, from my master.   4

Many were the rigors
And ascetic practices of the mind,
Many were the intellectual reflections
On scriptures;
Many more were such fetters,
Which had bound my soul;
It was the master alone
Who opened the door of salvation for me.
The Truth is above all,
Its practice is superior
To all other practices.   5

Consider everyone high,
Let no one appear low to thee.
For the one potter
Has made all vessels;
One source of light
Illumines the three worlds.
By His grace
Do we find the Truth;
What He once gives
None can take away.   6

When one meets a master,
Peace takes abode in him through love.
If we were to merge in our master,
We would know the unutterable Truth.
We would then drink nectar
And be in peace;
We would go to the Lord's court
Wearing robes of honour.   7

Within us reverberates
The music of the lute,*
And day and night, of its own,
Rings the Word.
Rare are they who know this;
Through the master alone
Comes this knowledge.
O Nanak, forget not the Name,
For one is released
Through practice of the Word.   8:14

Sri, p.62

---

* Music of the third spiritual region.

The Happy Union

Human life has been compared to a night that is sleepless and painful for a bride who is without her husband. The same night, however, would become delightful if her husband were with her. Through the imagery of a decorated bride without the company of her husband, Guru Nanak conveys that all the comforts and luxuries of life fail to give happiness and peace if the Lord is forsaken. All sense pleasures are false, for they are not only temporary but also mixed with pain.

Mundh rain duhelareea

Without her Spouse
The night for the bride
Is sleepless and painful.
She wears away pining for Him;
She becomes weak
Waiting for His return.
She says to herself,
"How shall I see Him with my own eyes?"
All her embellishments
And the sweet delicacies offered to her
Are false;
Of what avail are these to her?
Her youth bursting like heady wine
Turns sour,
But youth returns not;
Her bosom will not fill again.
Says Nanak: the bride will meet the Lord
Only when He wills;
Else her nights will be long
And without sleep.   *1*

Without her beloved Lord,
How will the wretched woman
Find fulfilment?
Ask your friends, O bride,
Is there a home without a groom?
Without the Name,
Love of the Lord is not awakened,
O friends.
Enshrine truth and contentment
In your mind,
And know your Spouse
Through the guru's Word.
Says Nanak:
A woman who forsakes not the Name
Abides in *sahaj* through the Name.   2

Come my friends,
Let us enjoy our Husband!
I'll ask my guru
And send my Lord
The love message through the Word.
Through my guru,
The true Word is revealed to me,
While the *manmukhs* come to grief.
My wandering mind becomes steady
When I realize the true One.
When one realizes the true One,
One is ever young;
The love of the Word
Keeps one fresh forever.
Nanak, from the true Lord's glance,
The state of *sahaj* is attained.
O my dear friends,
Endeavour then to meet Him.   3

My desire is fulfilled,
My Friend has come to my home.
At the union of Husband and wife
A song of rejoicing is sung.
By singing the song of joy,
In praise and love of the Groom,
The bride's mind is filled with delight.
Her friends are happy,
Her enemies are filled with envy.
By meditating on the true One,
True benefit is reaped.
With folded hands the wife prays:
Night and day let me remain lost
In my Lord's love;
Nanak, my desire has been achieved,
The Husband and wife now revel in love.   *4:1*

Gauri Purabi, pp.242–243

The Beloved Lord

The soul of man will attain union with the Lord if, as a beautiful bride, she has intense love for her Husband. The Lord is immaculate and is full of compassion. When the bride is immersed in the love of her Lord, all her sense organs together with her mind and intellect become pure. The Lord is pleased when the soul becomes attached to the Word. As she beholds her divine Spouse, she attains a state of rapture and bliss. It is in the nature of all things to move towards their source. The soul, too, has this natural urge, but the weight of karmas keeps her down. Once this weight is removed, she will instantly go to her source. Such a merger is intensely and eternally blissful.

Mundh joban baalareeye

O thou beauteous young bride,
Thy Lord is full of life.
When thou, His bride,
Art deeply in love with Him,
He is all compassion for thee.
Then He, thy Lord, meets thee in His mercy,
And then thou enjoyest His warm bed,
Filling thy seven seas* with nectar.
Show Thy compassion and kindness,
O merciful Lord,
That I may sing Thy praise
By immersing myself in the Word.
Beholding her divine Spouse, O Nanak,
The bride is in bliss
And her mind is filled with joy.   *1*

---

* The five *gyanindryas* (cognitive faculties), mind and intellect.

O thou bride of natural beauty,
Worship thy Lord with love.
I love my Spouse with body and mind;
I am intoxicated with His presence.
I am dyed in His love
And abide in the bliss of His Name.
If thou wert to know His virtues,
Thou wouldst know Him;
Then thine own virtues would abide in thee
And thy vices flee.
O Lord, I cannot live without Thee
Even for a moment;
Merely speaking or hearing of Thee
Gives me no solace.
Nanak calls: O my Beloved, O my Love,
My tongue and mind are saturated
With Thy nectar.   2

O my confidantes,
My Lord is a merchant-king.
I have purchased the Name of God from Him;
Its sweetness and value are limitless.
Invaluable is His worth
And He abides in the true home.
If she pleases Him, the bride too is blessed.
Some there are
Who enjoy dalliance with the Lord,
While I stand at His door and wail.
The Lord is the doer of deeds,
The all-powerful, the all-affluent,
Who sets right men's affairs.

Nanak, blessed is the bride
On whom falls the Lord's merciful glance
And who is embellished with the Word.   3

In my home rings the song of true joy;
The Lord, my friend, has come unto me.
Intoxicated with love, the Lord enjoys me.
I have captivated His heart
And given mine to Him.
I gave away my heart
And won the Lord as my groom.
As He pleases, so does He enjoy me.
I've surrendered my body and mind
To the Beloved
And I am blessed with the Word.
Within my home I have attained
The ambrosial fruit.
The Lord is not realized through intellect,
Recitation and cleverness;
He is attained through love,
If it be His will.
Nanak, the Lord is my friend;
I am no longer a stranger to Him.   4:1

Asa, Chhant, pp.435–436

Season of Love

The monsoon season in India, with the grandeur of its beauty, its dark clouds and flashes of lightning, the chirping of birds and the dancing of peacocks, is generally associated with love between the bride and the bridegroom. Using this analogy, Guru Nanak considers the human birth as the season for love of the Lord. Just as in the monsoon season a woman who does not enjoy the love of her husband is wretched, so also a man who does not realize God and enjoy union with Him during the span of his human existence remains unhappy. Even if he is provided with all the worldly comforts of life, he still feels a vacuum in his soul, which the pleasures of the senses cannot fill.

The latter part of the poem brings out the poignancy of the pain of separation of one who sees her Lord in a dream for a brief spell, but on waking up feels all the more acutely the pangs of separation. Likewise, man may have an intuitive vision of the Lord for a brief moment, but is all the more unhappy when the vision disappears. What is needed is permanent union of the soul with her Lord. The poem ends with a tribute to the master: Guru Nanak says that if someone were to bring about his union with the Lord, he would be prepared to offer his head to him and serve him without his head.

Moree runjhun laaya bhaine saawan aaya

The peacocks are crying with joy;
O sisters, the rainy season has come!
The fervent woman, O God, is enamoured
Of Thy glances which bind her
As if with a rope.

I am a sacrifice to a sight of Thee, O God;
To Thy Name I am a sacrifice.
Since Thou art my Lord I am proud;
Without Thee what pride should I have?

O woman, break your couch with its frame
And your arms with their bracelets,
Since, notwithstanding your decorations,
The Lord is enamoured of others.

You need not a bangle dealer,
Or silver, or gold bracelets:
Burn the arm
Which embraces not the Bridegroom.

All my companions went
To enjoy the Bridegroom;
Whose door shall I,
Wretch that I am, approach?

O Lord, I think myself well behaved
And very clever,
Yet I have no charm to please Thee.
I plaited my tresses with cosmetic
And filled the parting of my hair
With vermilion;
Yet when I went before Thee
I was not accepted –
I shall die of grief.

I am weeping; the whole world weeps;
Even the birds of the forests weep for me.

One thing weeps not for me – the separation
Which parted me from my Beloved.
He came to me in my dreams
But went away again,
At which I wept to the full.
I cannot go to Thee, Beloved,
Nor send anyone to Thee.
Return, O happy sleep,
Perhaps I may again behold my Lord.

What shall I give him, says Nanak,
Who tells me of Thee, O God?
I will cut off my head
And give it to him to sit on;
Without my head I will serve him.
Why do I not die and give up my life
Since my Lord has chosen another?   *1:3*

Vadhans, pp.537–558

The Sinner's Vow

The mind of the sinner is filled with fear. He is afraid of the punishment and the pain that will be inflicted on him.

And yet he has infinite faith in the power of the forgiveness of the merciful Lord. He says he will henceforth serve Him with all his might and with great devotion. When his end comes, he will surely be redeemed.

He vows to practice the Name, which will serve as his boat to ferry him across the sea of life. For none is true other than the Lord. There is none else to whom one can turn for succour.

Guru Nanak ends the hymn by praying to the Lord to grant him the boon of His Name, and Nanak will serve Him forever.

Jeeo darat hai aapna

My mind is beset with fears,˙
To whom shall I cry for help?
I shall serve the dispeller of sorrow,
He is forever and ever bountiful.   *1*

My Lord reveals Himself
Ever fresh, forever new;
He is forever and ever bountiful.   *1:P*

Night and day will I serve the Lord.
When my end comes, He will be my Redeemer.
By hearing the Word, O my friend,
I shall be ferried across to the other shore.   *2*

˙Of its sins.

O merciful Lord,
Thy Name shall ferry me across.
To Thee shall I sacrifice my life forever.   *1:P*

In all the world Thou alone art True,
There is none besides Thee.
On whom falls Thy grace
Will alone serve Thee.   *3*

Beloved, without Thee
How shall I survive?
Grant me the boon
That I cling to Thy Name.
My Love, there is no other
To whom I can turn.   *1:P*

O Lord, Thee alone shall I serve,
Of Thee alone will I beg;
Forever will Nanak be Thy servant.
Every joint and limb of my body
I dedicate to Thee.   *4*

Yea, every limb and every joint
I offer to my Lord.   *1:P:4:1*

Dhanasari, p.660

The Inept Bride

This poem has been written in a spirit of humility and prayer. Guru Nanak has used the analogy of the bride, devoid of all merit, for the inept aspirant who seeks union with the Lord. If the bride has no virtues and is full of vice, how can she ever hope to consummate her marriage?

Guru Nanak says that the Spouse is sought after by many, and each of them is more virtuous than the other. What chance, then, has a worthless wife of being accepted by her Husband?

Continuing the analogy, Guru Nanak says that the bride is running after gold and silver and other worldly treasures, not realizing that even these come from her Lord. Man is fascinated by His creation and forgets the Creator.

Even when old age descends and hair turns grey, the ignorant man continues to waste his precious human life and still fails to make any preparation for his journey to the hereafter.

Guru Nanak concludes with a prayer to the Lord: Just as You have showered the blessing of Your presence on others, so may You bless me also one day.

Manjh kuchajee amaavan dosare

I am vile, and countless are my sins,
How shall I go revel in my Lord's love?
One excels the other in merit and beauty,
Who is there to know my name?
Those who revel in His love
Delight in the mango-shade,
But I imbibe none of their virtues:
On whom shall I put the blame?
How shall I expand upon Thy merits, O Lord?
Which of Thy names shall I utter?

Not one of Thy virtues can I reach;
A hundred times I am a sacrifice unto Thee.
Gold and silver, pearls and rubies,
These are Thy gifts and I am lost in them.
Temples made of clay and decorative stones
Have led me astray
And I sat not by the side of my Lord.
Over the sky the cranes shriek,[*]
The herons have come and sat on me.[†]
I am now to leave for my inlaws' house;[‡]
With what face shall I turn up there?
I slept through the night
And it turned into morn,
And having lost the way,
I became separated from my Lord.
Now a heap of sorrows await me.
Thou art all virtue,
I am without merit;
Nanak hath but this prayer:
Thou, O Lord, hast blessed Thy brides
With Thy presence for all these nights;
Is there not a night also for me?   1

                                        Suhi, p.762

---

[*] Old age has come.
[†] Hair has turned grey.
[‡] The hereafter.

The Meritorious Bride

This hymn is the complement of "The Inept Bride." Guru Nanak enumerates in it the qualities of a competent and successful bride. The title denotes a person who is devoted to the Lord, lives in His will and is engaged in the practice of the Word.

When the Lord is with one, he is at peace with himself and the world. He has surrendered himself to the Lord and is content in whatever condition the Lord keeps him. He also realizes that everything occurs according to His will.

If He so wills, He appears as a delightful person and if His will is otherwise, He assumes a dreadful form. He is unfathomable.

Guru Nanak concludes this small poem with the prayer that the Lord might bestow on him the guru's Word, for through that alone will he attain Him.

Jaa too taa mai sab ko

If Thou art with me,
I have everything;
Thou art my Lord,
The source of all joy.
In Thy presence abides all bliss,
In Thy presence is all my glory.

If it be Thy will,
Give me the honour of a king;
If it be Thy will,
Make me a wretched beggar.

If it be Thy will,
Make me a mighty ocean
Flowing over dry land;

If it be Thy will,
Make a lotus flower
Bloom in the sky.

If it be Thy will,
We cross the terrible sea of life;
If it be Thy will,
We drown in midstream.

If it be Thy will,
Thou appearest high-spirited,
Full of virtue and merit,
Worthy of all praise.

If it be Thy will.
Thou seemest terrible,
Throwing one
Into the never-ceasing cycle
Of birth and death.

O Lord, Thou art unfathomable,
Immeasurable;
Speaking of Thee,
I fall into self-oblivion.
What shall I ask,
Pray, what shall I utter,
Save that I hunger and thirst
For a glimpse of Thee?
Through the guru's Word
The Lord is attained;
For this boon Nanak truly prays.   2

Suhi, pp.762–763

The Lost Opportunity

In this hymn surcharged with love for the Lord, man has been compared to a bride, God to her bridegroom, and the span of human life to a night. The night is meant for the newly married woman to play the game of love with her husband and for their love to be consummated. Instead, she wastes the opportunity by occupying herself with frivolous activities of the world. When she could have enjoyed a life of rapture and bliss with her Lord, she accumulated a heavy load of sins. The master, in his compassion, offers to serve as a middle man, but the foolish bride, in the insolence of her youth, does not heed his words of wisdom.

Near the end of the night, the bride realizes her folly and humbly prays to the master to arrange her union with the Lord. The master, in his mercy, accedes to her request, and eventually the woman lives in everlasting bliss, as she wins the love and affection of her Lord.

Bhar joban mai mat peeerai

Intoxicated with the wine of youth,
I knew not that I was but a guest
In my parents' home.
I am a sacrifice unto Thee, O Lord.
Soiled as I was with sins,
No virtue could enter my mind
Without the master's help.
Devoid of virtue, lost in delusion,
I wasted away my youth in vain.
My Spouse was at the door of His abode
And I saw Him not,
I tasted not my Lord's bliss.
I asked not the path from the master,
And in sleep the night passed away.

Thus I was widowed in youth, O Nanak;
Without the benign warmth of the Lord,
The bride withered.   *1*

O father, marry me to my Lord,
I pine for Him,
I belong to Him
Whose Word pervades the three worlds,
And in all ages,
I am a sacrifice unto Him.
The Lord of the three worlds
Enjoys the virtuous bride
But keeps away from the unvirtuous.
As is the desire,
So is the hope fulfilled
By the all-pervading Lord.
The Lord's bride is eternally blissful;
She is widowed not,
Nor wears she soiled robes.
O Nanak, I love my true Spouse,
My Beloved,
Who remains the same age after age.   *2*

O father,
Have the auspicious moment calculated
That I may speed to my inlaws;
And let the auspicious moment
Be determined by His will,
For His command will not be undone.
Whatever is the writ of our deeds
Decreed by the Lord,
No one can erase.
My Bridegroom is self-dependent
And pervades all the three worlds.

Maya laments in despondency,
For she envies the love
Between the bride and the Bridegroom.
The bride lives in the bliss of the Word,
O Nanak, in the Lord's palace;
She clings to the feet of the master
And cherishes the Lord.   3

My father has sent me
To such a distant land,
The land of my Lord,
That I shall not have to return
To my parents' world.
Now I revel in my Lord's presence;
The Lord enjoys me
And I look radiant in His home.
The true Lord wanted me
And so my Beloved
United me with Himself
And perfected my understanding.
How fortunate was the moment
That I met Him!
How blessed the place of our union!
How grateful I am to my master
Who imparted this wisdom to me!
Truth and contentment
I have gathered in my lap,
And the Lord loves me
For my true speech.
I shall not suffer separation from Him,
O Nanak, through the grace of my master
I have merged in Him.   4:1

Suhi, Chhant, pp.763–764

Couplets on Love

Here is an assortment of love couplets from the *Var of Rag Suhi* and *Shaloks left over from the Vars.* They depict various moods of love: the pangs of separation, the longing for union, the frustration of unrequited love and the ecstasy of consummated love. In the couplets from the leftover *shaloks*, Guru Nanak brings out not only the truth that God is to be realized through love, but that He is to be realized within oneself, and not in temples, mosques and churches.

Iko kant sabaaya jiti dar khareeaah

All who stand at the Lord's door
Have only Him as their Spouse;
They ask of Him from those
Who are imbued with His love.   2

Sabhe kantai rateea

When all are immersed in His love,
Oh why am I alone in separation?
I am so full of evil
That my Husband turns not
His mind to me.   3

Hau balihaaree tin kau

I am a sacrifice unto those
Whose mouths are filled with His praise,
For they enjoy
The nuptial love of their Lord,
While I pass my nights
Separated from Him.   4

Shalok

Jinee na paaio prem ras

They who obtain not the elixir of love,
Know not the taste of God;
They are like the guest in an empty house,
Who goes as empty-handed as he came.   *1*

Var Suhi, p.790

Tan na tapaai tanoor jeo

Heat not thy body like a furnace
And burn not thy bones like fuel.
What hath turned thy head?
What is wrong with thy feet?
Behold thy Spouse within thyself.   *18*

Sabhnee ghatee soh wasai soh bin ghat na koe

In the bodies of all abides the Lord;
Without the Lord there is no body.
But the fortunate bride is she
To whom the Lord becomes manifest,
By the master's grace.   *19*

Jau tau prem khelan kaa chaao

If you seek to play the game of love,
Then come to my lane
With your head on your palm.
Once you set your foot on the path,
Lay down your head without any reluctance.   *20*

Shalok, Varan te Vadhik, pp.1411–1412

Love Intoxicated

In this stanza from *Dakhani Onkar*, Guru Nanak has described the state of one who in his intensity of love for the Lord has become impervious to public opinion. Comparing him to a bride who has thrown away her veil to meet her lord and who is no longer afraid that her mother-in-law will create trouble between herself and her husband, Guru Nanak says that the devotee does not care for the world and has gotten rid of ignorance (the mother-in-law) which was a veil between him and the Lord. Now the devotee revels in the bliss of the Word and all his suffering has ended. He attained this blissful state through his master's grace.

Laaj maranti mar gaee

All shyness and hesitation have died away;
I have cast off my veil and walk fearlessly.
My mother-in-law has lost her moorings,
She can no more create doubt and delusion
And stand between me and my Love.
My Beloved has sent for me for a love tryst,
In my mind is the joy of the Word;
In the embrace of the Beloved
I am intoxicated with love.
All cares and worries have departed
Through the grace of my Master.   12

Ramkali, Dakhani Onkar, p.931

Thou
hast
not far
to go

S T E P S

Trace the rest

STEP
? Eucl # 443 ?

452-453

He brings us
to the door CHHS)
everywhere, through
small, will others
leave

Vaisakh

In this English rendering of one of the spring months from the *Barah Maha* of Guru Nanak, replete with imagery of the spring season and the lovelorn bride waiting for her husband, Guru Nanak has brought out the significance of human birth and the opportunity offered to man to realize the Lord within himself by forming contact with the Word.

Vaisaakh bhala saakha ves kare

Beauteous *Vaisakh*,
When the bough adorns itself anew,
The wife awaits her Lord,
Her eyes fixed on the door:
"Come, my Love, come,
Have compassion for me,
Thou alone, my Love,
Can help me cross
The turbulent waters of life,
Come home.
Without Thee I am as worthless as a shell;
Cast Thou a glance upon me,
Let our eyes mingle,
Then I shall become priceless
Beyond measure."
Nanak says:
Thou hast not far to go for the Lord,
Know Him within thee,
Thou art His mansion.
Nanak, *Vaisakh* will beautiful be,
If thy soul becomes attuned to the Word.   6

Tukhari, Barah Maha, p.1108

ENDNOTES

Section One: Life

1. *The Panjab Past and Present*, III:39. Translated by W.H. McLeod (hereafter cited as *P.P.P.*).
2. John Malcolm, *Sketch of the Sikhs*, p.17.
3. Khushwant Singh, *Hymns of Guru Nanak*, p.299.
4. Max Arthur Macauliffe, *The Sikh Religion*, I:lxxxvii.
5. Ibid., I:xxx.
6. W. Hew McLeod, *Guru Nanak and the Sikh Religion*, p.20.
7. According to Ganda Singh, the name of the author was Zulfiqar Adistani Azur Sasani; he was popularly known as Mobid and is wrongly called Mohsin Fani (*P.P.P.*, III:11).
8. Macauliffe, *The Sikh Religion*, I:vii, xvi.
9. Khushwant Singh, *Hymns*, p.30.
10. Ibid., p.143.
11. Macauliffe, *The Sikh Religion*, I:29.
12. I Corinthians 15:31.
13. Ganda Singh in *P.P.P.*, III:19.
14. Gurbux Singh in *Essays in Honour of Dr. Ganda Singh*, pp.107–108.
15. G.H. Westcott, *Kabir and the Kabir Panth*, p.1.
16. Sher Singh, *The Philosophy of the Sikhs*, p.114.
17. A.S. Garden: "All that was best and most tolerant in [Ramanand's] system was then taken up by Kabir in the Punjab in the sixteenth century – with him and with his great disciple Nanak originated the reforming movement of the Sikhs" (*Encyclopaedia of Religion and Ethics*, IV:287).

    J.N. Farquhar: "Nanak, the founder of the Sikh sect, was a disciple of the famous Teacher Kabir" (*Modern Religious Movements in India*, p.336).
18. Beale, *An Oriental Biographical Dictionary*, p.292.
19. Indubhushan Banerjee, *Evolution of the Khalsa*, p.73.

20. For instance, Dr. Ganda Singh and Bhai Jodh Singh, *P.P.P.* III:19 (English) and III:59 (Punjabi).

21. *Puratan Janamsakhi*, p.39.

22. McLeod, *Guru Nanak*, pp.108–109, 67; Khushwant Singh, *Hymns*, p.33; Teja Singh and Ganda Singh, *A Short History of the Sikhs*, I:5.

23. Macauliffe, *The Sikh Religion*, I:147.

24. Ibid., I:163.

25. Ibid., I:174.

26. *P.P.P.*, III:34–35.

27. Ibid., 45. Trans. Ganda Singh.

28. Ibid., 34–35.

29. Macauliffe, *The Sikh Religion*, I:43–44.

30. Ibid., 47–50. *Puratan Janamsakhi*, however, makes no mention of it.

31. Macauliffe, *The Sikh Religion*, I:52–56.

32. Ibid., 50–52. This incident is not mentioned in the *Puratan Janamsakhi*.

33. Trans. Harbans Singh, *Guru Nanak and Origins of the Sikh Faith*, p.116.

34. Meharban Sodhi, *Janamsakhi Sri Guru Nanak*, p.139 (hereafter cited as *Meharban Janamsakhi*).

35. Anil Chandra Banerjee, *Guru Nanak and His Times*, p.128.

36. *P.P.P.*, III:21.

37. Macauliffe, *The Sikh Religion*, I:64–65.

38. With the exception of *Meharban Janamsakhi*.

39. An Oriya manuscript by Ishwar Das, preserved by the Oriental Society, Cuttack.

40. Ibid., Ch. 61.

41. Ibid., Ch. 64.

42. Ram Narayan Misra. Invocation in the Bengali commentary on *Dasam Sikandha*.

43. Macauliffe, *The Sikh Religion*, I:84–92, 101–106.

44. Ibid., 106–109.

45. Ibid., 132–138; McLeod, *Guru Nanak*, pp.138–140.

46. Teja Singh and Ganda Singh, *Short History*, I:9.

47. Macauliffe, *The Sikh Religion*, I:146–147; McLeod, *Guru Nanak*, pp.114–117; Kirpal Singh, *Papers on Guru Nanak*, pp.179–187.

48. S. Karunaratan, "Guru Nanak and Ceylon."

49. Teja Singh and Ganda Singh, *Short History*, I:9–10.
50. Macauliffe, *The Sikh Religion*, I:157–163; McLeod, *Guru Nanak*, p.141.
51. *P.P.P.*, III:325–333.
52. Macauliffe, *The Sikh Religion*, I:171–172; McLeod, *Guru Nanak*, p.78.
53. McLeod, *Guru Nanak*, p.77.
54. A Sikh commander came across an inscription in Baghdad during the first world war and it was given publicity in 1918. Another inscription recording the Guru's presence in Baghdad was also reported by an Indian traveler. These discoveries have practically put an end to the controversy started by Trumpp and still maintained by McLeod.
55. *P.P.P.*, III:37–40.
56. Macauliffe, *The Sikh Religion*, I:174–180.
57. A.C. Banerjee, *Times*, pp. 139–140.
58. Ibid.
59. Adi Granth, *Asa*, p.360:11–12.
60. *Sacred Writings of the Sikhs*, pp.87–88.
61. McLeod, *Guru Nanak*, p.137.
62. *P.P.P.*, III:40.
63. Ibid.
64. "It is stated in several Sikh works that Mardana's body was cremated" (Macauliffe, *The Sikh Religion*, I:182), so presumably it was the ashes that were consigned to the river.
65. *Meharban Janamsakhi*, trans. Harbans Singh, *Origins*, p.73.
66. *Puratan Janamsakhi*, ed. Bhai Vir Singh, p.123.
67. *Meharban Janamsakhi*, II:67.
68. Ibid.
69. *Puratan Janamsakhi*, p.125.
70. Trans. Harbans Singh, *Origins*, pp.196–197.
71. *Puratan Janamsakhi*, pp.132–133, trans. Harbans Singh, *Origins*, p.197.

Section Two: Teachings

72. Genesis 1:27.
73. *Ham kuza o ham kuza-gar o ham gil-i-kuza.* (Rumi: *Masnavi*)
74. *Chashm band o gosh band o lab biband, gar na beenee sirr-i-haq bar man bikhand.* (Rumi: *Masnavi*)

75. David Hume, *Treatise of Human Nature*, I:iv:6.
76. Ibid.
77. Plato, *The Republic*, ed. F.M. Comford, p.211.
78. Plato, *The Dialogues of Plato*, trans. Jowett.
79. W.T. Stace, *Mysticism and Philosophy*, p.329.
80. Bhagavad Gita, II:12.
81. Ibid., 20.
82. Bhai Gurdas, *Kabbitt* 204.
83. Ibid., 213.
84. John 1:1.
85. *Bishnaw yak kalaam-i-naamaqtu', aaz hadoos o fanaa buwad marfu'.* (Niaz)
86. *Charkh raa dar zer-i-paa aar ai shujaa'a, bishnaw az farq-i-falak baang-i-samaa'a.* (Rumi: *Masnavi*)
87. *Naghmaha nek shunidam wo nidaaha waafar, ka'aba o butkhaana banazdam shuda har do kaafir.* (Rumi: *Masnavi*)
88. *Praan Sangli.*
89. *Kathopanishad*, 6:4.
90. Ibid., 13.
91. *Mootoo qabl an tu mootoo.* (*Adhadith-i Mathnawi*)
92. *Khez bayastaan baya pesh az ajal, dar nigar shahi o mulk-i-bekhalal.* (Rumi: *Masnavi*)
93. *Sirr-i-mant ra qabl az mant in buwad, kaz pai murdan ghanimatha rasad.* (Rumi: *Masnavi*)
94. *Je toon maran maran ton pahlaan, eh marna phal paavega.* (Bulleh Shah: *Kafian*)
95. John 3:3.
96. John 10:18.
97. *Bamai sajjaada rangeen kun garat peer-i-mughaan goyad, ke saalik bekhabar nabuwad z raah-o-rasm-i-manzilha.* (Hafiz)
98. *Pir raa biguzeen ke be peer een safar, hast bas pur aafaat o khauf o khatar, har ke oo be murshidi dar raah shud, oo z ghaulan gumrah o dar chah shud, gar nabaashad saayaa-i-peer ai fasool, pas tura sargashta darad baang-i-ghool, ghaulat az raah afganad andar guzand, az tu waahi tu dareen raah bas budand.* (Rumi: *Masnavi*)
99. Puran Singh, *The Spirit of Oriental Poetry*, p.101.
100. Ibid., pp.101–102.
101. Bhai Nand Lal Goya, *Zindagi Nama*, verses 494–496.

102. *Gar ayaan khaahi z khaak-i-paai eshaan surma saaz, zaanke eshaan kor-i-maadar zaad raa rahbaan kunand.* (*Diwan-i-Shams-i-Tabriz*)

103. *An paadshaah-i-aazam darbasta bood mohkam, posheed dalq-i-aadam, yaa'ani ke bar dar aamad.* (*Diwan-i-Shams-i-Tabriz*)

104. *Khaamosh panj naubat bishnaw z aasmaane, kaan aasmaan beroon zaan haft o een shash amad.* (*Diwan-i-Shams-i-Tabriz*)

105. Sasani, *Dabistan-i-Mazahib.* Translated in *P.P.P.*, III:46.

106. Some historians do not consider this *saakhi* to be authentic.

GLOSSARY

ak   a plant that grows wild, usually in low hilly country.

amritsar   'pool of nectar'.

Anahad Shabd   'unstruck sound'; "unstruck music, music of the spheres; celestial symphony; divine music heard within the soul by the mystics" *(Sacred Writings of the Sikhs)*. See also *Shabd*.

attributes   See *gunas*.

Babar (1483–1530)   Mughal conqueror of India; Muslim rule in India 1526–1857; Babar's sack of Sayidpur (Eminabad) in 1520, referred to by Guru Nanak in *Babar Vani (Rag Asa)*.

Bein, River   See *Kali Bein*.

bhagat   'devotee'.

bhuyangma   coiled energy situated above the rectal chakra.

bin   musical instrument whose sound resembles that of an oboe or bagpipe. When the saints speak of the sweet music of the *bin* they are referring to the sound of the fifth region.

Brahm or Brahman   Lord of the second region; in Vedanta, the absolute Lord.

Brahma   God of creation in the Hindu trinity of creator-preserver-destroyer (Brahma, Vishnu, Shiva).

Brahmin   the highest caste in the Hindu four-caste system. They are the priestly caste, whose function is the acquisition and imparting of knowledge.

Buddha, Bhai   highly respected and spiritually elevated disciple who lived to see the first six Gurus in the line of Guru Nanak.

caste   The four castes of the Hindu system are Brahmin (priests), Kshatriya (rulers and warriors), Vaisya (traders and farmers) and Sudra (manual, unskilled workers).

chakra   'wheel'; energy centres within the body.

chakvi   a female goose which, according to Indian folklore, is parted from its mate by the darkness and therefore fervently longs for daybreak and reunion.

chatrik   In Indian folklore the *chatrik* or rainbird is always longing for the drops of rain that fall during the constellation *swanti*; it will die of thirst rather than drink any other water.

Daswan Dwar   'tenth door'; third stage in the spiritual journey within; includes Sunn and *Mahasunn*.

Dharam Rai   'Lord of Justice'. See *Kal*.

dharamshala   'religious house'; free guest house endowed by religious body; also a Hindu or Sikh temple.

dhoti   cloth worn around the waist by men; the usual garb of the Hindu priest.

dhyan   inner contemplation.

eighty-four or chaurasi   the cycle of 84 lakh (8,400,000) life forms into which the soul may have to incarnate as a result of its karmas; the wheel of transmigration, the cycle of birth and death.

eye centre   the seat of the mind and soul in the human body, located in the forehead above and behind the physical eyes, through which the soul enters the inner regions. When the attention is totally withdrawn to the eye centre – a process known as 'dying while living' – the soul enters the inner spiritual regions and returns to the body at will. The eye centre is referred to as the 'single eye' in the Bible – "If thine eye be single, thy whole body shall be full of light" (*Matt.* 6:22). The Indian mystics refer to the eye centre variously as *til* (sesame), *tisra til* (third eye), *sui duar* (eye of needle), *dibb chakshu* (divine eye), *dibb drishti* (divine eye or vision), *nuqta-i-suvaida* (black spot), *daswan* (tenth), *til ghar* (home of the eye), *ghar mandir* (temple of the home), *ghar* (home), *dar* (door), *sodar* (that door), *mukat duar* (door of liberation), *dar ghar* and *ghar dar* (door of the house), etc.

faqir   Muslim term for saint; also, ascetic, religious mendicant.

gayatri   highly revered Vedic *mantra* recited silently, morning and evening, by devout Hindus.

ghee   clarified, unsalted butter.

Gopis   'milkmaids'; devotees of Lord Krishna.

Gorakh   Gorakhnath was the founding teacher of a yogic school; Machindera is thought to have been his master and father. Some followers of Gorakhnath slit their ears and make Shiva the special object of their worship.

gunas   the three attributes or qualities of *prakriti*, the primordial matter out of which the creation proceeds: *sattva* (pleasure, light), *rajas* (action, delusion) and *tamas* (inertia, pain, darkness).

Gurdas, Bhai   devotee and scholar, contemporary of Guru Arjan, traditionally supposed to be his maternal uncle; scribe of the Adi Granth, dictated to him by Guru Arjan c. 1604. His own compositions, the *Varan* and *Kabbitt*, are not included in the Adi Granth, but apparently were called 'the key to the Adi Granth' by Guru Arjan.

gurdwara   'door of the guru' or 'by means of the guru'; Sikh temple.

gurmukh   'one whose face is turned towards the guru'; one who has completely surrendered to the guru; a highly advanced soul; sometimes used for the saint or perfect master.

haji   one who has performed the *haj* or pilgrimage to Mecca.

hansa   'swan'. In the Indian spiritual tradition, the highly evolved souls in the regions beyond Brahm are called swans or *hansa*; they are described as living on the shores of Lake Mansarovar, feeding on pearls *(moti)*, and with such a high degree of discrimination that they can separate milk from water.

Indra   in Hindu mythology, the king of the gods; also, the rain god.

ira   current on left of the central current or *sushumna* in the spinal column of the finer body.

Ishwar   'highest lord'. In the Vedantic tradition, Ishwar is *sagun brahman*, qualified personal God, creator; cf. *nirgun brahman*, the absolute, unqualified Lord. See also *Brahm*.

janamsakhi   'birth story'; term used to denote life stories of Guru Nanak.

janeu   sacred thread worn by Brahmins and other high-caste Hindus.

jat   agriculturalist subcaste.

jogi   one who practices *yoga*.

Ka'aba   the shrine at Mecca which houses the Black Stone; the most sacred spot for Muslims.

Kabir Sahib   fifteenth century mystic who lived at Benares, a low-caste weaver by birth. A selection of his compositions is included in the Adi Granth.

Kal   'time', 'death'; the Negative Power, the ruler of the three perishable worlds (physical, astral, causal); also called Dharam Rai, the Lord of Judgment, Yama, the Angel of Death.

Kali Bein   rivulet that flows by the side of Sultanpur, scene of Guru Nanak's enlightenment experience.

kaliyuga   the fourth cycle of time, known as the dark age or iron age; it is the age in which we now live. See also *yuga*.

Kalma   'Word'. See *Shabd*.

kamadhen, kamadhenu   the mythical cow which is believed to fulfill all one's wishes.

karma   'action'; the law of action and reaction; the debits and credits resulting from our deeds. *Pralabdh karma*: the fate or destiny we experience in this life; the past actions that are responsible for our present condition. *Kriyaman karma*: the debits and credits created by our actions in this life, to be reaped in future lives. *Sinchit karma*: the balance of unpaid *kriyaman karmas* from all our past lives; the store of karmas.

khalsa   'pure one'; term used by the tenth Guru, Gobind Singh, for his followers; he defined a *khalsa* as 'one who has seen the light within'.

khani   fourfold classification of living beings according to whether they are born via womb, egg, sweat, or seasonal change.

khapar   vessel resembling a cup or skull, used by *jogis* for the alms they receive.

kirtan   devotional music; singing hymns from the scriptures to the accompaniment of instruments; esoterically, listening to the *Shabd* within.

koel   Indian cuckoo, whose call is associated with spring. It is believed that the *koel* longs for the mango blossom.

Krishna   believed to be one of the incarnations of Vishnu. The celebrated Bhagavad Gita, 'song of the Lord', is said to have been taught by Krishna on the battlefield of the Mahabharata.

Kshatriya   the second highest caste in the Hindu system; warriors, kings, administrators.

kungu   'saffron'. See *tilak*.

lakh   one hundred thousand.

langar   free community kitchen sponsored by a religious body, where men and women of all castes, creeds and nationalities eat together in brotherhood and equality.

lokas   'regions'; the fourteen grand divisions or regions that the universe is traditionally divided into.

M   abbreviated form of *mohilla*, used in the Adi Granth to indicate the authorship of compositions by the Gurus. *M.1*, means Guru Nanak; *M.2*, Guru Angad (the second in the house of Nanak); *M.3*, Guru Amar Das; *M.4*, Guru Ram Das; *M.5*, Guru Arjan; *M.9*, Guru Tegh Bahadur. In giving the sources for hymns, the same system has been followed: *Asa, M.1* means a composition by Guru Nanak in *Rag Asa*; etc.

manes   See *pittripuja*.

manmukh   'one who faces the mind'; someone who obeys the dictates of the mind; a devotee of the mind and the ways of the world.

mantra shakti   power *(shakti)* that comes from reciting or repeating specific formulas or *mantras*, usually from the Vedas.

maya   'illusion', 'delusion', 'deception', 'unreality'; the phenomenal universe. All that is known through the senses is *maya*; it appears, but is not; it conceals the vision of God, reality, from our sight; also, another name for the goddess Shakti.

mehrab   arch of the mosque; direction in which Muslims turn to pray.

mina   'deceitful'; Prithi Chand's followers: "Guru Ram Das stigmatized Prithi Chand [Guru Arjan's older brother] as *mina* or 'deceitful', a name given to a robber tribe in Rajputana. Prithi Chand's followers came to be known as 'Mina'" (Macauliffe, *The Sikh Religion*. I: lxxx).

mullah   Muslim priest.

Nam   'Name'; creative power. See *Shabd*.

namaz   the prayers said by devout Muslims at certain fixed times of the day.

Narad Rishi   a sage of ancient India to whom a number of couplets in the Rig Veda are attributed.

naths   a sect of *yogis*, especially *hath-yogis*.

nawab   governor in India under the Moghul empire.

nirvana   liberation from the cycle of birth and death; *mukti*.

panthi   'one who follows a path'; *Nanak-panthi*, 'one who follows the path of Nanak'.

passions   The five passions are lust *(kam)*, anger *(krodh)*, greed *(lobh)*, attachment *(moh)* and pride *(ahankar)*; also called the 'five demons', 'five thieves', 'five robbers', etc.

pauri   'step', 'ladder'; a stanzaic form used in the Adi Granth.

pilgrimage places   There are 68 places of Hindu pilgrimage in India, including mountaintops, rivers and temples. The rivers Ganga (Ganges) and Jamuna are considered holy, and the confluence or *'triveni'* of Ganga, Jamuna and Saraswati at Prayag (Allahabad) is an important place of Hindu pilgrimage, one of the many that Guru Nanak visited on his missionary journeys.

pingula or pingala   current on the right of the central current or *sushumna* in the spinal column of the finer body.

pir   spiritual teacher or master in the Sufi tradition; also used for Muslim priest.

pittripuja   According to the Hindu tradition, one is born with four debts or duties: towards the gods; the rishis or holy men; one's ancestors; and one's fellow beings. These duties are fulfilled by a lifetime of worship (rituals, etc.), studying the scriptures, oblations and charity. The Latin word *manes*, 'respected souls of the departed', is used in connection with the various rituals and traditions associated with *pittripuja*, particularly the oblation ceremony Guru Nanak witnessed at Hardwar, and also the traditional giving of alms and free meals to propitiate the gods and ameliorate the condition of one's dead relatives in their afterlife.

pranayam   yogic practice of holding and controlling the breath.

pundit   'learned man'; Hindu priest.

Puranas   'old ones'; 18-volume Hindu scripture, religio-historical stories describing the lives and deeds of gods, heroes and great kings.

Purusha   'primal being'; creator.

qazi   expounder of Muslim law.

Quran or Koran   the holy book of the Muslims, revealed to Prophet Mohammed.

rag   musical mode or scale in the Indian system. The compositions in the Adi Granth are nearly all arranged according to *rag*, indicating thereby the basic tune and mood of the piece.

rainbird   See *chatrik*.

Ram   Hindu name for God.

Ram Chandra   son of King Dasaratha, the hero of the *Ramayana*; believed to be an incarnation of Vishnu.

Ram Das, Guru   the fourth Guru in the line of Guru Nanak; also the father of Guru Arjan, the fifth Guru.

sacred thread   See *janeu*.

saffron   See *tilak*.

sahaj   'easy', 'natural'; esoterically, that state of meditation in which the soul, having realized its own true nature, gravitates easily and naturally towards complete merging in God. This state begins in Par Brahm and reaches its culmination in Sach Khand.

Sahaj Yoga   See *Surat Shabd Yoga*.

sakhi   'story'. See also *janamsakhi*.

saligram   spherical stone idol traditionally worshipped by Brahmin priests.

samadhi   a state of concentration in which all consciousness of the outer world is transcended; a state of deep meditation.

samvat   'era'. See *Vikram Samvat*.

sangat   congregation.

sannyasin or sannyasi   an order of Hindu ascetics who renounce the world and put on the yellow robe as a mark of renunciation.

Satguru   'perfect master', 'true master'; a master or spiritual teacher who has access to the fifth spiritual region, Sach Khand.

seva   'service'.

Shabd   'Word', 'sound'; creative power; source of all creation, the one reality behind all appearances; manifests as sound and light in the spiritual regions; referred to by many names: *Nam* (name), *Anahad Shabd* (unstruck melody or sound), *Bani* (voice), *Dhun* (sound), *Hukam* (command), *Nad* (heavenly sound), *Sat Nam* (true name), *Kalma* (word), *Logos* (word), etc. Hymns from a scripture are also called *shabd*; collectively they are known as *bani*.

shakti   'power', 'strength'; mother of Brahma, Vishnu and Shiva; highest form of *maya*.

shalok   'couplet'; a verse form used in the Adi Granth.

sheikh   'chief'; Muslim holy man; descendant of disciples of Prophet Mohammed; Muslim courtesy title.

Shiva   God of destruction in the Hindu trinity of creator-preserver-destroyer (Brahma, Vishnu, Shiva); also called Mahesh and Mahadeo.

sidh or siddha   yogis who are popularly supposed to have acquired a high degree of perfection in supernatural powers. *Sadhak* is one who is aspiring to be a *sidh*.

simran   'repetition'; repetition of the five holy names according to the instructions of a perfect master.

sukhmana or sushumna   the central path starting from the eye centre and leading upwards to the higher spiritual regions, located and traversed by means of the spiritual practice taught by a perfect master. This is not to be confused with the *sushumna* of the yogis, which is the central canal along the spine, the current on the left being called *ira* and the one of the right, *pingula*.

Sunn   'void', 'emptiness', 'vacuum'; name of the third spiritual region, also called Daswan Dwar.

Surat Shabd Yoga   'union of soul with *Shabd*'; the spiritual practice by which the current of consciousness is applied to hearing the sound or *Shabd Dhun* within; merging the mind and soul in *Shabd*; also called *Sahaj Yoga, Shabd Yoga, Shabd Abhyas*.

Swami or Soami   'Lord'; the supreme Lord; also a title given to religious teachers.

swan   See *hansa*.

tantric creed   practice of tantra, a lately developed esoteric yogic sect prevalent in both the Hindu and Buddhist traditions.

tattwa   'element'. The entire universe is made up of five *tattwas*: earth *(prithvi)*, water *(jal)*, fire *(agni)*, air *(vayu)* and ether *(akash)*.

tilak   a mark made on the forehead mostly out of vermilion, saffron or sandalwood paste. In medieval times it was believed that a tilak made on the forehead of a dying person would lead to salvation.

Triloki   'three worlds'; the physical, astral and causal worlds, the realm governed by Kal, also known as Brahmand.

tulsi   'holy basil'; beads worn as a necklace by sadhus, and used as a rosary.

udasi   'detached'; term used for the journeys that Guru Nanak undertook to spread his teachings, because he travelled like a person who has renounced the world.

Vaishnavite   worshipper of Vishnu, the god of preservation.

var   'heroic ballad'; a verse form used in the Adi Granth, but with a spiritual, not mythological content.

Vedas   'knowledge'; revealed knowledge, as embodied in the four sacred books of the Hindus: the Rig Veda, Sama Veda, Yajur Veda and Atharva Veda.

Vikram Samvat   'Vikram era', one of the two eras commonly used in India besides the Christian (A.D.) and Muslim (Hijri) eras; it supposedly dates back to the great king, Vikram. Subtract 57 years from v.s. to obtain A.D.

Vishnu   god of preservation in the Hindu trinity of creator-preserver-destroyer (Brahma, Vishnu, Shiva).

Vyas, Rishi   ancient sage, founder of the Vedant system of philosophy; supposed to have lived on the banks of the River Beas, in whose memory the river was apparently named.

worlds   See *Triloki*; *lokas*.

yajna or yagya   'sacrifice'; a ritual or religious ceremony of the Hindus, which in ancient India included the sacrifice of some animal.

Yama   'God of Death'; See *Kal*.

yoga   'union'; a system of exercises or spiritual practice that leads to or aims at the union of the soul with God.

yogi or yogin   one who practices *yoga*.

yuga   'age' or cycle of time. Hindu tradition divides time into four *yugas*, of which *kaliyuga* is the fourth.

SELECTED BIBLIOGRAPHY

* denotes references in Punjabi
† denotes references in Punjabi and English

Bala Janam-Sakhi.* Amritsar: Bhai Chatar Singh Jiwan Singh.

Banerjee, Anil Chandra. *Guru Nanak and His Times.* Patiala: Punjabi University, 1971.

Banerjee, Indubhushan. *Evolution of the Khalsa.*

Beale, Thomas William. *An Oriental Biographical Dictionary.* N.d., rev. and enl. Reprint. Ludhiana: Kalyani Publishers, 1972.

Diwan Singh. *Guru Nanak and the Indian Mystic Tradition.* Ludhiana: Lahore Book Shop, 1981.

Goya, Nan Lal. *Zindagi Nama.*

Gurbux Singh. "Persian Writings on Guru Nanak." In *Essays in Honour of Dr. Ganda Singh,* edited by Harbans Singh and N. Gerald Barrier. Patiala: Punjabi University, 1976.

Harbans Singh. *Guru Nanak and Origins of the Sikh Faith.* Bombay: Asia Publishing House, 1969.

Hymns of Guru Nanak. Translated by Khushwant Singh. New Delhi: Orient Longman (Sangam), 1978.

Hymns of Guru Nanak.† Translated by Manmohan Singh. Patiala: Language Department, 1972.

Joginder Singh. *Sikh Ceremonies.*

Karunaratan, S. "Guru Nanak and Ceylon." Patiala: Punjabi University, 1969.

Kirpal Singh. *Japji.* Delhi: Ruhani Satsang, 1959.

Kirpal Singh. *Papers on Guru Nanak* (Punjabi History Conference). Patiala: Punjabi University, 1969.

Macauliffe, Max Arthur. *The Sikh Religion: Its Gurus, Sacred Writings and Authors.* 6 vols. New Delhi: S. Chand and Co., 1963.

Maini, D.S. *Studies in Punjabi Poetry.* New Delhi: Vikas Publishing House, 1979.

Malcolm, John. *Sketch of the Sikhs.* London: 1812.

McLeod, W.H. *Guru Nanak and the Sikh Religion.* Delhi: Oxford University Press, 1976.

Meharban Sodhi. *Meharban Janamsakhi.*ˣ

Otto, Rudolph. *Mysticism East and West: A Comparative Analysis of the Nature of Mysticism.* Translated by Bertha L. Bracey and Richenda C. Payne. London: Theosophical Press, 1987.

The Panjab Past and Present, vol. III.ˣ Patiala: Punjabi University, 1969.

Puran Singh. *The Sisters of the Spinning Wheel.* 2d ed. Patiala: Punjabi University, 1977.

———. *The Spirit of Oriental Poetry.* 2d ed. Patiala: Punjabi University, 1969.

*Puratan Janam Sakhi.*ˣ Edited by Shamsher Singh Ashok. Amritsar: S.G.P.C., 1969.

Selections from the Sacred Writings of the Sikhs. Translated by Dr. Trilochan Singh, Bhai Jodh Singh, Kapur Singh, Bawa Harkishan Singh, Khushwant Singh. Revised by George S. Fraser. London: George Allen and Unwin, 1973.

*Shabdarath, Sri Guru Granth Sahib.*ˣ 4 vols. Amritsar: S.G.P.C., 1979.

*Sri Guru Granth Kosh.*ˣ Edited by Bhai Vir Singh and Gyani Hazara Singh. Amritsar: Khalsa Tract Society, 1899.

Sri Guru Granth Sahib. 4 vols. Translated by Gopal Singh. Chandigarh: World Sikh University Press, 1978.

Stace, W. T. *Mysticism and Philosophy.* London: MacMillan & Co, 1961.

Teja Singh and Ganda Singh. *A Short History of the Sikhs.*

Westcott, G.H. *Kabir and the Kabir Panth.* Calcutta: Susil Gupta, 1953.

INDEX OF FIRST LINES (PUNJABI)

The Adi Granth reference is in parentheses, followed by the page number of the translation given in Section Three.

477

ADDRESSES FOR INFORMATION AND BOOKS

INDIAN SUB-CONTINENT

INDIA
The Secretary
Radha Soami Satsang Beas
Dera Baba Jaimal Singh
District Amritsar, Punjab 143204

NEPAL
Mr. Dal Bahadur Shreshta
Radha Soami Satsang Beas
P. O. Box 1646
Gongabu, Dhapasi
Kathmandu
☎+97-1-435-7765

PAKISTAN
Mr. Sadrang Seetal Das
Lahori Mohala, Larkana
Sindh

SRI LANKA
Mr. Chandroo Mirpuri
39/3 Horton Place, Colombo 7

SOUTHEAST ASIA

FOR FAR EAST
Mrs. Cami Moss
RSSB-HK, T.S.T.,
P.O. Box 90745
Kowloon, Hong Kong
☎+852-2369-0625

MALAYSIA
Mr. Selvarajoo Pragasam
No. 15 Jalan SL 10/4
Bandar Sungai Long, Selangor
43000 Kajang

THAILAND
Mr. Harmahinder Singh Sethi
Radha Soami Satsang Beas
58/32 Rachdapitsek Road, Soi 16
Thapra, Bangkok Yai, Bangkok 10600
☎+66-2-868-2186 / 2187

INDONESIA
Mr. Ramesh Sadarangani
Jalan Pasir Putih IV/16, Block E 4
Ancol Timur, Jakarta
DKI Jakarta 14430

PHILIPPINES
Mr. Kay Sham
Science of the Soul Study Centre
9001 Don Jesus Boulevard
Alabang Hills, Cupang
Muntinlupa City, 1771
☎+63-2-772-0111 / 0555

SINGAPORE
Mrs. Asha Melwani
Radha Soami Satsang Beas
19 Amber Road, Singapore 439868
☎+65-6447-4956

ASIA PACIFIC

AUSTRALIA
Mr. Pradeep Raniga
P.O. Box 642
Balwyn North, Victoria 3104

NEW ZEALAND
Mr. Tony Waddicor
Science of the Soul Study Centre
P. O. Box 5331, Auckland
☎+64-9-624-2202

483

GUAM
Mrs. Hoori M. Sadhwani
115 Alupang Cove
241 Condo Lane, Tamuning 96911

HONG KONG
Mr. Manoj Sabnani
Radha Soami Satsang Beas
3rd Floor, Eader Centre
39-41 Hankow Road
Tsimshatsui, Kowloon
☎+852-2369-0625

JAPAN
Mr. Jani G. Mohinani
Radha Soami Satsang Beas
1-2-18 Nakajima-Dori
Aotani, Chuo-Ku, Kobe 651-0052
☎+81-78-222-5353

TAIWAN, R.O.C.
Mr. Haresh Buxani
Science of the Soul Study Group
Aetna Tower Office, 15F., No. 27-9
Sec.2, Jhongjheng E.Rd.
Danshuei Township, Taipei 25170
☎+886-2-8809-5223

NORTH AMERICA

CANADA
Mr. John Abel
#701-1012 Beach Avenue
Vancouver, B.C. V6E 1T7

Science of the Soul Study Centre
2934 -176ᵗʰ Street
Surrey, B.C. V3S 9V4
☎+1-604-541-4792

Mrs. Meena Khanna
149 Elton Park Road
Oakville, Ontario L6J 4C2

MEXICO
Mr. Jorge Villaseñor
Av. De Las Amapolas #39
Condominio Rancho Contento
Zapopan, Jalisco, C.P. 45010

UNITED STATES
Mr. Hank Muller
20038 Indigo Lake Drive
Magnolia, TX 77355

Dr. Vincent P. Savarese
2550 Pequeno Circle
Palm Springs
CA 92264-9522

Dr. Frank E. Vogel
275 Cutts Road
Newport, NH 03773

Dr. Douglas Torr
P.O. Box 2360, Southern Pines
NC 28388-2360

Science of the Soul Study Centre
4115 Gillespie Street
Fayetteville, NC 28306-9053
☎+1-910-426-5306

Science of the Soul Study Centre
2415 East Washington Street
Petaluma, CA 94954-9274
☎+1-707-762-5082

CARIBBEAN

FOR CARIBBEAN
Mr. Sean Finnigan
R.S.S.B. Foundation
P. O. Box 978, Phillipsburg
St. Maarten, N. A.
☎+599-547-0066

BARBADOS, W.I.
Mrs. Jaya Sabnani
1 Sunset Drive South
Fort George Heights
St. Michael BB111 02

CURACAO, N.A.
Mrs. Reshma Jethmalani
Science of the Soul Study Centre
Kaya Seru di Milon 6-9
Santa Catharina
☎+599-9-747-0226

GRENADA, W.I.
Mr. Prakash Amarnani
P.O. Box 726, St. Georges

GUYANA
Mrs. Indu Lalwani
115, Garnette Street
Newtown Kitty, Georgetown

HAITI, W.I.
Mrs. Mousson Finnigan
P.O. Box 2314
Port-au-Prince

JAMAICA, W.I.
Mrs. Reshma Daswani
17 Colombus Height
First Phase, Ocho Rios

ST. MAARTEN, N.A.
Mr. Haresh Balani
R.S.S.B. Foundation
P. O. Box 978
Phillipsburg
☎+599-547-0066

ST. THOMAS
Mrs. Hema Melwani
P.O. Box 600145,
USVI-VI00801-6145

SURINAME
Mr. Chandru Samtani
15 Venus Straat
Paramaribo

TRINIDAD, W.I.
Mr. Chandru Chatlani
20 Admiral Court
Westmoorings-by-Sea, Westmoorings

FOR CENTRAL & SOUTH AMERICA

Mr. Hiro W. Balani
Paseo De Farola, 3, Piso 6
Edificio Marina, Malaga, Spain 29016

CENTRAL AMERICA

BELIZE
Mrs. Milan Bhindu Hotchandani
5789 Goldson Avenue, Belize City

PANAMA
Mr. Ashok Tikamdas Dinani
P.O. Box 0302, 00830 Colon

SOUTH AMERICA

ARGENTINA
Mrs. Estela M.I.
Calle Guemes 249, Acassuso
Buenos Aires 1641

BRAZIL
Mr. Guillerme Almeida
SQN 315, Bloco C, Apto. 306 Brasilia
DF 70-774-030

CHILE
Mr. Vijay Harjani
Pasaje Cuatro No. 3438
Sector Chipana, Iquique

COLOMBIA
Mrs. Emma Orozco
Calle 45, #99-25, Medellin 49744

ECUADOR
Dr. Fernando Flores Villalva
Radha Soami Satsang Beas
Calle Marquez de Varela
OE 3-68y Avda. America
P.O. Box 17-21-115, Quito
☎+5932-2-555-988

PERU
Mr. Carlos Fitts
P.O. Box 18-0658
Lima 18

VENEZUELA
Mrs. Helen Paquin
Radha Soami Satsang Beas
Av. Los Samanes con
Av. Los Naranjos Conj
Res. Florida 335
La Florida, Caracas 1012

EUROPE

AUSTRIA
Mr. Hansjorg Hammerer
Sezenweingasse 10, A-5020 Salzburg

BELGIUM
Mr. Piet J. E. Vosters
Driezenstraat 26, Turnhout 2300

BULGARIA
Mr. Deyan Stoyanov
Foundation Radha Soami Satsang Beas
P. O. Box 39, 8000 Bourgas

CYPRUS
Mr. Heraclis Achilleos
P. O. Box 29077, 1035 Nicosia

CZECH REPUBLIC
Mr. Vladimir Skalsky
Maratkova 916, 142 00 Praha 412

DENMARK
Mr. Tony Sharma
Sven Dalsgaardsvej 33, DK-7430 Ikast

FINLAND
Ms. Anneli Wingfield
P. O. Box 1422, 00101 Helsinki

FRANCE
Mr. Pierre de Proyart
7 Quai Voltaire, Paris 75007

GERMANY
Mr. Rudolf Walberg
P. O. Box 1544, D-65800 Bad Soden

GIBRALTAR
Mr. Sunder Mahtani
RSSB Charitable Trust Gibraltar
15 Rosia Road
☎+350-412-67

GREECE
Mr. Themistoclis Gianopoulos
6 Platonos Str. 17672 Kallithea, Attiki

ITALY
Mrs. Wilma Salvatori Torri
Via Bacchiglione 3, 00199 Rome

THE NETHERLANDS
(HOLLAND)
Mr. Henk Keuning
Kleizuwe2, Vreeland 3633AE

Radha Soami Satsang Beas
Middenweg 145 E
1394 AH Nederhorst den Berg
☎+31-294-255-255

NORWAY
Mr. Manoj Kaushal
Langretta 8
N-1279 Oslo

POLAND
Mr. Vinod Sharma
Ul. 1go Sierpnia 36 B, M-100
PL-02-134 Warsaw

PORTUGAL
Mrs. Sharda Lodhia
Torres das Palmeiras, Lote 68, 11° C,
2780-145 Oeiras

ROMANIA
Mrs. Carmen Cismas
C.P. 6-12, 810600 Braila

SLOVENIA
Mr. Marko Bedina
Brezje pri Trzicu 68, 4290 Trzic

SPAIN
Mr. J. W. Balani
Fundacion Cultural RSSB
Fca Loma del Valle S/N
Cruce de Penon de Zapata
Alhaurin De la Torre, Malaga 29130
☎+34-952-414-679

SWEDEN
Mr. Lennart Zachen
Norra Sonnarpsvägen 29
SE-286 72 Asljunga

SWITZERLAND
Mr. Sebastian Züst
Weissenrainstrasse 48
CH 8707 Uetikon am See

UNITED KINGDOM
Mr. Narinder Singh Johal
Haynes Park, Haynes
MK45 3BL Bedford
☎+44-1234-381-234

AFRICA

BENIN
Mr. Jaikumar T. Vaswani
01 Boite Postale 951
Atlantique, Cotonou 01

BOTSWANA
Dr. Krishan Lal Bhateja
P. O. Box 402539, Gaborone

CONGO
Mr. Prahlad Parbhu
143 Kasai Ave. Lubumbashi

GHANA
Mr. Murli Chatani
Radha Soami Satsang Beas
P. O. Box 3976, Accra
☎+233-242-057-309

IVORY COAST
Mr. Konan N'Dri
Boite Postale 569, Abidjan 08

KENYA
Mr. Surinder Singh Ghir
35 Mutty Court
(Kipepu RD), Nairobi

LESOTHO
Mr. Sello Wilson Moseme
P. O. Box 750, Leribe 300

LIBYA (G.S.P.L.A.J.)
Mr. Roshan Lal
P.O. Box 38930, Bani Walid

MADAGASCAR
Mr. Francis Murat
Lote 126B, Ambohiminono
Antanetibe, Antananarivo 101

MAURITIUS
Dr. I. Fagoonee
17 Manick Avenue
La Louise, Quatre Bornes

NAMIBIA
Mrs. Jennifer Carvill
P. O. Box 449
Swakopmund 9000

NIGERIA
Mr. Nanik N. Balani
G.P.O. Box 5054, Marina, Lagos

RÉUNION
Ms. Marie-Lynn Marcel
5 Chemin 'Gonneau, Bernica
St Gillesles Hauts 97435

SIERRA LEONE
Mr. Kishore S. Mahboobani
82/88 Kissy Dock Yard,
P O Box 369, Freetown

SOUTH AFRICA
Mr. Gordon Clive Wilson
P. O. Box 47182, Greyville 4023

Radha Soami Satsang Beas
P.O. Box 5270, Cresta 2118
☎+27-11-792-7644

SWAZILAND
Mr. Peter Dunseith
P. O. Box 423, Mbabane

TANZANIA
Mr. D.N. Pandit
P.O. Box 1963, Dar-Es-Salaam

UGANDA
Mr. Sylvester Kakooza
Radha Soami Satsang Beas
P. O. Box 31381
Kampala

ZAMBIA
Mr. Chrispin Lwali
P.O. Box 12094
Nchanga North Township
Chingola

ZIMBABWE
Mr. G.D. Wright
Pharmanova, P. O. Box 1726
Harare

MIDDLE EAST

BAHRAIN
Mr. Mangat Rai Rudra
Flat No. 12, Building No. 645
Road No. 2107
Manama 321

ISRAEL
Mr. Michael Yaniv
Moshav Sde Nitzan 59
D.N. Hanegev 85470

KUWAIT
Mr. Vijay Kumar
Yousef AL Badar Street Salmiya
Block 10, Flat #8, Bldg 28

U.A.E.
Mr. Daleep Jatwani
Radha Soami Services Centre
P.O. Box 37816, Dubai
☎+971-4-339-4773

BOOKS ON THIS SCIENCE

SOAMI JI MAHARAJ
Sar Bachan Prose (The Yoga of the Sound Current)
Sar Bachan Poetry (Selections)

BABA JAIMAL SINGH
Spiritual Letters

MAHARAJ SAWAN SINGH
The Dawn of Light
Discourses on Sant Mat
My Submission
Philosophy of the Masters, in 5 volumes
Spiritual Gems
Tales of the Mystic East

MAHARAJ JAGAT SINGH
The Science of the Soul
Discourses on Sant Mat, Volume II

MAHARAJ CHARAN SINGH
Die to Live
Divine Light
Light on Saint John
Light on Saint Matthew
Light on Sant Mat
The Master Answers
The Path
Quest for Light
Spiritual Discourses, in 2 volumes
Spiritual Heritage
Thus Saith the Master

BOOKS ABOUT THE MASTERS
Call of the Great Master—Daryai Lal Kapur
Heaven on Earth—Daryai Lal Kapur
Treasure Beyond Measure—Shanti Sethi
With a Great Master in India—Julian P. Johnson
With the Three Masters, in 3 volumes—Rai Sahib Munshi Ram

INTRODUCTION TO SPIRITUALITY
A Spiritual Primer—Hector Esponda Dubin
Honest Living—M. F. Singh
The Inner Voice—C. W. Sanders

Liberation of the Soul—J. Stanley White
Life is Fair: The Law of Cause and Effect—Brian Hines

BOOKS ON MYSTICISM

*A Treasury of Mystic Terms, Part I: The Principles of Mysticism
(6 volumes)*—John Davidson
The Holy Name: Mysticism in Judaism—Miriam Caravella
Yoga and the Bible—Joseph Leeming

BOOKS ON SANT MAT IN GENERAL

In Search of the Way—Flora E. Wood
Living Meditation: A Journey beyond Body and Mind
—Hector Esponda Dubin
Message Divine—Shanti Sethi
The Mystic Philosophy of Sant Mat—Peter Fripp
Mysticism: The Spiritual Path, in 2 volumes—Lekh Raj Puri
The Path of the Masters—Julian P. Johnson
Radha Soami Teachings—Lekh Raj Puri

MYSTICS OF THE EAST SERIES

Bulleh Shah—J. R. Puri and T.R. Shangari
Dadu: The Compassionate Mystic—K. N. Upadhyaya
Dariya Sahib: Saint of Bihar—K. N. Upadhyaya
Guru Nanak: His Mystic Teachings—J. R. Puri
Guru Ravidas: The Philosopher's Stone—K. N. Upadhyaya
Kabir: The Great Mystic—Isaac A. Ezekiel
Kabir: The Weaver of God's Name—V. K. Sethi
Mira: The Divine Lover—V. K. Sethi
Saint Namdev—J. R. Puri and V. K. Sethi
Saint Paltu: His life and teachings—Isaac A. Ezekiel
Sarmad: Martyr to Love Divine—Isaac A. Ezekiel
Sultan Bahu—J. R. Puri and K. S. Khak
Tukaram: The Ceaseless Song of Devotion—C. Rajwade
Tulsi Sahib: Saint of Hathras—J. R. Puri and V. K. Sethi

BOOKS FOR CHILDREN

The Journey of the Soul—Victoria Jones

For Internet orders, please visit: www.rssb.org

For book orders **within** India, please write to:

Radha Soami Satsang Beas
BAV Distribution Centre, 5 Guru Ravi Dass Marg
Pusa Road, New Delhi 110005